Mary Gubser's

Quick
BREADS
SOUPS & STEWS

Quick
BREADS
SOUPS & STEWS

196 DELECTABLE QUICK BREADS AND CLASSIC

SOUPS TO PAIR WITH THEM *for* AN ALMOST

LIMITLESS NUMBER *of* SUPERB MEALS

by Mary Gubser

ILLUSTRATED BY PAT BIGGS

EDITED BY CAROL HARALSON

COUNCIL OAK BOOKS TULSA OKLAHOMA

gift 3/22

Council Oak Books
Tulsa, Oklahoma 74120
1-800-247-8850

©Copyright 1991 by Mary Gubser. All rights reserved
Printed in the United States of America
99 98 97 96 95   8 7 6 5 4

Illustration: Pat Biggs
Cover and book design: Carol Haralson

ISBN: 0-933031-33-5
Library of Congress Catalogue Card Number 90-081820

To Pat Biggs, my niece, artist, and confidant

Acknowledgments

With such a variety of both breads and soups, recipe testing for this book became an exciting and demanding experience. Laura Gubser, my youngest daughter-in-law, despite having the responsibility for two children, two dogs, two rabbits, six birds, multiple fish, and the management of Mary's Bread Basket, willingly assisted me in testing.

To my son, Michael Gubser, I am most grateful for excellent advice and special recipes. Many companies, mills, and friends have unhesitantly given suggestions, ideas and recipes. I thank in particular The Kansas Wheat Commission; Great Grains Milling Company; Arrowhead Mills; War Eagle Mills; Judy Bell of Portland, Oregon; Kathy Major of Tulsa, Oklahoma; Mary Jane Kaho of Tulsa, Oklahoma, Taos, New Mexico and Minnesota; Terry Davis, chef at Mary's Bread Basket, Tulsa, Oklahoma; Robert Libey, chef at Michael Gubser's Kitchen; Annie Y. Gubser, Chevy Chase, Maryland; Rosalie Talbot of Taos, New Mexico; and Denise Minard, Paris, France.

I also offer my humble thanks to my tasters for both approving and rejecting. They were Dora Malone, Kent and Diane Atkinson, Anne and Troy Cradduck, Jesse and J. R. Enloe, Clara Walrod, Harry and Carthel Burt, and one hundred citizens of Claremore, Oklahoma.

MARY GUBSER

CONTENTS

Quick Breads

Soups & Stews

Bread & Soup: Ancient Foods

Bread and soup are ancient foods. Long before the arrival of Europeans on this continent, native Americans were preparing stews and quick breads. Indians on the Great Plains relished a dish of stewed meat and in the American Southwest the Zuni and other tribes made a variety of breads with corn flour, water, and "lime yeast," baking them over hot coals or among the ashes of the hearth. For early European settlers, quick breads, soups, and stews, usually made from wild game, were culinary mainstays. Travelers carried leather pouches of jonnycake and thousands of western-bound wagons rumbling from the Alleghenies to the Pacific carried barrels of flour and sacks of cornmeal. When campfires blazed beneath the stars, the aroma of cornbread, biscuits or sourdough loaves wafted up from iron skillets and improvised rock ovens.

Two hundred years later, the pace and demands of life still yield little culinary leisure for many of us. And yet we long for *real* food, for food of excellent quality that tastes good and nourishes us both physically and spiritually. Most supermarkets offer an increasing range of processed (and overprocessed), prepackaged (and overpackaged) foods. Their convenience may be welcome. But they are not the only answer to the need for something delicious and *fast* for dinner. Excellent hot bread can be ready in thirty minutes or less, as you assemble a simple main course or heat a wonderful stew made and frozen beforehand. While soups may take longer than quick breads to prepare, they keep beautifully in the refrigerator or freezer, can be made in quantity, and require little attention while cooking. And many soups are actually surprisingly fast to prepare.

And there is yet another reason why this is the perfect moment for the return of good hot homemade breads and soups. As we come to the end of the twentieth century we are more and more aware of how the excesses of past decades have tired and tried Mother Earth.

This is the moment to learn new ways of dealing gently with our world. When you make quick bread at home, not only do you bring pleasure and sustenance to yourself and others, but you also avoid contributing to the expense of resources that are invested in the processing, packaging, and transportation of commercially prepared foods. And you can be sure of what is in that lovely, fragrant loaf, because you yourself put it there. A panful of golden muffins from your own kitchen need not contain stabilizers, flavor enhancers, or preservatives. It only contains the fine ingredients you chose, and your skill, concern, and affection.

Perhaps more than any other foods, quick breads and soups lend themselves to endless variation, experimentation, and personal expression. The recipes included here comprise a sound contemporary North American repertoire of two ancient and beloved foods. They are also an excellent starting point for your own innovations. And not only can you improvise on the individual recipes, creating soups and breads to suit your taste, your family's preferences, the vegetables and fruits of the season, but you can also combine breads with soups for a wonderful variety of bread-and-soup meals. Try any of the popovers or scones with light soups or fruit soups, for example, or any of the cornbreads with soups and stews containing beans and grains, or meat. Try seafood soups with crepes or quick yeast breads. Try creamy soups with muffins. The variations are so many. May you have health and joy in the making of bread and soup!

Cooking for the Twenty-first Century

Bread and soup, foods from the ancient past, are perfect foods for the future as well because they offer us a chance to protect our health while helping to protect the health of the planet. Delicious, hot breads made from whole grains are one of the original dishes found "low on the food chain." Producing fruits, grains, and vegetables uses less than 5% of the raw materials required by meat production. Half of American agricultural land is used to grow feed for livestock; cattle raised for beef in the U.S. eat more than enough grain and soybeans to sustain the 60 million people who die each year of starvation. It takes 16 pounds of grain and soybeans to make one pound of beef – but a pound of good grain makes much more than a pound of delicious bread. And when you do enjoy a portion of

excellent U.S. beef, less becomes more when accompanied by succulent vegetables in a hot stew. And when you have finished dining on roasted beef or fowl,
you are left with the bones – the essential ingredient for making a broth that can
become the basis for several nourishing and delicious meals.

The kitchen, classically the heart and hearth of the home, is a perfect place to do
some simple daily things that can help make us part of the solution to current
global problems. You may wish to

Use reuseable containers to store food instead of reaching for the plastic wrap or
aluminum foil. Use biodegradable waxed paper to wrap portable foods. The
United States produces over 50 billion pounds of plastic a year, most of which
will find its way into the 100 pounds of trash thrown away weekly by the average
North American family.

Keep kitchen cloths handy to wipe up spills. They can be washed and reused
indefinitely. Use cloth napkins instead of paper; they are pretty and effective as
well as being more economical, both in private and global terms.

Avoid purchasing foods that are overpackaged or packaged in styrofoam. The U.S.
yearly produces enough styrofoam cups, for example, to circle the planet 436
times – and *all* the styrofoam we produce will be orbiting the sun with us for the
next 500 years or more because it is not biodegradable.

Ask for paper bags at the grocery store. Plastic bags are made from petroleum, a
nonrenewable resource, and do not break down in the environment. Many will
wind up in the ocean where they are deadly to marine animals. But paper bags
are costly too – it takes one 15-20-year-old tree to make 700 grocery bags. If your
purchase is small, don't take a bag at all – save the tree. Or bring a cloth bag with
you when you shop.

Recycle your glass and aluminum. Making new glass objects from recycled glass
takes up to 32% less energy than producing glass from new raw materials,
reducing related air pollution by 20% and water pollution by 50%. Glass that is
not recycled may take up to a thousand years to completely self-destruct.
Unrecycled aluminum will still be around 500 years from now, and if you throw
away two aluminum cans, you are tossing away more energy than is used daily by
each of a billion human beings in poorer countries. An aluminum can that is

recycled ordinarily appears back in the store in 6 weeks in its new form. And while you are at it, why not recycle your newspapers, too. If everyone recycled one-tenth of their newspapers, we would save about 25 million trees a year.

These facts come from the Earth Works Group. To find out more, look for the informative *50 Simple Things You Can Do To Save the Earth*, from the Earthworks Press in Berkeley, California.

The kitchen is a wonderful place to start any worthwhile endeavor, as the cooking-hearth was in many ways the beginning place of the race. In the pages that follow Mary Gubser invites you to return to the hearth, to the beginning, to a loaf of bread, to a simmering kettle of aromatic stew – finding there ancient pleasures and seasoned practices well-beloved of many, many generations, and, we hope, generations to come.

CAROL HARALSON

Quick
BREADS

The Delectable Muffin

B ite-size, medium-size or gargantuan, baked in classic tins or intriguing molds, hot homemade muffins add a special harmony to any meal. They are delicious plain or enriched with a hidden delight such as a bit of jam, a whole pecan, luscious fruits, spices, cheese or aromatic herbs. And what a pleasure occasionally to sit down in a simple restaurant to a basketful of assorted hot muffins! For muffins and other quick breads have been "rediscovered."

Although you can make good muffins with cold ingredients, ideally muffins should be made with ingredients at room temperature, especially at high altitudes. Bring eggs to room temperature by leaving them out of refrigeration for 15 minutes or by placing them in warm water. Flour from the freezer can be brought to room temperature in the oven, using the pilot light or a setting of 150°. Or place flour, eggs, and milk in the microwave at the lowest setting for a minute or less, *just* to take the chill off.

Quick breads do not belie their name; the more swiftly you mix, the better your muffins will be. To avoid too much beating, combine the dry ingredients in one bowl and the liquids in another, blending each very well. Make a well in the dry ingredients, add the liquid mixture and stir rapidly, using firm quick strokes, just until the flour mixture is moistened.

MUFFIN MAKING

1. Preheat the oven and coat a muffin pan with butter or vegetable spray.

2. Combine dry ingredients in one bowl and liquid ingredients in another.

3. Make a well in the dry ingredients and pour in the liquid ingredients.

4. Stir rapidly just until the dry ingredients are moistened.

5. Spoon the batter into the muffin cups, filling each three-quarters full.

6. Bake.

7. Enjoy!

MUFFIN TIPS

When there are empty muffin cups, fill each with one-fourth cup water to avoid burning the pan.

Remove muffins from the pan when they are cool enough to handle to prevent them from becoming soggy.

Freeze leftover muffins in heavy plastic containers for another meal. To reheat, place the frozen muffins on a small baking sheet in a preheated 350° oven, uncovered, for 20 minutes.

Leftover muffins are delicious split, toasted and buttered for breakfast.

Too much beating overdevelops the gluten in the flour, making it so strong the leavening agent cannot satisfactorily raise the batter. This is the cause of undesirable "tunnels" in muffins. Don't worry if the muffin batter looks lumpy — it should. Spoon the batter into prepared muffin pans and pop them into a preheated oven. If a spoon seems messy, try distributing the batter with a third-cup measure. Rapid action produces the perfect muffin.

Most muffins require a baking temperature of 400° to 450° in order to finish rising and to keep berries and nuts from sinking to the bottom. By the time the batter is mixed and in tins, the oven should be the correct temperature.

Recipes using white flour have been tested with all purpose flour available at any supermarket. My first choice is unbleached white flour, which is also easily attainable and can be used in the same proportions as all purpose flour. When baking with whole-grain flours, use the stone ground versions if possible. Find them in health food stores, the health food departments of supermarkets, or through Sources of Supply (page 276). Most recipes call for unsifted flour. If flour is to be sifted, the recipe will say so. Butter, vegetable shortening, and light oil all are acceptable and may be interchanged.

Any recipe using eggs and butter can be converted for low cholesterol and low sodium diets. Egg substitutes such as Fleischman's Egg Beaters are excellent. Just follow the directions on the box for amount per egg. Occasionally one-eighth to one-fourth cup of flour may need to be added if the batter seems too liquid. Or use just egg whites – I find them most successful. When two eggs are specified, use three to four egg whites as a substitute. Double acting baking powder and baking soda are the primary leavening agents for muffins. Low sodium baking powders are available in health food stores. If you are on a salt free diet, eliminate the salt or cut its measurement in half – this will not affect the final result.

Some muffins start with a special batter prepared as if for a cake, with butter and sugar creamed together and the remaining ingredients added gradually. Explicit directions will be given with these recipes. Standard muffin pans vary in size with cups measuring 2 ¼", 2 ½" or 3" in diameter. Most recipes will make twelve 2½" muffins, twenty-four petite ones (which measure 1" across) or eight Texas size. Texas-size cups are frequently made of paper and measure about 4" in diameter. Custard cups that flare slightly at the top are useful for larger muffins. I have used as my standard the 2½" muffin tin, as it seems to be the most obtainable. Paper cups are permissible but they do stick to muffins and must be placed in muffin cups to hold their shape. I prefer not to use them. Restaurants often use paper, mainly for convenience.

Techniques for making these little breads are delightfully easy and equipment is inexpensive. If you are a beginner, start with the Perfect Basic Muffin, trying different variations until you perfect your technique, and then you will be ready to bake any muffin that suits the menu or moment

A PERFECT BASIC MUFFIN

2 cups all purpose flour
3 teaspoons baking powder
3 tablespoons sugar
¾ teaspoon salt
2 large eggs, beaten
1 cup milk
¼ cup butter or margarine, melted

Preheat oven to 425°. Brush twelve 2½" muffin cups with melted butter or coat with vegetable spray. Combine the flour, baking powder, sugar and salt in a medium size mixing bowl, blending thoroughly. Beat eggs in a separate bowl and add the milk and butter. Make a well in the dry ingredients with a rubber spatula and pour in the milk mixture. Quickly stir several times just until the dry ingredients are thoroughly moistened. Batter will still be lumpy — and that is fine. Fill the prepared muffin cups three-fourths full. Bake immediately until a light golden color, about 20 minutes. Serve hot with butter and a favorite jam or preserves.

Variations on the Muffin Theme

Variations on the Perfect Basic Muffin are almost inexhaustible. Consider your favorite flavors, what will harmonize with the meal you are planning, or what you have on hand. Here are a few ideas...

RAISIN-LEMON MUFFINS: To the dry ingredients add ¾ cup currants or raisins that have been scalded with hot water and dried plus the grated rind of one lemon. Proceed as directed.

CHEDDAR CHEESE MUFFINS: Add ¾ cup grated Cheddar cheese to the dry ingredients. Follow directions for Perfect Basic Muffin.

CRYSTALLIZED GINGER MUFFINS: Chop ½ cup crystallized ginger and add to the dry ingredients. Follow directions as specified.

PECAN MUFFINS: Add ½ cup chopped pecans to the dry ingredients. Proceed as directed. Fill each muffin cup one-half full and place a whole pecan on top of each. Cover the pecans with the remaining batter. Bake as directed.

CINNAMON-BROWN SUGAR MUFFINS: Combine ½ cup brown sugar, packed, 1 teaspoon cinnamon and ½ cup chopped pecans or walnuts. Mix thoroughly. Fill each muffin cups one-third full and top with a sprinkling of the brown sugar mixture. Top each with the remaining batter and bake as directed. If brown sugar mixture is left, cover and refrigerate for future use.

SAUSAGE IN THE MUFFIN: Cook and drain 12 small smoky sausages. Fill each muffin cup one-third full of batter. Place a sausage on top of the batter in each cup and spoon remaining batter over to cover. Bake as directed.

BANANA MUFFINS

This baker's dozen of wonderfully moist banana muffins is transformed easily with added flavors. Be certain the bananas are very ripe.

2 cups all purpose flour
1 teaspoon baking soda
½ teaspoon salt
½ cup butter or margarine
1 cup sugar
3 large eggs
3 large, ripe bananas
½ cup coarsely chopped pecans or walnuts
½ cup raisins, rinsed in hot water and dried

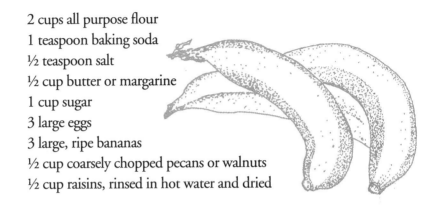

Preheat oven to 375°. Brush twelve muffin cups plus one custard cup or small ramekin with melted butter or coat with vegetable spray. Sift flour, baking soda and salt together and set aside. In the large mixing bowl of an electric mixer, cream the butter and sugar until light and fluffy. Add the eggs one at a time, beating well after each addition. Either throw the peeled bananas into a food processor and pulse several times or mash with a fork in a small bowl. Add to the batter, mixing well. Slowly blend in the dry ingredients until well mixed. Fold in the nuts and raisins. Fill muffin cups and ramekin three-fourths full. Bake approximately 20 to 25 minutes.

CINNAMON BANANA MUFFINS: Add 1½ teaspoons cinnamon to the dry ingredients. Proceed as directed. Mix ¼ teaspoon cinnamon with one tablespoon sugar. After the batter is placed in the muffin cups, sprinkle the cinnamon-sugar over tops of the muffins. Bake as directed.

WHOLE WHEAT-ORANGE BANANA MUFFINS: Substitute one cup whole wheat flour for one cup white flour. Add the grated rind of one large orange to the dry ingredients. Proceed as directed.

ORANGE STREUSEL MUFFINS

The true essence of orange was elusive, but after eight experiments I finally caught it in a muffin. This lovely muffin and its variations are delicious with a cup of hot tea.

2 cups all purpose flour
½ teaspoon salt
2 teaspoons baking powder
¼ cup sugar
Grated rind of 1 large orange
2 large eggs
½ cup orange juice
1 tablespoon lemon juice
½ cup milk
¼ cup butter or margarine, melted
  STREUSEL:
½ cup cold butter
½ cup all purpose flour
½ cup sugar
Grated rind of 1 large orange

Preheat oven to 425°. Brush twelve 2½" muffin cups with melted butter or coat with vegetable spray. Combine the flour, salt, baking powder, sugar and orange rind in a mixing bowl, blending thoroughly. In a separate bowl beat the eggs, orange juice and lemon juice together. Add to the dry ingredients with the milk and melted butter, stirring rapidly with a rubber spatula until just moistened. Fill each muffin cup three-fourths full. Top each muffin with about one tablespoon of streusel. Bake muffins 20 minutes until lightly golden.
STREUSEL: Place all ingredients for the streusel in a food processor and whirl until the butter is thoroughly cut into the dry ingredients. The remainder of the streusel may be placed in a covered container and frozen for future use.

Orange Streusel Muffin Variations

CRANBERRY-ORANGE MUFFINS: Whirl one cup fresh cranberries in a food processor or chop by hand and add to the dry ingredients for Orange-Streusel Muffins. Proceed as directed.

BLUEBERRY-ORANGE MUFFINS: Clean one cup fresh blueberries. Frozen blueberries may be used but extend the baking time by five to ten minutes. After the Orange Streusel Muffin batter is completed, fold in the blueberries. Proceed as directed.

DATE-ORANGE MUFFINS: With kitchen scissors snip one cup dates and add to the dry ingredients for Orange Streusel Muffins. Stir well and proceed as directed.

COCONUT-ORANGE MUFFINS: Measure one cup moist coconut and add to the dry ingredients for Orange-Streusel Muffins. Proceed with recipe as directed.

FRESH STRAWBERRY MUFFINS

Fresh strawberries and almonds combine to make an irresistible muffin. The recipe is also excellent with fresh raspberries. Almond Streusel may be added as a final embellishment.

1 cup chopped fresh strawberries
¾ cup plus 1 tablespoon sugar
2 cups all purpose flour
3 teaspoons baking powder
½ teaspoon salt
2 medium eggs
¼ cup butter or margarine, melted
¾ cup buttermilk
2 teaspoons lemon juice
½ cup coarsely chopped blanched almonds

Preheat oven to 400°. Brush twelve 2½" muffin cups with melted butter or coat with vegetable spray.

Sprinkle the one tablespoon of sugar over the strawberries and set aside. In a mixing bowl combine the flour, remaining sugar, baking powder and salt, blending well. Separately beat together the eggs, butter, buttermilk and lemon juice. Make a well in the dry ingredients and quickly stir in the liquid mixture until just moistened. Drain berries and fold into the batter with the almonds. Fill muffin cups three-fourths full. If desired, sprinkle tops of muffins with Almond Streusel. Bake 25 minutes.

ALMOND STREUSEL: Combine ¼ cup flour, ¼ cup sugar, ¼ cup cold butter and ¼ cup blanched almonds. Whirl in a food processor until well blended. Butter and almonds should be finely ground into the dry ingredients. This may be done by hand; chop the almonds finely and add to the remaining ingredients with a pastry blender.

APRICOT AND GRAND MARNIER MUFFINS

Apricots and Grand Marnier, an orange-flavored liqueur, give this muffin a sensual quality that is perfect for an intimate dinner before a crackling fire.

> 1 cup chopped dried apricots
> Boiling water
> 2 cups sifted all purpose flour
> 3 teaspoons baking powder
> ½ teaspoon salt
> ¼ teaspoon baking soda
> ½ cup sugar
> 2 large eggs, beaten
> 2 tablespoons Grand Marnier
> 1 cup sour cream

Preheat oven to 400°. Brush twelve 2½" muffin cups with melted butter or coat with vegetable spray. Place apricots in a small unbreakable bowl and cover with boiling water. Let sit for five minutes and drain. In a mixing bowl combine the flour, baking powder, salt, baking soda and sugar, stirring until well mixed. Add the drained apricots. In a separate bowl combine the eggs, Grand Marnier and sour cream, whisking until smooth. Make a well in the dry ingredients and stir in the sour cream mixture with a rubber spatula until just moistened. Spoon the batter into the muffin tins three-fourths full and bake approximately 20 minutes.

ORANGE CURRANT MUFFINS

Currants, nuts and fresh orange juice are a satisfying trio of flavorings for moist, luscious muffins. No jam or preserves are needed for these muffins and even butter may be foregone so they are just right for tea time.

> 2 cups all purpose flour
> ½ cup sugar
> 2 teaspoons baking powder
> ¼ teaspoon baking soda
> 1 cup orange juice, freshly squeezed or
>   made from frozen concentrate
> Grated rind of 1 large orange
> 3 tablespoons butter or margarine, melted
> 1 large egg
> ½ cup currants, scalded and dried
> ½ cup coarsely chopped walnuts or pecans

Preheat oven to 400°. Brush twelve 2½" muffin cups with melted butter or coat with vegetable spray. Combine the flour, sugar, baking powder and baking soda in a mixing bowl. Stir well to mix thoroughly. In a separate bowl beat the orange juice, grated rind, butter and egg together. Add the liquid ingredients to the dry mixture, stirring rapidly with a rubber spatula until just moistened. Fold in the currants and nuts. Fill each muffin cup three-fourths full and bake 20 minutes. Serve warm.

BLUEBERRY LEMON MUFFINS

Blueberries and lemons have an affinity that melds in a perfectly luscious muffin. Top with Lemon Streusel for extra zest and sweetness.

2 cups all purpose flour
⅓ cup sugar
3 teaspoons baking powder
½ teaspoon salt
Grated rind of 1 lemon
¾ cup milk
¼ cup butter or margarine, melted
2 large eggs
4 tablespoons lemon juice
1½ cups fresh or frozen blueberries

Preheat oven to 400°. Brush twelve 2½" muffin cups with melted butter or coat with vegetable spray. The recipe will also make 24 miniature muffins.

Combine the flour, sugar, baking powder, salt and lemon rind in a mixing bowl, stirring until well blended. In a separate bowl beat together the milk, butter, eggs and lemon juice. Sprinkle two teaspoons of flour over the berries and fold into the batter. Spoon the batter into the prepared muffin cups, filling three-fourths full. Top with Lemon Streusel if desired. Bake approximately 18 minutes. If berries were frozen, baking time will be several minutes longer. To make miniature muffins, fill cups almost full and bake about 15 minutes.

LEMON STREUSEL: In a food processor, combine ½ cup sugar, ½ cup all purpose flour, ½ cup cold butter, and the grated rind of 1 large lemon. Whirl until well mixed. Butter should be cut into the dry ingredients until it resembles coarse cornmeal. Or place all ingredients (first slicing the butter) in a bowl and blend with a pastry blender. Remaining streusel may be frozen for future use.

BRANDIED PEACH MUFFINS

This luxurious muffin is both luscious and gratifying even though a bit expensive. Brandied peaches are available in specialty stores and fine supermarkets. They are usually sold in beautifully packed glass jars. Save the juice for especially tasty yogurt or ice cream.

> One 18-ounce jar brandied peaches
> 1 large egg, beaten
> Grated rind of 1 large orange
> ¼ cup light oil
> 1 cup flour
> 1 cup rolled oats
> 2 teaspoons baking powder
> 1 teaspoon cinnamon
> ½ cup raisins, scalded and drained

Preheat oven to 400°. Coat twelve 2½" muffin cups with vegetable spray. Drain the peaches, reserving the juice for other uses. Chop the peaches on a board and set aside. Blend together the egg, grated rind and oil. In a large mixing bowl combine the flour, oats, sugar, baking powder and cinnamon and blend thoroughly. Make a well in the center and pour in the liquid ingredients. Mix quickly, just until the dry mixture is well moistened. Fold in the peaches and raisins. Using a fourth-cup measure fill the muffin cups three-fourths full. Bake 20 to 25 minutes. Serve warm or cold. As with other muffins, these will freeze if there are any left.

Brandied Peaches

To make this old-fashioned treat yourself, select firm, ripe peaches and weigh them. Wash them and rub off the fuzz. Put them in a syrup made of 1 cup sugar and 1 cup water per pound of peaches. Simmer 5 minutes. Drain and pack in sterile canning jars. Pour 4 tablespoons of brandy into each jar, then fill with hot syrup. Cover with new, clean two-part lids. Process 15 minutes in boiling water bath. Allow to mature for 3 months before using.

Making Applesauce

When good, tart apples such as Northern Spys, Russets or Granny Smiths are in season, make applesauce! Wash, quarter and core the apples, place them in a saucepan and cover with water. Simmer until tender, then put them through a food mill or ricer. Return the apple pulp to the saucepan, add sugar to taste (plus lemon juice or cinnamon if desired) and cook gently 3 minutes. Applesauce freezes beautifully.

APPLESAUCE MUFFINS

Homemade and canned applesauce work equally well in these moist muffins. They make a special after-school treat and are just right for those wonderful times when the grandchildren spend the night.

2 cups all purpose flour
3 teaspoons baking powder
1 teaspoon cinnamon
½ teaspoon nutmeg
½ teaspoon salt
½ cup brown sugar, packed
2 eggs, beaten
½ cup milk
¼ cup butter or margarine, melted
¾ cup applesauce
½ cup chopped pecans or walnuts

Preheat oven to 400°. Brush twelve 2½" muffin cups with melted butter or coat with vegetable spray. In a mixing bowl combine the flour, baking powder, cinnamon, nutmeg, salt and brown sugar. Stir until well blended. In a separate bowl mix the eggs, milk, butter and applesauce. Make a well in the dry ingredients and stir in the applesauce mixture with quick strokes just until well moistened. Fold in the nuts. Spoon the batter into the muffin cups, filling them three-fourths full. Bake 20 to 25 minutes.

CRANBERRY MUFFINS WITH MARMALADE

Fresh cranberries and a secret spot of marmalade — be certain to use sweet marmalade — will please guests for a Sunday morning brunch.

2 cups fresh cranberries, coarsely chopped
2 cups all purpose flour
½ cup sugar
3 teaspoons baking powder
½ teaspoon salt
2 eggs, beaten
1 cup milk
¼ cup butter or margarine, melted
Sweet orange marmalade

Preheat oven to 425°. Brush twelve 2½" muffin cups with melted butter or coat with vegetable spray.

Chop cranberries in a food processor or in a wooden bowl with a curved knife and set aside. In a mixing bowl blend the flour, sugar, baking powder and salt. In a separate bowl combine the eggs, milk and butter. With a rubber spatula quickly stir the liquid ingredients into the dry mixture with swift strokes. Fold in the cranberries until just blended. Fill each muffin cup one-half full of batter. Top with one tea-spoon of marmalade and cover each with the remaining batter. Bake 20 to 25 minutes. Serve hot.

Storing Cranberries

To have cranberries all year round, buy plenty of them when they are harvested in the fall and tuck them into heavy plastic freezer bags in the sacks in which they are purchased. Stored at 0°, they will keep nicely for a year.

CHRISTMAS CANDIED FRUIT MUFFINS

Christmas aroma floats through the house while these muffins bake.
Prepare them ahead to freeze and they will be ready for Christmas morning.
The recipe doubles easily for large gatherings.

2 cups all purpose flour
3 teaspoons baking powder
2 tablespoons sugar
½ teaspoon salt
¼ teaspoon cinnamon
¼ teaspoon nutmeg
1 cup chopped candied fruits
   (pineapple, orange and lemon rind)
¼ cup chopped candied red cherries
Grated rind of 1 large orange or lemon
2 medium eggs
1 cup milk
3 tablespoons butter or margarine, melted
Red candied cherries, cut in half for topping

Preheat oven to 425°. Brush twelve 2½" muffin cups with melted butter or coat with vegetable spray.

Sift flour, baking powder, sugar, salt, cinnamon and nutmeg into a mixing bowl. Add the candied fruits, the ¼ cup of red cherries and the grated rind, stirring to mix well. Separately combine the eggs, milk and butter, beating to blend well. Add the milk mixture to the flour mixture stirring just until well mixed. Fill muffin cups three-fourths full. Top each muffin with half a cherry and press down lightly. Bake 20 to 25 minutes until lightly golden. To defrost frozen muffins, place them in an ovenproof serving dish, cover with foil, and heat at 375° until defrosted and piping hot, about 25 minutes.

GINGERBREAD MUFFINS

Serve these aromatic muffins with Honey Butter (page 141) for a special treat.

3 cups sifted all purpose flour
1½ teaspoons baking soda
1 teaspoon cinnamon
¼ teaspoon allspice
1 teaspoon ginger
½ teaspoon salt
1 cup butter or margarine
½ cup brown sugar
2 medium eggs
¾ cup molasses
1 cup hot water

Preheat oven to 375°. Brush eighteen 2½" muffin cups with melted butter or coat with vegetable spray. Resift flour with baking soda, cinnamon, allspice, ginger and salt. Set aside. Cream the butter and brown sugar together in the large bowl of an electric mixer. Blend in the eggs and molasses. Add the flour mixture to the butter mixture until well mixed. Slowly add the hot water, stirring well. Spoon batter into prepared muffin cups, filling them two-thirds full. Bake approximately 25 minutes. These muffins are equally good hot or at room temperature.

The Aromatic Ginger Root

Ginger comes from the rhizome of Zingiber officinale, a native of India or Maylasia. Before the second century A.D. the Romans were importing large quantities of it over the Red Sea from India for cookery. The English have always savored it. Queen Elizabeth is credited with originating "Gingerbread Men" when she asked her cook to make the bread in the form of little portaits of her favorite retainers.

YOGURT MUFFINS

This wholesome muffin has just a hint of nutmeg.

¼ cup butter or margarine
¾ cup sugar
¼ teaspoon salt
½ teaspoon nutmeg
2 medium eggs
¾ cup plain yogurt
½ teaspoon baking soda
1⅓ cups all purpose flour
⅓ cup currants, scalded and dried

Preheat oven to 450°. Brush twelve 2½" muffin cups with melted butter or coat with vegetable spray. In a mixing bowl cream together the butter, sugar, salt and nutmeg until fluffy. Separately combine the eggs, yogurt, baking soda and flour, beating until smooth. Add the flour mixture to the butter mixture, stirring until just well moistened. Fold in the currants with quick strokes. Fill each muffin cup three-fourths full and bake 15 to 20 minutes. Bake petite muffins 15 minutes or until lightly golden.

Yogurt

Yogurt is milk fermented with a friendly bacteria. It originated thousands of years ago as a way of preserving milk. You can make your own yogurt by adding a package of yogurt culture (from a health food store) or a tablespoon of plain yogurt containing active cultures to a quart of milk in a clean, warm container. Cover the mixture and keep it at 110° F. for 8 to 12 hours using the pilot light of an oven or the heated containers of a special yogurt-making kit.

LEMON MUFFINS

Delicate and lightly flavored with fresh lemon, these muffins have the tender texture of cake.

1½ cups all purpose flour
2½ teaspoons baking powder
½ teaspoon salt
½ cup butter or margarine
½ cup sugar
3 egg yolks
4 tablespoons lemon juice
Grated rind of 1 lemon
3 egg whites
¼ cup sugar plus ½ teaspoon cinnamon

Preheat oven to 375°. Brush twelve 2½" muffin cups with melted butter or coat with vegetable spray. In a bowl combine the flour, baking powder and salt, blending well. Cream the butter and sugar in bowl of an electric mixer until light and fluffy. Add the egg yolks, stirring to mix well. Combine the lemon juice and grated rind, and add alternately to the butter mixture with the dry ingredients. Begin and end with the dry mixture. Beat the egg whites until softly stiff and fold into the muffin batter. Fill muffin cups three-fourths full and if desired sprinkle a little sugar mixed with cinnamon atop each muffin. Bake 20 minutes.

The Zest of Lemon

Lemon zest is the grated yellow outer rind of the lemon (do not grate the bitter white inner pith). Its essential oil evaporates quickly, so grate it at the last minute. To get more juice from lemons, soak them in hot water or heat them for a minute or less in the microwave, then roll them on a hard surface under the heel of your hand before cutting and squeezing.

TEA MUFFINS

These light, airy, melt-in-your mouth muffins may be baked in regular or miniature muffin tins for a party. Their texture is similar to that of a lovely cake and they are adaptable to several flavorings.

1 cup butter, room temperature
1 cup sugar
4 egg yolks
½ cup apricot nectar, pineapple juice or orange,
 lemon or lime juice
2 tablespoons Triple Sec liqueur
2 cups all purpose flour
2½ teaspoons baking powder
1 teaspoon salt
4 egg whites
¼ cup sugar
¼ teaspoon nutmeg

Preheat oven to 375°. Brush eighteen 2¼" muffin cups with melted butter or coat with vegetable spray.

Cream the butter and sugar together in a large bowl of an electric mixer. Add the egg yolks and blend well. Combine your choice of juice with the Triple Sec. Mix the flour, baking powder and salt together. Add the juice mixture alternately to the butter mixture with the dry ingredients, beginning and ending with the dry mixture. Beat the egg whites until softly stiff and fold into the muffin batter. Fill muffin cups two-thirds full, being certain to place three tablespoons of water in each empty muffin cup. Mix the ½ cup sugar with the ½ teaspoon nutmeg and sprinkle atop each muffin if desired (the topping is optional). Bake about 20 minutes. The recipe will make twice as many miniature muffins which will bake in about 15 minutes or until very lightly golden.

ORANGE-CHOCOLATE MUFFINS WITH ALMONDS

Indeed a sumptuous muffin, half orange and half chocolate, that certainly will charm any guest.

2 cups all purpose flour
½ cup sugar
3 teaspoons baking powder
½ teaspoon salt
¾ cup toasted, chopped blanched almonds
2 eggs, beaten
¾ cup orange juice
⅓ cup butter or margarine, melted
2 ounces semi-sweet chocolate, melted
Grated rind of 1 large orange

Preheat oven to 400°. Brush twelve 2½" muffin cups with melted butter or coat with vegetable spray.

In a mixing bowl combine the flour, sugar, baking powder and salt. Stir in the almonds, leaving ¼ cup to sprinkle over tops of muffins. Combine the eggs, orange juice and butter. Stir into the dry ingredients until just well mixed. Remove half the batter to a second bowl. To one-half the batter add the melted chocolate, mixing rapidly until smooth. To the other half of the batter add the grated orange rind, mixing well. Holding the muffin tin slightly tipped, spoon in the orange batter on one side of each muffin cup. Fill the other side with chocolate batter. By lightly touching the batter you can keep each under control — and they certainly do not have to be perfect. Sprinkle tops with remaining almonds. Bake muffins 20 minutes.

To toast almonds, spread the nuts in a cake tin and place them in a 300° oven. Toast about 15 minutes, stirring occasionally. Watch carefully to avoid burning.

PEANUT BUTTER AND GRAPE JELLY MUFFINS

Here are the children's favorites — peanut butter and grape jelly — all jumbled together. Use either chunky or creamy peanut butter.

2 cups sifted all purpose flour
2 tablespoon sugar
3 teaspoons baking powder
½ teaspoon salt
1 large egg
1 cup milk
¼ cup butter or margarine, melted
⅓ cup peanut butter
½ cup chopped peanuts (optional)
Grape jelly

Preheat oven to 400°. Brush twelve 2½" muffin cups with melted butter or coat with vegetable spray.

Combine the flour, sugar, baking powder and salt in a mixing bowl, stirring well. In a separate bowl, blend the egg, milk and butter. Using a rubber spatula, swiftly beat the liquid mixture into the dry ingredients just until moistened. Quickly beat in the peanut butter and peanuts if desired. If the children dislike the chopped peanuts, forget them. Fill each muffin cup one-half full. Top with one teaspoon of grape jelly and cover each with remaining batter. Bake muffins 20 to 25 minutes.

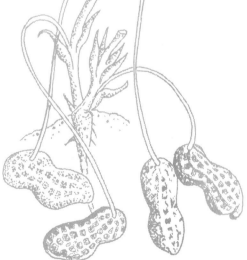

CHEDDAR CHEESE AND GARLIC MUFFINS

Rich with sharp Cheddar cheese and fragrant with garlic, these muffins are perfect for a backyard feast featuring barbecued ribs or chicken — and they are fun to make.

2 cups sifted all purpose flour
3 teaspoons baking powder
¼ teaspoon baking soda
½ teaspoon salt
2 tablespoons sugar
1 large egg
1 cup buttermilk
3 tablespoons light oil
1 cup sharp Cheddar cheese, coarsely grated
1 garlic clove, peeled and finely chopped
1 teaspoon chopped fresh or frozen chives

Preheat oven to 425°. Brush twelve 2½" muffin cups with melted butter or coat with vegetable spray.

In a mixing bowl combine the flour, baking powder, baking soda, salt and sugar blending well. In a separate bowl beat the egg, buttermilk and oil together. Add the liquid ingredients to the dry ingredients with light quick strokes. Fold in the cheese, garlic and chives. Fill muffin cups three-fourths full. Bake muffins 20 to 25 minutes. Serve piping hot.

The Inimitable Garlic

Garlic, or Allium sativum, is a member of the onion family, is so ancient that its origins are uncertain. It was known to the Chinese in 2000 B. C. and has been used both as medicine and food by them ever since. An inscription in an Egyptian pyramid states that the 100,000 workers who built it were fed on garlic, onions and leeks valued at 1,600 talents of silver – strong food! For those who enjoy it, garlic is the very soul of many aromatic dishes.

GREY POUPON MUFFINS

My neighbor walked across the yard to our picnic table, stood in an elegant pose and said, "You do have Grey Poupon Muffins, do you not? I caught a beautiful aroma and wondered if you could spare two?" "But, of course," I said, as nonchalant as possible in blue jeans, "take four!"

2 cups all purpose flour
3 teaspoons baking powder
½ teaspoon salt
2 eggs, beaten
1 cup milk
¼ cup butter or margarine, melted
1 tablespoon Grey Poupon Dijon Mustard or other prepared
     Dijon-style mustard, domestic or imported
½ cup finely chopped cooked ham

Preheat oven to 425°. Brush twelve 2½" muffin cups with melted butter or coat with vegetable spray. Combine the flour, baking powder and salt in a mixing bowl, blending well. In a separate bowl mix the eggs, milk and butter. Add the Grey Poupon mustard to the milk mixture and whisk with a fork until smooth. Make a well in the flour mixture and add the Grey Poupon mixture, stirring quickly with a rubber spatula until dry ingredients are moistened. Fold in the ham. (If the ham is salty, you may wish to omit the salt listed in the ingredients.) Fill the prepared muffin cups and bake about 20 minutes.

Dijon Mustard

Mustard is made from the seeds of two flowering plants, Brassica hirta and Brassica juncea. The most famous mustard producing area is Dijon, France. Dijon mustard from France is characteristically pastel in color and piquant in taste. Grey Poupon brand mustard is not made in France but is made in the style of Dijon mustards.

RO-TEL MUFFINS

A brash little muffin guaranteed to send top of head upwards!

2 medium eggs
1 cup buttermilk
1 cup Ro-Tel brand diced tomatoes and green chilies*
2 cups white cornmeal
1 teaspoon baking soda
¾ teaspoon salt

Preheat oven to 425°. Brush twelve 2½" muffin cups with melted butter or coat with vegetable spray. Combine and stir well the eggs, buttermilk and Ro-Tel brand tomatoes and green chilies. Set aside. In a separate mixing bowl blend the cornmeal, baking soda and salt. Make a well in the dry mixture and add the buttermilk mixture, stirring quickly with a rubber spatula just until moistened. Fill muffin cups three-fourths full and bake about 18 minutes. Serve piping hot with lots of fresh butter!

*Ro-Tel brand tomatoes and chilies are available in supermarkets, mainly in the Southwest.

Ro-Tel

Ro-Tel brand tomatoes and tomatoes with green chiles have been produced since the early 1940s in Donna, Texas using tomatoes from the Rio Grande Valley of Texas, jalapeño chiles from west Texas and Mexico, and spices. They are sold in most places in the country but are less available on the Northeast Coast. They are a quick spicy addition to many dishes, and a particular boon in mid-winter when good canned tomatoes may be preferable to the tough, flavorless ones available fresh in the supermarkets. If you cannot obtain them, you can flavor these muffins with chopped canned tomatoes plus chopped fresh or canned hot green chiles such as jalapeños, or the milder canned or fresh green chiles.

SPICY CORN MUFFINS

Highly aromatic Spicy Corn Muffins have the tang of the Southwest.

6 slices bacon
1 cup onion, finely chopped
1 cup all purpose flour
1 cup cornmeal
3 tablespoons sugar
3½ teaspoons baking powder
½ teaspoon salt
2 medium eggs
1 cup milk
3 tablespoons butter or margarine, melted
1¼ cups sharp Cheddar cheese, grated
¼ cup pickled jalapeño chilies

Preheat oven to 425°. Brush twelve 2½" muffin cups with melted butter or coat with vegetable spray.

Sauté the bacon until crisp and drain on paper towels. Pour off all but two tablespoons of the bacon grease and sauté the chopped onions until just limp, about five minutes. Break the bacon into small pieces and combine with the onions in a clean bowl.

Combine the flour, cornmeal, sugar, baking powder and salt in a mixing bowl blending well. Separately beat together the eggs, milk and butter. Add the milk mixture to the dry ingredients beating until just moistened. Stir in the bacon, onions, one cup of the cheese and the jalapeños. Fill muffin cups three-fourths full and top with the remaining cheese. Bake 20 minutes or until crusty brown.

CAJUN MUFFINS

Cajun muffins with bits of spicy sausage — guaranteed to cure anything!

2 cups all purpose flour
3 teaspoons baking powder
¼ teaspoon baking soda
2 tablespoons sugar
2 teaspoons Cajun seasoning*
1 large egg
1¼ cups buttermilk
3 tablespoons butter or margarine, melted
½ cup cooked sausage, cut in small pieces

Preheat oven to 425°. Brush twelve 2½" muffin cups with melted butter or coat with vegetable spray.

In a mixing bowl combine the flour, baking powder, baking soda, sugar and Cajun seasoning and blend very well. Separately stir together the egg, buttermilk and butter. Make a well in the dry ingredients and add the liquid mixture, stirring quickly with a rubber spatula. Fold in the sausage. Fill muffin cups three-fourths full and bake 20 minutes.

*There are several varieties of Cajun seasonings on the market, many of which are loaded with salt. I chose Chef Paul Prudhomme's Cajun Vegetable seasoning and was very pleased with the result. It lent just the right amount of spice to this muffin. No extra salt is needed since both the seasoning and the sausage add saltiness. This is a marvelous little muffin to have with scrambled eggs and broiled tomatoes for breakfast or a light supper.

WHOLE GRAIN MUFFINS: SPECIAL GOODNESS

The Origin of Wheat

The great glaciers of ice slowly receded as the last ice age ended. Mammoths roamed the forests where Paris now stands and warm winds blew in the Fertile Crescent that reached from northern Iran to Egypt, creating an ideal climate for wild grasses. In the land of the Kurds close to Iran two grasses, emmer and einkorn, began to take permanent root. Emmer was the stronger of the two. Gradually through thousands of years prehistoric people learned a primitive agriculture. When moving from winter caves to upland pastures they discovered that the previous year's refuse piles had sprouted. While the men hunted, women learned to plant the magical seeds of grass in holes made with a stick. The Neolithic traveler carried emmer seeds in pouches to middle and western Europe and as far as the British Isles.

Twelve thousand years ago rough cakes of bread were made of barley, millet and wheat baked on rocks. The Assyrians began to cluster around the Tigris and Euphrates rivers and slowly they learned to irrigate and to cultivate barley, millet and wheat. Each step took centuries, but slowly emmer was developed into wheat and civilization took a step forward, creating villages clustered close to the rivers. The men who crossed the Bering Straight had fire but no wheat. Through centuries of slow immigration they finally reached central California and here there is evidence they made a rough bread of grass seeds, cooked on rocks, similar to that of the Europeans. But their biggest discovery hundreds of years later was the tiny plant corn, in South America.

Four thousand years ago wheat had become the staple and economic mainstay of Egypt. The Pharaohs had conquered much of the Fertile Crescent feeding their soldiers well with bread and beer. The laborers who built the pyramids were paid in bread and beer. The tax system was based on wheat. Egyptians discovered that yeast spores would make dough rise and after thousands of years of unleavened bread rough with ground grasses, the risen loaf became known.

Millet, oats, barley, wheat, rye and rice fed the ancient world. It was prehistoric man's choice as to which of these grasses he liked the best and could grow best. Wheat and rye became the favorites for the fruit of these plants could withstand strong winds and other climatic extremes. In fact the fruit of wheat clung so strongly to the stalk that it could be removed only by shaking and trampling — so threshing was invented.

Of all the grains, only wheat and rye had gluten that would rise when it was mixed with yeast. From Egypt wheat was transported to the Roman Empire, where the strains of emmer were perfected even further and became the predominate grain of the Mediterranean world. Bread with wheat, one of humankind's first great chemical triumphs, is today still the most popular food of the western world.

Muffins made with whole grains and high protein flours have a sturdy texture and wonderfully earthy quality that makes them especially good with full-meal soups and stews. Try using stone ground flours for your whole-grain muffins — they will enhance the flavor as well as add ing a wholesome essence.

RAISIN BRAN MUFFINS

A classic muffin that has become a favorite with breakfast on a chilly morning or to accompany a cold supper in the summer. Choose crisp, flaky bran cereal for these muffins.

> 1¼ cups all purpose flour
> 1½ cups crisp dry ready-to-eat bran cereal
> 3 teaspoons baking powder
> ½ teaspoon salt
> ⅓ cup sugar
> 1 cup raisins, scalded and dried
> ½ cup coarsely chopped walnuts (optional)
> 2 medium eggs, beaten
> 1 cup milk
> ¼ cup butter or margarine, melted

Preheat oven to 425°. Brush twelve 2½" muffin cups with melted butter or coat with vegetable spray. Combine the flour, cereal, baking powder, salt and sugar. As the cereal is added, crush lightly with your hands. Mix well and stir in the raisins and nuts, if desired. In a separate bowl combine the eggs, milk and butter. Make a well in the dry ingredients, add the liquid mixture and stir quickly with a rubber spatula until just moistened. Do not mind a lumpy batter. Fill the muffin cups three-fourths full using a spoon or third-cup measure. Bake in a preheated oven 20 to 25 minutes or until golden in color. Serve hot. If there are leftover muffins, split, brush with melted butter and toast for breakfast — they are delicious without any addition of jam or jelly.

QUINOA MUFFINS

Quinoa (pronounced keen-wa) has a greater abundance of protein than any other grain, as well as a complement of essential amino acids that is close to ideal. Grown by the Incas hundreds of years ago in the Andes, the grain flourishes at 12,500 feet. When the Spanish arrived among the Incas quinoa was revered as "the mother grain." But after a disagreement with the Indians, the European intruders forbade them to eat quinoa. The grain almost disappeared and was unknown to North Americans until recently. Quinoa is now available in health food stores and mills and in some supermarkets (see Sources of Supply). For this muffin, I toasted the quinoa lightly, which makes the crust of the muffin crunchy and crisp while the inside is quite moist. I designed it with simple ingredients so that the true grain flavor would predominate. Quinoa is also delicious just boiled in chicken broth with a bit of butter.

> 1 cup all purpose flour
> 1 cup stone ground whole wheat flour
> ½ teaspoon salt
> 3 teaspoons baking powder
> ¼ teaspoon baking soda
> 1 cup toasted quinoa
> 1¼ cups buttermilk
> ¼ cup butter or margarine, melted
> 3 tablespoons honey
> 2 eggs

Preheat oven to 425°. Coat twelve 2½" muffin cups plus one custard cup with vegetable spray.In a mixing bowl combine the two flours, salt, baking powder and baking soda, blending well. Heat a heavy dry skillet (do not add butter or oil) and add half the quinoa. Stir and toast the grain briefly. It will begin to turn golden and have a marvelous aroma. Repeat with the remaining quinoa. Stir quinoa into the dry ingredients. In a separate bowl, beat together the buttermilk, butter, honey and eggs. Make a well in the dry mixture and quickly stir in the liquids just until dry ingredients are moistened. Fill the muffin cups and custard cup three-fourths full. Bake 25 to 30 minutes.

OATMEAL-CURRANT MUFFINS

1 cup all purpose flour
¼ cup brown sugar
3 teaspoons baking powder
½ teaspoon salt
1 cup old fashioned rolled oats
1½ cups milk
1 cup dried currants, scalded, drained and dried
3 tablespoons butter or margarine, melted
1 egg, beaten

Preheat oven to 425°. Brush twelve 2½" muffin cups with melted butter or coat with vegetable spray.

Combine the flour, sugar, baking powder and salt in a mixing bowl. In a saucepan stir the oats and milk over medium heat until the mixture is warm. Remove from the burner and add the currants, butter, and egg, blending well. Add the liquid mixture to the dry ingredients, stirring quickly with a rubber spatula. Fill muffin cups three-fourths full. Bake 20 minutes or until a light golden color. Serve piping hot.

Currants

The currant, which grows on a handsome bushy shrub, was probably first cultivated before 1600 in Denmark. It seem to have first appeared in England in Elizabethan times and about the same time in France. The English love currants, especially the black ones, too bitter to eat fresh but prized for jams and jellies. There are over 100 species of currants but few are grown in the United States because, oddly, the currant bush serves as a host to a parasitic fungus that doesn't harm the currant but is fatal to white pine trees. If you can get fresh currants, their tart, flavorful acidity should be greatly savored. Dried currants are more available than fresh.

CRUNCHY MILLET MUFFINS

If you've never had the pleasure of using whole millet, do try this recipe for it is pleasingly crunchy and filled with protein. Serve Crunchy Millet Muffins hot with honey butter — equal parts of soft butter and honey whisked together in a bowl.

1 cup all purpose flour
1 cup whole wheat flour
3 teaspoons baking powder
½ teaspoon salt
½ cup whole millet*
1 cup milk
¼ cup honey
⅓ cup butter or margarine, melted
2 medium eggs, beaten lightly

Preheat oven to 400°. Brush twelve 2½" muffin cups with melted butter or coat with vegetable spray.

Combine the flours, baking powder, salt and millet in a mixing bowl. In a separate bowl blend the milk with the honey, butter and eggs. With a rubber spatula stir the liquid mixture into the dry ingredients until just well moistened. Fill the muffin cups three-fourths full. Bake 20 to 25 minutes.

*Whole millet may be purchased in health food departments of supermarkets or in health food stores.

WHEAT GERM MOLASSES MUFFINS

An unusually savory muffin redolent with the flavor of molasses. If molasses is a bit too pungent for your taste, substitute honey.

1¾ cups sifted all purpose flour
1 cup toasted wheat germ
2 tablespoons sugar
1 teaspoon salt
1 teaspoon baking powder
½ teaspoon baking soda
½ teaspoon cinnamon
1 egg, beaten
1 cup milk
½ cup molasses
¼ cup light oil

Preheat oven to 400°. Brush twelve 2½" muffin cups with melted butter or coat with vegetable spray.

Combine the dry ingredients in a mixing bowl, blending well. In another bowl stir together the egg, milk, molasses and oil. Add to the dry ingredients stirring with a rubber spatula until the mixture is well moistened. Fill each cup three-fourths full. Bake 20 minutes. Try these muffins with apple butter!

Molasses

Molasses is a liquid byproduct of sugar manufacturing. If it comes from the first boiling, it is light molasses, if from the second boiling, it is dark molasses. Blackstrap molasses, the strongest in flavor, comes from the third boiling.

RYE MUFFINS

For centuries coarse rye bread was the main sustenance of peasants in Europe and Russia. During early colonial days rye immigrated to America where it grew better on the rocky ground of New England than did wheat. Certain flavors have an affinity with rye and one of my favorites is grated orange rind. Try these muffins for breakfast with orange marmalade.

1 cup rye flour
1 cup whole wheat flour
½ teaspoon salt
4 teaspoons baking powder
¼ cup brown sugar
Grated rind of 1 orange
½ cup each of raisins and walnuts
2 eggs, lightly beaten
1 cup milk
¼ cup butter or margarine, melted

Preheat oven to 425°. Brush twelve 2½" muffin cups with melted butter or coat with vegetable spray.

In a mixing bowl combine the rye and whole wheat flours with the salt, baking powder, sugar, grated rind, raisins and nuts. In a separate bowl blend the eggs, milk and butter. Add the liquid mixture to the dry ingredients, stirring rapidly with a rubber spatula until just moistened. Fill the muffin cups three-fourths full. Bake 20 to 25 minutes or until a golden brown.

WHOLE WHEAT MUFFINS

A simple, wholesome muffin using only whole wheat flour that is easy to prepare. It is tastier if made with stone ground whole wheat flour.

1¾ cups whole wheat flour
3 teaspoons baking powder
¼ teaspoon baking soda
¼ cup honey, molasses or brown sugar
½ teaspoon salt
1 large egg, beaten
1½ cups buttermilk
¼ cup light oil

Preheat oven to 425°. Brush twelve 2½" muffin cups with melted butter or coat with vegetable spray.

If using brown sugar, blend the sugar with the flour, baking powder, baking soda and salt. If honey or molasses is used, mix with the egg, buttermilk and oil. Blend the dry ingredients in a separate bowl. Pour the liquid ingredients into the dry mixture, stirring quickly with a rubber spatula. Fill the muffin cups three-fourths full. Bake muffins 20 to 25 minutes; they will be dark golden when done.

NOTE: ½ cup coarsely chopped walnuts or ½ cup raisins may be stirred into the dry ingredients. Proceed as directed.

GOLDEN CORN MUFFINS

This classic muffin may be found in all regions of the country but particularly in the New England states where pioneers first learned to cook with cornmeal. Such cornbread has been a staple for 300 years. In the early days it was made with honey or maple syrup, the only available sweeteners.

1½ cups all purpose flour
2 teaspoons baking powder
¼ teaspoon baking soda
4 tablespoons sugar
1 cup yellow cornmeal
1½ cups buttermilk
1 egg, beaten
¼ cup butter or margarine, melted

Preheat oven to 425°. Brush twelve 2½" muffin cups with melted butter or coat with vegetable spray.

Combine the flour, baking powder, baking soda, sugar and cornmeal in a mixing bowl, blending well. In a separate bowl stir the buttermilk, egg and butter together. Make a well in the dry ingredients and pour in the liquid mixture. Stir quickly with a rubber spatula just until the dry ingredients are moistened. Fill muffin cups three-fourths full. Bake 20 to 25 minutes or until a lovely yellow golden color. Serve hot with your favorite preserves.

FOR CORNBREAD STICKS: Prepare heavy iron bread stick molds by placing ¼ to ½ teaspoon vegetable shortening in each groove. Place molds in a preheated 425° oven until piping hot. Fill each groove with batter and return immediately to the oven. Bake about 20 minutes or until crispy and lightly browned on the edges. The recipe will make 15 to 18 sticks but if you have only one mold such as mine with nine grooves, bake the remaining batter into muffins — or buy another corn stick pan! Bake muffins as directed in the original recipe.

Some Variations
on the Beautiful Golden Corn Muffin:

CORN MUFFINS WITH BLUEBERRIES: Clean and dry one cup fresh blueberries. (Frozen blueberries work well but if you use them, allow 5 minutes extra baking time.) After the batter has been stirred, fold in the blueberries quickly. Bake as directed. Makes twelve 2½" muffins or twenty-four miniature muffins. Blueberries can also be added to cornbread sticks.

CORN MUFFINS WITH CRANBERRIES: Rinse and blot dry one cup fresh cranberries, then whirl in a food processor and add to the batter as described with the blueberry muffins. Bake as directed. Try serving these with sweet marmalade — delicious!

CORN MUFFINS WITH BACON AND PEPPER: These are especially good with barbecue, beef stew or bean soup. Sauté four slices of bacon until crisp. Drain on paper towels. When cool, crumble into pieces. When combining the dry ingredients eliminate two tablespoons of the sugar and add 3 to 6 tablespoons freshly ground black pepper. Prepare the batter as directed and fold in the crumbled bacon. Bake at 425° for 20 to 25 minutes.

CORN MUFFINS WITH BACON AND CHEDDAR CHEESE: Sauté four slices of bacon until crisp, drain on paper towels and crumble when cool. Add to the liquid ingredients of the Golden Corn Muffin recipe. Grate one cup of sharp Cheddar cheese and add to the dry ingredients. Prepare and bake as directed.

MOLASSES OR MAPLE SYRUP CORN MUFFINS: Add ¼ cup molasses or maple syrup to the liquid ingredients, eliminating two tablespoons of the sugar. Add ¼ cup more all purpose flour to the dry ingredients. Follow directions as directed.

All variations make twelve 2½" muffins.

HIGH PROTEIN CORN MUFFINS

From Arrowhead Mills in Hereford, Texas comes an unusually high protein muffin. Almonds and apples give a delicious and sophisticated flavor.

1 cup Arrowhead Mills High-Lysine Cornmeal*
1 cup whole wheat flour
4 teaspoons baking powder
½ teaspoon salt
2 eggs, beaten
1 cup buttermilk
3 tablespoons honey
3 tablespoons light oil
½ teaspoon almond extract
1 large tart apple (Granny Smith), peeled, cored and grated
½ cup sliced almonds

Preheat oven to 400°. Brush twelve 2½" muffin cups with melted butter or coat with vegetable spray.

Combine the cornmeal, flour, baking powder and salt together blending well. Beat eggs, buttermilk, honey, oil and almond flavoring in a separate bowl and stir in the grated apple. Make a well in the dry mixture and add the liquid ingredients, stirring with a rubber spatula until well moistened. Fill the muffin cups three-fourths full. Sprinkle with almonds on top of each muffin, pressing them into the batter so they will adhere. Bake 20 to 25 minutes.

*High-lysine cornmeal, developed by Purdue University, contains 70% more amino acid than regular cornmeal and has a nutty, naturally sweet flavor and crunchy texture. Look for it in health food stores and in the health food departments of supermarkets.

ARROWHEAD OAT BRAN MUFFINS

With the exciting discovery that the bran, or outer layer, of oats may help lower serum cholesterol, this ancient grain has come into its own and every bakery and cereal manufacturer extols its glories. I am most grateful to Arrowhead Mills for permission to use the following excellent recipe. I will give you the original recipe and then show how to change ingredients to lessen cholesterol content even more.

2½ cups oat bran
2 cups milk
2 eggs
¼ cup light oil
¾ cup honey
2½ teaspoons Arrowhead Mills Ezekiel flour*
½ cup unbleached white flour
2½ tablespoons baking powder
1 teaspoon salt (optional)
1 teaspoon cinnamon
1 cup raisins, scalded, dried and coarsely chopped
¾ cup walnuts or pecans, chopped

Preheat oven to 400°. Coat 18 to 20 2½" muffin cups with melted butter or vegetable spray. Whirl the oat bran in a food processor for two minutes to make the bran finer. Place the bran in a mixing bowl and combine with the milk, eggs, oil and honey. Stir very well. To the food processor add the two flours, baking powder, optional salt, cinnamon, raisins and nuts. Pulsate several times until the raisins are coarsely chopped and ingredients well mixed. Add the dry mixture to the oat bran mixture, stirring rapidly until thoroughly blended. Allow mixture to rest for five minutes — it will begin to bubble and become thicker. Fill each cup three-fourths full. Bake muffins about 18 minutes or until they begin to brown lightly. Although these are not high-rising muffins, they are quite moist and their texture is delightful.

*Ezekiel flour, available in health food stores, is a mixture of wheat, barley, beans, millet, lentil and spelt, a form of wheat.

Oat Bran Muffin Variations

Low-Fat, Cholesterol-Free Muffins

Substitute three egg whites for the two eggs in the Arrowhead Oat Bran Muffin recipe. Substitute ¼ cup soy or millet flour for the white flour and eliminate the Ezekiel flour. Instead of whole milk, try using skim milk. Start the day with one of these muffins and a bowl of fresh fruit. Not only a delectable breakfast but one that has staying power until the next meal.

Sugar Free Oat Bran Muffins

Eliminate the honey in the Arrowhead Oat Bran Muffin recipe. Use two cups of orange juice in place of the milk and substitute three egg whites for the whole eggs. One of the purposes of eggs is to bind ingredients together and certainly egg whites alone will accomplish this purpose. When the flour, baking powder, cinnamon, nuts and raisins are placed in the food processor as directed, add three ripe bananas and whirl all together. Add this mixture to the oat bran/orange juice mixture and stir very well. Let sit five minutes and proceed as directed.

WHOLE WHEAT DATE MUFFINS

An irresistibly appetizing muffin for breakfast on a cold winter's morning.

> 1 cup sifted all purpose flour
> 3 teaspoons baking powder
> ¼ teaspoon baking soda
> ½ teaspoon salt
> 1 cup whole wheat flour
> 1 cup chopped pitted dates
> 2 medium eggs
> 2 tablespoons milk
> 1 cup sour cream
> ⅓ cup brown sugar, packed

Preheat oven to 400°. Brush twelve 2½" muffin cups with melted butter or coat with vegetable spray.

Combine the white flour, baking powder, baking soda, salt and whole wheat flour in a mixing bowl stirring to mix well. Add the dates, blending thoroughly. In a separate bowl combine the eggs and milk, beating until well mixed. Add the sour cream and brown sugar; continue to beat, preferably with a whisk, until the sugar is incorporated. Stir the liquid mixture into the dry ingredients just until well moistened. Spoon the batter into muffin cups three-fourths full. Bake in preheated oven 20 to 25 minutes.

Phoenix dactylifera – The Date

Dates are an essential of life in the arid regions of the Middle East and North Africa. The hardy date palm survives with little water and yields a concentrated food that can be eaten fresh or dried. It also gives desert-dwellers a source of fiber for baskets, mats, and ropes, and a lovely cooling shade in an otherwise sunbaked environment. The fresh date harvest occurs from late summer to mid-fall, but dried dates are generally obtainable all the year long.

GREAT GRAINS MUFFINS

Alvin Rustebakke, a grain merchant in Scobey, Montana, grinds some of the finest flours available. Through Alvin I have obtained the recipe for this wonderful classic bran muffin whose batter may be tucked in your refrigerator to be used when needed. Stone ground whole wheat flour is used in abundance.

2 cups boiling water
2 cups wheat bran
5 cups stone ground whole wheat flour
1 tablespoon salt
5 teaspoons baking soda
1 cup butter or margarine
1 cup brown sugar, packed
4 large eggs
4 cups buttermilk
1½ cups chopped dates, pecan or walnuts (optional)

Pour boiling water over the wheat bran in a mixing bowl and set aside to cool while preparing remaining ingredients.

In a large mixing bowl combine the flour, salt and baking soda, blending very well. Set aside. Cream the butter and sugar together in the bowl of an electric mixer until light and fluffy. Add the eggs one at a time to the butter-sugar mixture, beating well after each addition. Stir in the dry ingredients alternately with the buttermilk. Last, add the soaked bran and stir until thoroughly mixed.

The batter may now be stored in a covered container in a refrigerator for about ten days. The total recipe will make five to six dozen 2½" muffins. When preparing twelve muffins remove sufficient batter (about three cups) and add the optional dates or nuts. The muffins are excellent just plain and make marvelous miniature breads. Preheat oven to 350° and bake muffins 20 to 25 minutes. If the batter is cold, the baking time will be longer.

KANSAS CRACKED WHEAT MUFFINS

Kansas leads the nation in production of fine wheat. Working with Sharon Davis of the Kansas Wheat Commission, I had the opportunity to test recipes with freshly ground wheat. Sharon graciously gave me permission to use this excellent cracked wheat muffin recipe.

1 cup cracked wheat
1½ cups hot milk
1 large egg
¼ cup butter or margarine, melted
¼ cup honey, molasses or brown sugar
¾ cup all purpose flour
½ cup whole wheat flour
3 teaspoons baking powder
½ teaspoon salt

Preheat oven to 400°. Brush twelve 2½" muffin cups with melted butter or coat with vegetable spray.

Combine the cracked wheat and hot milk in a small bowl and stir well. Set aside to cool. In a bowl beat the egg, butter and honey together. In a large mixing bowl combine the two flours, baking powder and salt, blending well. Add the egg mixture to the cracked wheat mixture, stirring to mix well. Make a well in the dry ingredients and quickly stir in the cracked wheat mixture just until dry ingredients are moistened. Fill muffin cups three-fourths full and bake approximately 20 minutes. These muffins are excellent hot out of the oven or cooled, split, toasted and spread with orange marmalade for breakfast.

Cornbread & Spoon Bread

*O*n the slopes of the high Andes Mountains in South America, a tiny pod appeared many thousands of years ago. No one knows the origin of this miraculous little plant but the prehistoric Incas discovered its usefulness and gradually nurtured it into prolific growth. By the time the Spanish arrived the pod was highly developed agriculturally and was cultivated with the help of an ingenious and elaborate irrigation system that conducted water hundreds of miles from the mountains to the arid regions bordering the Pacific ocean.

This tiny pod was the beginning of corn. Totally dependent on man to propagate and flourish, corn can be devastated by weeds and lack of nourishment if left alone. Corn spread slowly as single villages grew it, saved its seeds, and passed them on to the next village, creating a delayed evolution with no predictable pattern. Through this slow process corn gradually migrated through South and Central America, then to Mexico and into North America. Thousands of years passed before corn reached the area of New England but the grain was there and developed when the Pilgrims landed in the New World. Research shows that Indians of both North and South America knew how to produce breads, puddings, popped corn, hominy, grits — the only idea we have added is ironing out cornflakes! Over hundreds of years Indians learned to enrich the soil;

MAKING CORNBREAD

1. Preheat the oven.

2. Butter, oil or spray with vegetable spray a baking pan or cornbread mold.

3. Mix dry ingredients together in one bowl and liquids in another.

4. Pour liquid ingredients into dry ingredients and mix together very quickly, just until dry ingredients are moistened.

5. Spoon cornbread batter into prepared pan.

6. Bake until golden.

the Incas with bat manure, the New England Indians with fish. Every American child knows the story of how Indians taught the Puritans to plant corn, a grain strange to the Europeans. However, adjusting to this golden grain did not take long. Settlers soon understood its nourishing and hardy properties and corn became integral to American life.

With the exception of elegant spoon breads, fast mixing is the key to excellent cornbreads. Dry ingredients are mixed together in one bowl; liquids in a second. The two are combined with a few quick strokes and immediately poured into a prepared pan. Cornbread is usually baked in a very hot oven.

Spoon breads should be called soufflés for they are light and airy and are mixed and baked quite differently from regular cornbread. Cornmeal for spoon breads is usually cooked in milk or water until thick, then mixed with eggs, a leavening agent and more liquids. Delicate, quivery spoon breads are a charming favorite for special meals.

Both commercial and stone ground cornmeal are available in supermarkets and health food stores. When traveling by car, stop in at old mills and purchase excellent stone ground grains of all kinds. Look for these mills in areas where there are swift streams, for the settlers who established them were dependent upon water power to turn the wood paddle wheel that drove the heavy round millstone. Visiting a traditional mill is a fascinating adventure into the past. At such mills you can usually purchase cornmeal ground from whole corn with nothing deleted and no preservatives added. Stone ground and commercial cornmeal are interchangeable in recipes but stone ground cornmeal imparts exceptionally fine flavor.

White cornmeal seems to be preferred by many cooks in the southern states where recipes have been handed down since the colonial era. My mother made hot water cornbread only with white cornmeal; in all other breads yellow corn-meal was used. The only explanation given me was that the breads had been taught by her mother and grandmother in east Texas. And frankly I cannot imagine enjoying a yellow hot water cornbread. It just isn't done!

The following cornbreads use both sweet milk and buttermilk with leaven-ing agents to match. If the recipe includes buttermilk, baking soda will be added along with baking powder. Dry buttermilk is acceptable; reconstitute according to the directions on the box. Butter, margarine or light oil can be used. Most cornbreads incorporate eggs but if you are seriously concerned about cholesterol, use an egg substitute or egg whites. Cornbreads baked in a heavy iron skillet will have a marvelous crunchy crust on the bottom. I prefer soufflé bowls for the spoon breads, and sturdy baking pans for regular breads and muffins. Recipes will designate exact sizes. If baking in glass, remember to reduce the heat by twenty-five degrees.

BUTTERMILK CORNBREAD

Here are recipes for both buttermilk and sweet milk cornbread with variations that are interchangeable between the two. Each has its own wonderful flavor. Buttermilk imparts a delightfully moist texture and special lightness.

¾ cup cornmeal
¾ cup all purpose flour
½ teaspoon baking soda
2 teaspoons baking powder
3 tablespoons sugar
¾ teaspoon salt
2 large eggs, lightly beaten
1½ cups buttermilk
¼ cup butter or margarine, melted

Preheat oven to 450°. Brush an 8" square baking pan with melted butter or coat with vegetable spray.

Combine the cornmeal, flour, baking soda, baking powder, sugar and salt in a mixing bowl. Blend very well with a rubber spatula. In a separate bowl mix the eggs, buttermilk and butter. Pour the liquid into the dry ingredients, stirring quickly until just moistened. Spread the butter evenly in a prepared pan. Bake 25 to 30 minutes or until golden with touches of brown. Serves six.

SWEET MILK CORNBREAD

Buttermilk is not always available in some areas; the following excellent recipe can be used with skimmed, reconstituted powdered low-fat or whole milk.

1 cup all purpose flour
1 cup cornmeal
3 teaspoons baking powder
2 tablespoons sugar
¾ teaspoon salt
2 eggs, lightly beaten
1 cup milk
¼ cup butter or margarine, melted

Preheat oven to 450°. Brush an 8" square baking pan with melted butter or coat with vegetable spray.

Combine the flour, cornmeal, baking powder, sugar and salt in a mixing bowl, blending well. In a separate bowl stir together the eggs, milk and butter. Combine the two mixtures with rapid strokes to just moisten the dry ingredients. Pour the batter into the prepared pan and smooth evenly. Bake 20 to 25 minutes or until golden in color. If baking in glass reduce heat to 425°. Serves 6.

Cornbread Variations

Spider Cornbread

In the early days of our country cornbread was often baked in a heavy skillet with legs that resembled those of a spider. The skillet could be set in the big kitchen fireplace and the bread cooked quickly. Try Buttermilk Cornbread or Sweet Milk Cornbread in a heavy iron skillet. Thoroughly rub the inside of the skillet with vegetable shortening and pop it into an oven preheated to 450°. When it is smoking hot, remove from the oven and fill immediately with batter. Return to the oven and bake 20 minutes at 450°. The bread will be quite crusty and brown on the bottom. Serve in pie-shaped wedges. Serves six to eight.

Blueberry Cornbread

When fresh blueberries arrive during June and July, add 1½ cups, carefully cleaned of stems and leaves, to either of the above finished cornbread batters. Do not wash the berries for they should be thoroughly dry when added to a cornbread mixture. Fold the berries carefully until well distributed and transfer the batter to the prepared pan. Bake as directed. Frozen berries may be used but baking time will be approximately 10 minutes longer.

Designer Muffins and Cornbread Sticks

Available in kitchen stores are charming heavy cast iron muffin pans with cups shaped like leaves, fruits — or even dinosaurs! Spray inside and around the edges of each cup with vegetable spray and use either recipe for cornbread. One-half the recipe will make the muffins and the remaining batter may be poured into a prepared cornstick pan. Bake 15 to 20 minutes. Both the muffins and sticks will be quite brown and crispy on the undersides. Buttermilk Cornbread and Sweet Milk Cornbread recipes each make 8 designer muffins plus 9 cornbread sticks.

HOT WATER CORNBREAD

The hot water cornbread I had as a child was made simply with white cornmeal, boiling water, and salt for that was the way my grandmother prepared it on her east Texas farm. I've added eggs and baking powder — the result is easy and delicious and very much like a hush puppy.

1 cup white cornmeal
1 teaspoon salt
3 teaspoons baking powder
¾ cup boiling water
2 large eggs, beaten
¾ cup corn oil

Preheat oven to 450°. The bread may be cooked in either a heavy iron skillet or baking pan.

Combine the cornmeal, salt and baking powder, stirring to mix. Add the boiling water and whisk until smooth. Whisk in the beaten eggs. Pour the corn oil into the skillet and place in hot oven. When the oil is quite hot, but not smoking, remove the skillet and spoon in the cornmeal batter by large tablespoons. The batter will make 11 to 12 pones. When the batter is placed in the oil, it should sizzle — if not the oil is not hot enough. Place back in oven and bake 10 to 15 minutes. The breads will be crispy and crunchy on the outside and soft on the inside. Serve very hot.

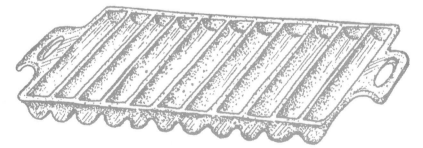

WAR EAGLE HUSH PUPPIES

These are marvelous hush puppies, especially if made with Zoe Medlin's stone ground cornmeal (refer to Sources of Supply). I've heard the origin of Hush Puppies so many times that it must be true. Hunters in the South always had dogs and when they whined while dinner was cooking over an open fire, the men rolled up bits of cornbread, fried them quickly and threw them to the dogs yelling, "Hush puppies!"

½ cup onion, finely chopped
1 clove garlic, peeled and minced
2 cups stone ground cornmeal
¾ cup all purpose flour
2 teaspoons baking powder
1 teaspoon salt
2 tablespoons sugar
1 large egg
1 cup milk

The ingredients may be stirred together in a mixing bowl and fried in deep fat but I've simplified the mixing and cooking method.

Place the onion and garlic in a food processor and pulsate until finely chopped. Separately mix the cornmeal, flour, baking powder, salt and sugar together. Add to the chopped onion mixture with the egg and milk. Whirl until the mixture is smooth. If the batter is too loose add a bit more flour to thicken.

Heat ¼ to ½ inch of corn oil in a heavy skillet until quite hot. Drop a tiny piece of batter into the oil and if it sizzles, the heat is correct. Dip into the batter with a tablespoon — make it heaping — and drop the batter into the hot oil. If the hush puppies brown too quickly, turn the heat down. Fry until crispy brown on one side and turn over a spatula to the other. Drain on paper towels and serve hot. Makes about 24 hush puppies.

CORN STICKS

Crispy outside and moist inside, these cornsticks have a double corn flavor. No butter is necessary for they are delicious alone.

1¼ cups all purpose flour
¾ cup cornmeal
2 teaspoons baking powder
½ teaspoon salt
2 tablespoons sugar
1 large egg
⅔ cup canned cream style corn
1 cup milk
2 tablespoons butter or margarine, melted

Preheat oven to 425°. The recipe will make 12 cornbread sticks. Place about one scant teaspoon of corn oil or vegetable shortening in each groove of a cornstick pan. Heat the pan in the oven until quite hot but not smoking.

Combine the flour, cornmeal, baking powder, salt and sugar in a mixing bowl, blending well. Separately beat the egg, canned corn, milk and butter together. Make a well in the dry ingredients and with a rubber spatula stir the milk mixture quickly into the dry mixture until well moistened. Remove hot pan from oven and fill each groove with batter. Bake 20 minutes until crispy golden brown.

BUTTERMILK KERNEL CORNBREAD

The combination of cornmeal and whole kernels of corn gives a doubly hearty flavor to this wonderful golden grain bread. The bread is delightful alone or accompanying a main entree such as sautéed chicken smothered in mushrooms.

¾ cup cornmeal
¾ cup all purpose flour
2 teaspoons baking powder
½ teaspoon baking soda
1 tablespoon sugar
1 teaspoon salt
2 eggs, beaten
1½ cups buttermilk
3 tablespoons butter or margarine, melted
1 cup fresh, frozen or canned whole corn kernels, drained

Preheat oven to 375°. Brush a two-quart casserole or soufflé dish with melted butter.

In a mixing bowl combine the cornmeal, flour, baking powder, baking soda, sugar and salt. In a separate bowl beat the eggs and add the buttermilk, butter and corn kernels. If canned corn is used, drain well. With a rubber spatula quickly combine the milk mixture with the dry ingredients, stirring until just well moistened. Transfer the mixture into the prepared casserole and bake 40 minutes or until golden and slightly firm to the touch. Serves 6 to 8.

CORNMEAL-WHOLE WHEAT BREAD

The addition of whole wheat flour to cornmeal gives a surprisingly rich depth to this bread. Try splitting a piece of hot bread, then splurging and slathering it with butter and spicy apple butter!

1⅔ cups cornmeal
1⅔ cups whole wheat flour
1½ teaspoons cream of tartar
½ teaspoon baking soda
3 tablespoons toasted wheat germ
¾ teaspoon salt
4 tablespoons brown sugar
1½ cups milk
¼ cup butter or margarine, melted
2 eggs, lightly beaten

Preheat oven to 425°. Brush a 9" square baking pan with melted butter or coat with vegetable spray.

Combine the cornmeal, whole wheat flour, cream of tartar, baking soda, wheat germ, salt and brown sugar, stirring until well mixed. In a separate bowl, combine the milk, butter and eggs. Pour the milk mixture into the dry ingredients, stirring rapidly with a rubber spatula until dry ingredients are well moistened. Spread the mixture into prepared baking pan and bake 20 to 25 minutes. Serves 8.

CORNBREAD WITH WHEAT GERM AND OAT BRAN

Crunchy and filled with the aroma and flavor of three important grains, this cornbread is delicious and unusual.

1 cup cornmeal
2 tablespoons sugar
1 teaspoon salt
2 teaspoons baking powder
½ teaspoon baking soda
½ cup toasted wheat germ
½ cup oat bran
1½ cups buttermilk
1 large egg
3 tablespoons butter or margarine, melted

Preheat oven to 400°. Brush a 7x11" baking pan with melted butter or coat with vegetable spray.

In a mixing bowl combine the cornmeal, sugar, salt, baking powder, baking soda, wheat germ and oat bran. Stir until very well mixed. In a separate bowl or a large measuring container stir together the buttermilk, egg and butter. Pour the liquid ingredients into the cornmeal mixture, stirring quickly with a rubber spatula until well moistened. Pour the batter in the prepared pan and spread evenly. Bake 25 to 30 minutes. The bread will be dark golden brown and not as high-rising as regular cornbread but superb with a full meal soup. Serves 6 to 8.

CORNMEAL CAKES

Upon the first trial of these cakes my husband turned to me and said, "These are excellent." Then he ate two more. Not only are they good with maple syrup or preserves but they also make a great variation from the usual potato or rice when served with turkey or chicken hash.

1 cup cornmeal
½ teaspoon baking soda
½ teaspoon salt
1¼ cups buttermilk
2 tablespoons butter or margarine, melted
2 eggs, lightly beaten

Combine the cornmeal, baking soda and salt in a mixing bowl, blending well. In a separate bowl mix the buttermilk, butter and eggs. Stir the buttermilk mixture into the dry ingredients, mixing quickly but thoroughly. Place a griddle over medium heat and rub lightly with vegetable shortening. When the griddle is hot, spoon the batter onto its surface, using one tablespoon of batter per cake. Spread the batter a little and allow to cook until bubbles form. Then flip the cakes over and cook until golden brown. The cakes can be stacked on a warm plate and placed in a 150° - 200° oven until ready to serve. The recipe will make 18 cakes using one tablespoon of batter per cake. The cakes may be made larger if desired.

Maize, or Corn

What we call "corn" was known first to New World explorers as "maize," the word used for this glorious food, which is really the seed of a giant grass, by the inhabitants of the West Indies during Christopher Columbus's time. The word "corn" began as a general term for any small grain or grainlike object, including grains of salt (hence the name "corned" – or salted beef). The English use the word "corn" to refer to whatever grain is the staple of a people or region. Only in the United States is the word applied specifically to the seeds of the maize plant.

A LOAF OF CORNBREAD

Tekla Levy, who has traveled and lived in many areas of the country, became intrigued with the quantity of cornmeal consumed in Kentucky and Tennessee. Her interest resulted in this loaf, which has a lovely texture, slices well, and is exceptionally good with bean soup.

1½ cups yellow cornmeal
½ cup flour
⅓ cup sugar
½ teaspoon salt
½ teaspoon baking soda
1½ cups buttermilk
½ cup butter or margarine, melted

Preheat oven to 350°. Brush an 8x4x2" loaf pan with melted butter or coat with vegetable spray.

In a mixing bowl combine the cornmeal, flour, sugar, salt and baking soda, stirring well. In a separate bowl or a large measuring cup mix the buttermilk and butter together. Add the liquid ingredients to the dry mixture and stir quickly but very well. Let stand for 20 minutes. Pour the batter into the prepared pan, smoothing the top, and bake in preheated oven for about one hour or until the bread tests done. Slice on a serving board and serve hot. Serves 8 to 10 according to thickness of slices.

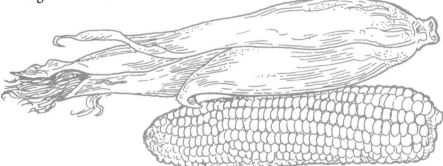

MAPLE CORN LOAF

This loaf with its lovely texture and light maple flavor reminds me of walking through the Green Mountains of Vermont or wandering beside one of the charming small lakes of New Hampshire.

1⅓ cups all purpose flour
⅔ cup cornmeal
3 teaspoons baking powder
½ teaspoon salt
2 large eggs
⅔ cup milk
⅓ cup maple syrup
½ cup butter or margarine, melted

Preheat oven to 375°. Coat an 8x4x2" loaf pan with vegetable spray.

Combine the flour, cornmeal, baking powder and salt in a mixing bowl, blending well. Separately beat the eggs and add the milk, maple syrup and butter. Add the liquid ingredients to the dry mixture, stirring quickly with a rubber spatula until thoroughly mixed. Pour the batter into the prepared pan, spreading evenly. Bake approximately 30 to 35 minutes and test for doneness. Serves 8.

MEXICAN CORNBREAD

No book on quick breads would be complete without the Texas version of Mexican cornbread. All recipes of this pungently flavored cornbread are similar but in this one I have added an ingredient creating a complete casserole dinner. Pair it with fresh chilled cucumber soup and fruit salad for a dinner that is easy and satisfying.

1 cup yellow cornmeal

I teaspoon salt

½ teaspoon baking soda

1 cup milk

2 eggs, beaten

½ cup melted margarine or bacon drippings

One 16-ounce can cream style corn

1 cup onion, finely chopped

½ pound ground meat, sautéed and drained

1 cup Cheddar cheese, grated and packed

4 canned jalapeño chilies, drained and chopped,
    or 4 fresh jalapeños, chopped

Preheat oven to 350°. Rub a 10" iron skillet with light oil or vegetable shortening. Combine the cornmeal, salt and baking soda in a mixing bowl and set aside. Separately mix the milk, eggs and margarine, then add the cream style corn, mixing well.

Place the prepared iron skillet in a preheated oven while finishing the cornbread. Add the milk mixture to the dry ingredients and stir quickly until well blended. Have the onion, meat, cheese and peppers prepared. (For the meat, simply sauté ground meat in a small amount of oil until browned. Drain on paper towels.) When the skillet is piping hot, pour in half the batter, spreading evenly. Sprinkle onion over the batter, then scatter the meat over the onion. Next add a layer of cheese, then the chopped chilies. Carefully spread the remaining batter over the filling. Bake 45 to 50 minutes until golden and resilient to the touch. Serve hot in pie-shaped wedges. Serves 8.

NOTE: You may eliminate the ground meat if you prefer. To cut calories use farmer's part skimmed milk cheese and skimmed milk in the batter. Strain bacon drippings if used.

GRITS SPOON BREAD

Grits make a firmer textured spoon bread than cornmeal but they impart a hearty flavor that is a favorite of mine. A topping of good Cheddar cheese gives even more zest to this lovely bread.

> 1 cup quick cooking grits (5-minute style)
> 2 cups milk
> ¼ cup butter or margarine
> 1½ teaspoons salt
> 3 eggs, beaten
> 1½ cups milk
> 3 teaspoons baking powder

Preheat oven to 350°. Brush a two-quart soufflé dish with melted butter or margarine.

In the top of a double boiler cook the grits in 2 cups of milk, stirring until creamy and thick. Remove the double boiler from the heat and add the butter and salt to the grits mixture, stirring well. Cool five minutes. Add the eggs, 1½ cups of milk and baking powder. Blend thoroughly and pour the mixture into prepared soufflé bowl. Bake about 40 minutes or until puffed and lightly browned. Serve on separate small plates with plenty of butter and your favorite preserves. Serves 6 to 8.

VARIATION: If desired, top the mixture the last 15 minutes of baking with 1 cup of grated Cheddar cheese. For cheese in the soufflé, add 1½ cups of grated Cheddar cheese to the mixture just before pouring into the dish. Bake as directed. No butter or preserves will be needed with the added cheese.

WHOLE KERNEL SPOON BREAD

Celebrate the first corn of summer with this delightful soufflé bread. It is also excellent made with golden canned or frozen corn.

> 1½ cups fresh corn kernels or a 12-ounce can
>   whole kernel corn, drained
> 2½ cups milk
> ¼ cup butter or margarine
> 2 tablespoons sugar
> ½ teaspoon salt
> ¾ cup yellow cornmeal
> 5 medium eggs, separated
> 1¼ cups Cheddar cheese, grated

Preheat oven to 350°. Brush a 2½-quart soufflé bowl or a casserole with melted butter.

Cut the fresh corn off the cobs, measure and set aside. If using canned corn, place in a sieve and allow to drain. Do not drain the fresh corn. Combine the milk, butter, sugar and salt in a saucepan. Place over medium heat and bring just to the boiling point. Slowly add the cornmeal, whisking constantly until the mixture thickens, about four to five minutes. Remove from burner. Beat the egg yolks lightly and add them to the cornmeal mixture with the cheese, stirring until well blended. Beat the egg whites in the bowl of an electric mixer until softly stiff. Fold the egg whites into the cornmeal mixture and then add the corn kernels. Transfer the mixture to the prepared bowl and bake about 40 minutes or until the top is lightly firm when touched. The top should be dark golden brown. Serve immediately. Serves 8 to 10.

WHITE CORNMEAL SOUFFLÉ

For those who love the purity of white cornmeal, this delightful soufflé is a perfect picture — served immediately out of the oven puffed and quivery, it is divine slathered with fresh unsalted butter.

3 cups milk
1 cup white cornmeal
1½ teaspoons baking powder
1 teaspoon salt
3 tablespoons butter or margarine, melted
4 large eggs, separated

Preheat oven to 350°. Brush a two-quart soufflé dish or casserole with melted butter. Scald the milk in a double boiler until it is steaming. Slowly pour in the cornmeal, stirring constantly with a wire whisk to avoid lumping. Continue stirring with a rubber spatula or wooden spoon until the mixture is thick, about 5 to 10 minutes. Remove the top of the double boiler from the burner and allow the mixture to cool 10 to 15 minutes. To the cornmeal mixture add the baking powder, salt, butter and egg yolks. Stir very well. Beat the egg whites until softly stiff. Fold into the batter. Be certain to scrape the bottom of the pan for sometimes the mixture thickens around the edges of the pan. Pour mixture into the prepared casserole and bake approximately 45 minutes. The soufflé will be quivery but firm to the touch. Serve immediately upon removing from the oven. If there is any left, reheat covered, the next morning for breakfast and serve with poached eggs. Serves 8.

NOTE: The recipe doubles easily. Doubled, it will take one hour to bake. Use a large ceramic baking dish that can be carried to the table in all its puffed glory. A doubled recipe will serve at least 12 — depending on the size of the servings.

OZARK THREE-LAYERED CORNBREAD

In a beautiful small valley of the Arkansas Ozarks, the War Eagle River winds through the hills. It curves past the historic War Eagle Mill that was burned to keep it out of Yankee hands, then later rebuilt into the present three-story building that vibrates excitingly when grain is ground. Zoe Medlin, a young miller, presides over this lovely area. Zoe is an excellent cook of whole grains and wild game. She conceived the following recipe that divides into three layers. It is just as enchanting as the Ozarks that Zoe loves so well.

1 cup yellow cornmeal
½ cup whole wheat flour
½ cup all purpose flour
2 teaspoons baking powder
½ teaspoon salt
1 large egg
¼ cup honey
¼ cup light oil or melted margarine
3 cups milk

Preheat oven to 350°. Brush a two-quart soufflé dish or casserole with melted margarine.

Combine the cornmeal, whole wheat and all purpose flour with the baking powder and salt, blending well. In a separate bowl beat the egg, honey, oil and milk together. Add the liquid ingredients to the dry ingredients (I found it best to use a whisk to avoid lumping for this bread is very much like a spoon bread). Transfer the batter to the prepared dish and bake about 50 minutes or until the top is springy when touched. The flours and cornmeal will separate into layers, creating a texture much like that of a lovely spoon bread. Serves 6 to 8.

BUTTERMILK SPOON BREAD

I could not resist trying a spoon bread with buttermilk. The result has a truly luscious, rather hearty flavor and texture. It is especially delicious made with stone ground cornmeal.

⅔ cup cornmeal
2 teaspoons baking powder
½ teaspoon baking soda
½ teaspoon salt
2 large eggs
1 cup buttermilk
1 cup sweet milk
2 tablespoons butter or margarine

Preheat oven to 450°. A two-quart soufflé dish or casserole will be needed.

Combine the cornmeal, baking powder, baking soda and salt in a mixing bowl. Beat the eggs in a separate bowl and add the buttermilk and sweet milk. Place the two tablespoons of butter or margarine in the soufflé dish and place in the preheated oven to allow the butter to melt. Add the liquid ingredients to the dry ingredients, stirring until just well moistened. Remove the hot buttered dish and pour the batter into it, spreading evenly. Return to the oven and bake 20 minutes. Reduce heat to 350° and bake 20 minutes more. Serve immediately. Serves 6.

SPOON BREAD

This bread contains the same ingredients as Elegant Spoon Bread but the eggs are incorporated using a faster method. I encourage trying a stone ground cornmeal with this spoon bread — the flavor is superb.

4 cups milk
1 cup yellow cornmeal
¼ cup butter or margarine
2 teaspoons salt
4 large eggs, beaten
1 teaspoon baking powder

Preheat oven to 400°. Brush a 2½-quart soufflé dish or casserole with melted butter. Measure three cups of the milk into the top of a double boiler. Scald the milk until a skin forms on top and steam is escaping. Add the cornmeal slowly to the hot milk, whisking constantly to keep the mixture smooth. When a thick mush has formed, remove from the burner and whisk again to avoid lumps. Whisk in the butter and salt. Add the remaining cup of milk to the beaten eggs and combine with the cornmeal mixture. Add the baking powder and stir very well. Pour the mixture into the prepared baking dish. Bake about 45 minutes. The spoon bread will be dark golden in color and will puff high. The puffiness will slowly subside but this does not harm the texture of the bread. Serve as soon as possible. Delicious with soft unsalted butter and your favorite preserves! Serves 6 to 8. The recipe may be doubled easily. Bake in a five-quart casserole for about an hour if doubling.

ELEGANT SOUTHERN SPOON BREAD

Why "spoon bread"? Apparently because this bread popular since pre-Civil War days is so light and soft that it must be served with a spoon. I love offering it at the table in all its puffed glory on individual small plates. Spoon bread is a classic favorite for brunch, luncheon or dinner and is often a base for creamed entrees, but it is equally perfect for barbecues.

4 cups milk
1 cup yellow cornmeal
¼ cup butter or margarine
2 teaspoons salt
1 teaspoon baking powder
4 large eggs, separated

Preheat oven to 350°. Brush a 2½-quart soufflé dish or casserole with melted butter.

Measure three cups of milk into the top of a double boiler. Scald the milk until a skin forms on top and steam is escaping. Add the cornmeal slowly to the hot milk, stirring constantly with a wire whisk. Change to a rubber spatula and continue stirring until the mixture is a thick mush (which takes only a few minutes). If the mixture should form lumps, whisk rapidly until smooth. Remove from the heat and whisk in the butter, salt and baking powder. Add the egg yolks, stirring well, and the remaining cup of milk. Beat the egg whites until softly stiff and fold them into the cornmeal mixture.

Pour the batter into the prepared soufflé dish. Bake 45 to 50 minutes. When the spoon bread is done it will be a lovely golden color. Its puffy height will slowly subside but this does not harm the texture of the bread. Serve as soon as possible after baking. Serves 6 generously.

A Perfect Loaf

Luscious quick loaf breads are eminently adaptable. A hot loaf completes a cozy fireside dinner or an afternoon tea. Slice and toast quick breads for breakfast or brunch. Sliced quick breads, sandwiched with a favorite spread and wrapped in waxed paper, make a perfect portable repast.

A variety of sweeteners is used in loaf breads, among them honey, brown sugar, maple syrup, molasses and granulated sugar. If necessary for special diets or tastes, the sugar content can be cut; for example, where two cups of sugar are required, use 1½ cups. Salt is strictly a personal taste. There are so many flavorful goodies in a loaf bread, salt is simply not necessary and the loaf's texture will not be harmed by totally eliminating it.

Butter and margarine may be used interchangeably. A few recipes employ a light corn or safflower oil (do not use the heavier olive oils) with a resulting fine texture. Eggs are important in many of the breads for lightness and to hold the batter together. If cholesterol counting is an important consideration, try using egg substitutes or just egg whites. When using an egg substitute, follow the manufacturer's direction for the amount per egg. With egg whites, use ½ cup egg whites in place of 3 eggs. Stir the egg whites lightly with a fork just to break them before adding other ingredients.

Regular commercial white all purpose flour such as Pillsbury or Gold Medal has been used for testing. If you prefer unbleached white flour, use it in the same quantities as all purpose flour. Whole grain stone ground flours are especially suitable for

LOAF BREAD TIPS

Loaf breads freeze beautifully. Make two or three loaves at a time so that you will always have some waiting in the freezer. Cool fully before wrapping in moistureproof materials for freezing. Thaw at room temperature in the same wrapper to retain moisture.

Flour for loaf breads need not be sifted, but if you are dipping right from the flour sack, be sure to stir vigorously with a fork before measuring it, to insure correct amounts.

health breads, not only for their nourishing quality but also for flavor that flows through the bread. Look for stone ground whole wheat, rye, millet, soy, buckwheat and barley flours — and cornmeal. Double acting baking powder is the main leavening agent for loaf breads. For a low salt diet, use a low sodium baking powder available in health food stores.

Two techniques are utilized to combine ingredients. In one method butter and sugar are creamed together and remaining ingredients are added as directed. In the second method, all dry ingredients are combined in one bowl and liquids in another, then the two are merged by swift mixing. Most of the recipes have been designed for a 9 x 5 x 3" loaf pan, allowing room for batter to expand. Recipes will specify when smaller pans are needed. Preparation of the pan is important for loaf bread has a tendency to stick to the pan. A vegetable spray is best — several excellent brands are available in supermarkets. Even if you brush a pan with melted butter, spray it with vegetable oil spray as well because the reaction of flour to oil is very effective in reducing sticking. If melted butter or margarine is used alone, brush the pan liberally. Cut a piece of oiled paper or baker's parchment to fit into the bottom of the pan. Insert it into the pan and brush again with melted butter.

Don't worry if your loaf bread cracks down the center – this is natural. Some cooks insist that the batter should sit in the pan for 20 minutes before baking but I have not found that waiting makes a difference in the finished loaf, so why waste those lovely 20 minutes?

Each recipe is definitive and clearly explained. A 9 x 5 x 3" loaf will serve 12 — more if sliced thinly. With a few exceptions, eggs used are those marked large — not jumbo. Directions always specify amount of time for baking but ovens do vary. Test at the end of the baking time with a cake tester or toothpick. If it comes out clean, the bread is finished. If not, bake the bread 10 to 15 minutes longer. With divinely elegant fruit and nut breads as well as nourishing health loaves, allow the loaf to completely cool before slicing. But if you cannot wait, slice away and simply eat the little crumbs of nuts and raisins that fall on the table. I admit there are times I cannot resist just a small taste right away!

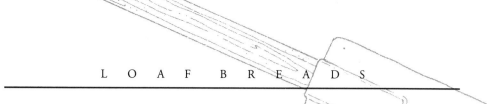

BASIC NUT BREAD

Basic Nut Bread is perfect for a beginning baker. As with many other breads, it is preferable to use ingredients that are at room temperature.

2 cups all purpose flour
3 teaspoons baking powder
½ teaspoon salt
1 cup sugar
⅔ cup butter or margarine
3 large eggs
1 teaspoon vanilla extract
¾ cup milk
1 cup coarsely chopped pecans or walnuts

Preheat oven to 350°. Brush a 9x5x3" loaf pan with melted butter or coat with vegetable spray.

Sift the flour, baking powder and salt together and set aside. In the bowl of an electric mixer combine the sugar and butter. Cream until light and fluffy. Add the eggs one at a time, beating well after each addition. Stir in the vanilla. Add the flour mixture alternately with the milk, beginning and ending with the dry ingredients and beating thoroughly after each addition. Fold in the nuts with a rubber spatula. Pour the batter into the prepared pan, spreading evenly. Bake one hour or until the bread tests done. Remove from the oven and cool in the pan on a wire rack for 10 to 15 minutes. When bread is removed from the pan, place on a rack and completely cool before slicing.

WHOLE WHEAT NUT BREAD: Try a delightful variation on the Basic Nut Bread that involves both a whole wheat flour and a different flavoring agent. Substitute 1 cup of whole wheat flour for the white flour, add 3 tablespoons of toasted wheat germ, and substitute brown sugar for the white sugar. Proceed with preparation as directed in the Basic Nut Bread.

DATE NUT BREAD

A moist, pleasurable bread enriched with dates and nuts and lightly flavored with aromatic orange juice. Excellent eaten alone but even more delicious topped with cream cheese touched with a bit of fresh or candied ginger (page 82).

2⅓ cups all purpose flour
2 teaspoons baking powder
½ teaspoon salt
½ cup butter or margarine
¾ cup sugar
1 teaspoon vanilla extract
¾ cup orange juice
Grated rind of 1 large orange
1 egg
1½ cups dates, chopped or snipped
1 cup pecans or walnuts, chopped

Preheat oven to 350°. Brush a 9x5x3" loaf pan with melted butter or coat with vegetable spray.

Combine the flour, baking powder and salt together in a small bowl and set aside. Cream the butter and sugar together until light and fluffy. Add the vanilla flavoring. Combine the orange juice, grated rind and egg, blending well. Add orange juice mixture to the butter mixture alternately with dry ingredients, beginning and ending with the dry mixture. Fold in the dates and nuts until well distributed. Pour the batter into prepared pan, smoothing evenly. Bake one hour or until bread tests done. Remove from the oven and cool in the pan on a wire rack for 10 minutes. Turn bread out on a wire rack to cool completely.

GRANOLA BREAD

Here is a favorite of mine, especially when made with my own granola (page 116). Several years ago I tested this bread at an altitude of seven thousand feet in Taos, New Mexico in a charming old kitchen with a tiny fireplace in the corner. At high altitudes ingredients must be at room temperature and baking time will be a bit longer.

> 2 cups all purpose flour
> 3 teaspoons baking powder
> ½ teaspoon salt
> ½ cup granola
> ½ cup raisins, scalded and dried
> 2 large eggs
> ⅓ cup plus 2 tablespoons soft butter or margarine
> 1 cup sugar
> Grated rind of 1 large lemon
> 2 tablespoons brandy
> ½ cup milk

Preheat oven to 350°. Brush an 8x4x2" loaf pan with melted butter or coat with vegetable spray.

In a small bowl combine the flour, baking powder, salt, granola and raisins, blending well. Set aside. In a large mixing bowl beat together the eggs, butter, sugar, lemon rind, brandy and milk. Slowly add the dry ingredients, mixing until just well blended. Pour the batter into a prepared pan, smoothing with a rubber spatula. Bake approximately one hour. Test for doneness. Remove from oven and cool bread in the pan on a wire rack for 10 minutes. Turn bread out on wire rack to finish cooling.

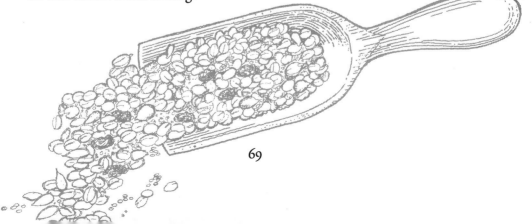

PEANUT BUTTER BREAD

What could be better for an afternoon snack than a slice of Peanut Butter Bread with soft cream cheese and grape jelly! Heat the cream cheese in a microwave oven for a few seconds and it will be perfect for spreading.

½ cup natural peanut butter
⅓ cup sugar
1 large egg
2 cups all purpose flour
4 teaspoons baking powder
½ teaspoon salt
1 cup milk
½ cup coarsely chopped toasted unsalted peanuts

Preheat oven to 350°. Brush a 9x5x3" loaf pan with melted butter or coat with vegetable spray.

In the large bowl of an electric mixer combine the peanut butter and sugar, creaming until well mixed. Add the egg and beat until smooth. Sift the flour, baking powder and salt together. Stir the dry ingredients into the peanut butter alternately with the milk beginning and ending with the flour mixture. Fold in the peanuts until well distributed. Pour the batter into the prepared loaf pan. Bake for one hour or until the bread tests done. Remove from the oven and cool bread in the pan on a wire rack 10 to 15 minutes. Turn the bread out on the rack and finish cooling.

Toasting Peanuts

Spread the nuts in a single layer in a baking pan. Preheat oven to 300°. Place nuts in the oven and set a timer for 15 minutes, shake the pan and check color of the nuts. Reset the timer (primarily not to forget the nuts!) and continue baking until nuts are a light color, about 15 minutes more. If the nuts scorch throw them out for the birds and squirrels and start over.

ORANGE MARMALADE BREAD

Devotees of orange marmalade will love this moist bread redolent with a poignant orange flavor. Excellent with morning coffee or tea!

3½ cups sifted all purpose flour
3 teaspoons baking powder
½ teaspoon salt
⅓ cup butter or margarine
1 cup sugar
2 eggs, lightly beaten
1 cup milk
1¾ cups sweet orange marmalade
1 cup chopped pecans or walnuts

Preheat oven to 350°. Brush a 9x5x3" loaf pan with melted butter or coat with vegetable spray.

Resift flour with baking powder and salt. Set aside. In the mixing bowl of an electric mixer cream the butter and sugar until light and fluffy. Add the eggs, blending well. Stir in the sifted flour mixture alternately with the milk beginning and ending with the dry ingredients. Blend in the marmalade and nuts. Pour the batter into the prepared pan and smooth with a rubber spatula. Bake approximately one hour and test for doneness. Remove bread from oven and let cook in the pan on a wire rack for 15 minutes. Turn bread out on the rack to finish cooling.

A Note About Nut Breads

If you plan to slice a nut bread loaf into thin slices, chop the nuts for the batter very finely. The resulting texture will allow for neater slicing.

CARROT WALNUT BREAD

Two favorite vegetables, carrots and zucchini, have given us popular, moist loaf breads. Because of the natural sweetness of carrots, carrot bread requires less sugar than zucchini bread and the added touch of orange is beautiful against a white serving platter.

1½ cups all purpose flour
½ teaspoon baking soda
½ teaspoon baking powder
1 teaspoon ground cinnamon
½ teaspoon ground nutmeg
¼ teaspoon ground allspice
¼ teaspoon salt
⅔ cup butter or margarine
1 cup sugar
2 large eggs
1½ cup carrots, cleaned and grated
¾ cup chopped walnuts
¾ cup chopped raisins

Preheat oven to 350°. Brush a 9x5x3" loaf pan with melted butter or coat with vegetable spray.

Combine in a bowl the flour, baking soda, baking powder, cinnamon, nutmeg, allspice and salt, stirring with a rubber spatula until very well mixed. Cream together the butter and sugar in bowl of an electric mixer until light and fluffy. Add the eggs and beat until creamy. Add the dry ingredients to the butter mixture gradually, blending well. Fold in the carrots and nuts. (The carrots can be grated in a food processor. Remove them and then chop the nuts and raisins together. Processor-chopped ingredients will yield a smoother slice of bread.) Spread the batter in the prepared pan and bake approximately one hour or until the bread tests done with a cake tester. Remove from the oven and cool in the pan on a wire rack 15 minutes. Turn bread out on rack to finish cooling.

PUMPKIN BREAD

During a short stay in the hospital I learned about this delicious and unusual pumpkin bread from a young nurse. Carole Cain opened a new world for me by sharing her knowledge of the West African coast, learned from her Liberian husband. Pumpkin bread seemed rejuvenated with her delightful combination of spices. I have added nuts and raisins for their sweetness and crunch.

3 cups all purpose flour, sifted
3½ teaspoons baking powder
1 teaspoon salt
½ cup butter or margarine
1 cup sugar
4 eggs
1 cup canned pumpkin puree
½ teaspoon Chinese five-spice powder*
¼ teaspoon cinnamon
½ cup chopped pecans or walnuts
½ cup dark or golden raisins, scalded and dried

Preheat oven to 350°. Brush a 9x5x3" loaf pan with melted butter or coat with vegetable spray. Resift flour with the baking powder and salt. Set aside. In the large bowl of an electric mixer cream the butter and sugar until light and fluffy. (In Liberia there are no electric mixers so all is performed by hand.) Add the eggs one at a time, beating until well blended. Stir in the pumpkin, five-spice powder and cinnamon. Gradually add the flour mixture to the pumpkin mixture until well blended. Fold in the nuts and raisins. Pour the batter into the prepared pan, smoothing with a rubber spatula. Bake about one hour, then test for doneness. Remove bread from the oven and cool in the pan on a wire rack for 15 minutes. Turn bread out on the rack to finish cooling.

*Five-spice powder is a blend of five ground spices favored in China and Southeast Asia. It usually includes star anise, cinnamon, peppercorns, fennel seeds and cloves. It may be purchased ready-made in the spice section of a supermarket.

BOURBON PECAN BREAD

Needless to say, the combination of pungent bourbon and southern pecans would entice any intrepid cook. The aroma while baking is so tantalizing that I wager you'll slice a small piece while the bread is still hot!

¾ cup golden raisins
⅓ cup bourbon
2 cups all purpose flour
1 teaspoon baking powder
½ teaspoon baking soda
½ teaspoon salt
1 cup sugar
½ cup butter or margarine
3 large eggs
¾ cup buttermilk
1 teaspoon vanilla extract
1 cup coarsely chopped pecans

Combine the raisins and bourbon in a small bowl and allow to marinate one hour. Drain, reserving the bourbon. Preheat oven to 350° and coat a 9x5x3" loaf pan with vegetable spray.

Blend the flour, baking powder, baking soda and salt in a bowl and set aside. Cream the sugar and butter in the bowl of an electric mixer until light and fluffy. Add the eggs one at a time, beating well after each addition. Add the dry ingredients alternately with the buttermilk to the butter mixture, beginning and ending with the flour mixture. Stir in the vanilla. Fold in the raisins, the bourbon and, last, the pecans. Mix until all is thoroughly incorporated. Pour the batter into the prepared pan and bake approximately one hour before testing for doneness. Remove the bread to a wire rack cooling in the pan 15 minutes. Turn bread out on the rack to finish cooling.

LEMON PISTACHIO BREAD

I will never forget one Christmas in the beautiful city of Beirut, Lebanon just before the civil war began there. One of my favorite stores sold nothing but nuts from a huge round copper bin with separate compartments for each variety. The nuts were sold warm, ready to serve with cocktails before the evening dinner. The pistachios were huge and flavorsome and I enjoyed using them with fruits, desserts and bread as well as eating them out of hand.

2 cups all purpose flour
3 teaspoons baking powder
½ teaspoon baking soda
½ teaspoon salt
½ cup butter or margarine
⅔ cup sugar
2 large eggs
Grated rind of 1 large lemon or lime
4 tablespoons lemon juice or lime juice
½ cup sour cream
1 cup coarsely chopped untoasted, unsalted pistachio nuts*

Preheat oven to 350°. Brush a 9x5x3" loaf pan with melted butter or coat with vegetable spray.

Sift the flour, baking powder, baking soda and salt into a mixing bowl. Set aside. In the large bowl of an electric mixer cream the butter and sugar together until light and fluffy. Add the eggs one at a time, beating well after each addition. Combine the grated rind, juice and sour cream. Add alternately to the butter mixture with the dry ingredients, beginning and ending with the flour mixture. Blend in the pistachios. Pour the batter into the prepared pan and bake approximately one hour or until the bread tests done. Remove from the oven and cool the bread in the pan 15 minutes on a wire rack. Turn the bread out on the rack to finish cooling.

*Import and health food stores have unsalted pistachios.

ALMOND ORANGE BREAD

This bread will be a favorite served with either Sweet Citrus Butter (page 141) or soft cream cheese beaten until fluffy with a touch of grated orange rind.

⅔ cup sugar
½ cup butter or margarine
2 large eggs
2 cups all purpose flour
3 teaspoons baking powder
½ teaspoon salt
¾ cup orange juice
Grated rind of 1 large orange
1 cup chopped blanched almonds

Preheat oven to 350°. Brush a 9x5x3" loaf pan with melted butter or coat with vegetable spray.

Cream the sugar and butter together in the large bowl of an electric mixer until light in color. Add the eggs one at a time, beating well after each addition. Sift the flour, baking powder and salt together. Add the flour mixture to the butter mixture alternately with the orange juice and grated rind, beginning and ending with the dry ingredients. Fold in the almonds. Pour the batter into the prepared pan, smoothing with a rubber spatula. Bake one hour and 10 minutes before testing for doneness. Remove from oven and cool bread in the pan on a wire rack for 15 minutes. Turn bread out on the rack to cool before slicing.

Festive breads freeze well for the holidays. Cool the loaf completely and wrap it closely in freezer-proof paper or plastic wrap before freezing. To serve, place the loaf on an ovenproof serving platter, cover with foil, and heat in a 350 oven for 30 minutes.

A HOLIDAY BREAD

Filled with fruits and nuts and fragrant with orange and cardamom, this gala bread fulfills the promise of the holidays.

1 cup sugar
½ cup butter or margarine
4 large eggs
2½ cups all purpose flour
½ teaspoon ground cardamom
2 teaspoons baking powder
½ teaspoon salt
1 cup milk
¼ cup chopped candied pineapple
¼ cup chopped candied orange rind
½ cup chopped red candied cherries
½ cup chopped pecans or walnuts
2 tablespoons orange juice
Grated rind of 1 large orange

Preheat oven to 350°. Brush a bundt pan with melted butter or coat thoroughly with vegetable spray. If you have a large, heavy mixer use the flat beater. If not, cream the sugar and butter in the large bowl of an electric mixer until light and creamy. Add the eggs one at a time, beating well after each addition. Combine the flour, cardamom, baking powder and salt together, mixing well. Add the flour mixture to the butter mixture alternately with the milk, beginning and ending with the dry ingredients. Fold in the candied fruits and nuts. Stir in the orange juice and rind and mix well. Pour the batter into the bundt pan, spreading evenly. Bake one hour and test for doneness. Remove from the oven and cool bread in the pan on a wire rack 15 minutes. Turn the bundt pan over and release the bread onto the wire rack. Allow to cool completely before slicing.

OPTIONAL TOPPING: Whisk 2 cups confectioners' sugar with ½ cup orange juice until smooth. Pour over the bread and decorate with red candied cherries cut in half.

SWEET LEMON BREAD

If you love lemon pie, lemon pudding, lemon anything, then this bread is for you. It is moist and luscious in flavor.

> 1½ cups all purpose flour
> 2 teaspoons baking powder
> ½ teaspoon salt
> ¾ cup butter or margarine
> 1½ cups sugar
> 3 large eggs
> ¾ cup milk
> 2 tablespoons lemon juice
> Grated rind of 1 large lemon
> ¾ cup chopped blanched almonds or pistachios
> TOPPING:
> ¼ cup sugar
> Juice of 1 large lemon

Preheat oven to 350°. Brush a 9x5x3" loaf pan with melted butter or coat with vegetable spray. Sift the flour, baking powder and salt together and set aside. In the large bowl of an electric mixer cream the butter and sugar together until fluffy. Add the eggs one at a time, beating well after each addition. To the butter mixture add the dry ingredients alternately with the milk, beginning and ending with the flour mixture. Stir in the two tablespoons of lemon juice and grated rind. Fold in the nuts and pour the batter into the prepared loaf pan, spreading evenly with a rubber spatula. Bake one hour and test for doneness. During the last 15 minutes, cover loosely with aluminum foil if the bread becomes too brown. Remove bread from the oven, leave in the pan and place on a wire rack. Combine the ¼ cup of sugar and juice of one lemon, stirring with a fork until the sugar is dissolved. Make tiny holes in the top of the bread with a cake tester or toothpick. Pour the lemon mixture slowly across the top of the bread, giving time for the topping to be absorbed into the warm loaf. Allow to set 15 minutes. Remove bread from the pan and finish cooling on the wire rack (although a little taste while still very warm is delicious!).

FRESH APPLE BREAD

A marvelous blend of ingredients highlighted with fresh apple makes this a delicious healthful bread. One thick slice is quite filling and makes a great quick lunch when paired with a green salad or mixed fruits.

1 cup brown sugar
½ cup light oil
1½ tablespoons brandy
1 teaspoon vanilla extract
2 large eggs
1 cup golden raisins, scalded and dried
½ cup candied pineapple
1 cup chopped pecans or walnuts
2 cups tart apples, peeled, cored and grated
2 cups all purpose flour
2 teaspoons baking soda
½ teaspoon salt
¼ teaspoon ground cinnamon
¼ teaspoon ground nutmeg

Preheat oven to 350°. Coat a 9x5x3" loaf pan with vegetable spray. In a large mixing bowl combine the brown sugar, oil, brandy and vanilla and stir well. Beat in the eggs until well blended. Add the raisins, pineapple, nuts and apples mixing until the fruit and nuts are evenly distributed. (Granny Smith apples are perfect for their tartness and can be successfully grated in a food processor.) Sift the flour, baking soda, salt, cinnamon and nutmeg together. Add the flour mixture to the fruit mixture with a rubber spatula until the dry ingredients are absorbed. Pour the batter into the prepared pan, spreading evenly. Bake one hour and test for doneness. If the bread becomes too brown, cover during the last 15 minutes with aluminum foil. It may be necessary to bake 10 to 15 minutes longer as this bread incorporates a large number of ingredients. Remove the bread from the oven and cool in the pan on a wire rack for 15 minutes. Turn the bread out on the rack to finish cooling before slicing.

HAZELNUT AND AMARETTO BREAD

While I was shopping one day with my youngest grandson, John, he told me that hazelnuts were his favorite nuts so he returned home with a sackful. Amaretto liqueur is a favorite of mine, especially for cooking. In the middle of the night I suddenly paired the two — why not try both in a loaf bread which should be delicate in texture and taste. I constructed these thoughts on paper and began mixing. Success!

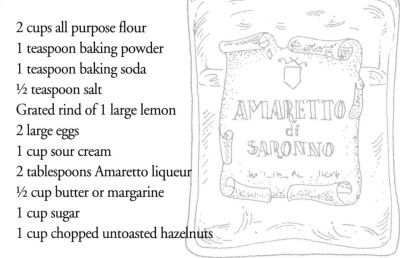

2 cups all purpose flour
1 teaspoon baking powder
1 teaspoon baking soda
½ teaspoon salt
Grated rind of 1 large lemon
2 large eggs
1 cup sour cream
2 tablespoons Amaretto liqueur
½ cup butter or margarine
1 cup sugar
1 cup chopped untoasted hazelnuts

Preheat oven to 350°. Brush a 9x5x3" loaf pan with melted butter or coat with vegetable spray. Sift the flour, baking powder, baking soda and salt together. Grate the lemon rind over the top of the flour mixture and set aside. In a small mixing bowl beat the eggs lightly, add the sour cream and Amaretto and blend well. Set aside. In the large bowl of an electric mixer beat the butter and sugar until light and creamy. Add the egg mixture and beat well until thoroughly mixed. Slowly blend in the dry ingredients, scraping the sides and bottom of the bowl to be certain all is absorbed. Fold in the chopped nuts. If a food processor is available, chop the hazelnuts using the steel blade. Because they are round hazelnuts are difficult to handle with a knife — they roll all over! Pour the batter into the prepared pan and smooth the top with a rubber spatula. Bake one hour and test for doneness. Remove from the oven and cool bread in the pan on a wire rack for 15 minutes. Turn loaf out on the rack to finish cooling. This loaf slices amazingly well while still warm.

GRAND MARNIER ORANGE NUT BREAD

The aromas of orange and Grand Marnier will float through the kitchen as this lovely bread bakes. Serve it plain or with a soft, creamy Brie at room temperature.

2¼ cups all purpose flour
3 teaspoons baking powder
½ teaspoon salt
½ cup butter or margarine
1 cup sugar
2 large eggs
Grated rind of 2 large oranges
1 cup orange juice
4 tablespoons Grand Marnier or Curaçao liqueur
½ cup chopped pecans
½ cup golden raisins, scalded and dried

Preheat oven to 350°. Brush a 9x5x3" loaf pan with melted butter or coat with vegetable spray.

Combine the flour, baking powder and salt together in a small bowl, blending together. Set aside. In the large bowl of an electric mixer cream the butter and sugar until smooth and fluffy. Beat in the two eggs and orange rind until well mixed. Combine the orange juice and Grand Marnier. Add the flour mixture to the butter mixture alternately with the orange and Grand Marnier, beginning and ending with the dry ingredients. Scrape the sides of the bowl and continue to beat until the mixture is smooth. Fold in the nuts and raisins. Pour the batter into prepared pan and spread evenly. Bake one hour and test for doneness. Remove from the oven and cool in the pan on a wire rack for 15 minutes. Turn bread out on the rack to finish cooling.

Some Spreads for Bread

~ Cream Cheese with Crystalized Ginger ~

I love the sweet piquancy of crystalized ginger. To an 8-ounce block of softened cream cheese add ⅓ cup of crystalized ginger sliced in tiny pieces. Do not chop in a food processor or you will lose much of the sugar as well as the ginger. Use a sharp knife on a bread board. Mix well and refrigerate until ready to use.

~ Cream Cheese Mixed with Fruits ~

Mix softened cream cheese with an equal amount of defrosted frozen raspberries or strawberries. Beat in the small bowl of an electric mixer until well blended. Transfer to a pretty bowl and use to top hot muffins or loaf breads. In the summer cut up strawberries, peaches or raspberries and mix with an equal amount of softened cream cheese. Refrigerate until ready to use.

~ Cream Cheese and Chutney ~

Chutney has a pungent, spicy flavor that is delicious mixed with cream cheese. To an 8-ounce block of cream cheese add ¼ cup of chutney. Mix well and taste, as you may wish to add more chutney. (All cream cheese mixtures should be made to your taste.) Stir the mixture well and refrigerate until ready to use. If you are a devotee of Brie or Camembert, allow the cheese to come to room temperature and pass it with a bowl of chutney to spread on bread — superb.

~ Cheese Spread ~

Soften cream cheese quickly by placing a block of it on a plate in a microwave oven. Heat approximately one minute on high. The cheese will be perfect for spreading or ready for mixing with other agreeable ingredients. Many flavors combine well with cream cheese. Try chopped parsley and chives, coasely ground black pepper, fresh chopped tarragon or any of your favorite herbs.

BRAZIL NUT BREAD

This exotic bread will swirl you away on a magic carpet to places fragrant with orange blossom water. Brazil nuts may be found in single packages in health food stores or in specialty shops. Do not attempt to chop these nuts but slice each with a sharp knife; the process is quick and easy.

2 cups all purpose flour
1 teaspoon baking soda
1 teaspoon baking powder
½ teaspoon salt
1 cup sour cream
2 large eggs
2 tablespoons orange blossom water
½ cup butter or margarine
1 cup sugar
½ cup candied orange peel, chopped
1 cup sliced Brazil nuts

Preheat oven to 350°. Brush a 9x5x3" loaf pan with melted butter or coat with vegetable spray.

Sift the flour, baking soda, baking powder and salt together and set aside. In a small mixing bowl, beat together the sour cream, eggs and orange blossom water. Set aside. In the large bowl of an electric mixer cream the butter and sugar until light and fluffy. Add the sour cream. Beat well and scrape the sides of the bowl. Slowly add the flour mixture, stirring until smooth. Fold in the orange peel and Brazil nuts until well distributed. Pour the batter into prepared pan and smooth with a rubber spatula. Bake one hour. Test for doneness and if necessary bake 10 to 15 minutes more. Remove from oven and cool bread in the pan on a wire rack 15 minutes. Turn bread out on rack to finish cooling.

CRANBERRY BANANA BREAD

Instead of the usual orange and cranberries I decided to try another combination in this loaf and it proved to be irresistibly pleasing. Serve sliced with soft cream cheese lightly flavored with grated orange rind.

4 cups sifted all purpose flour
2 teaspoons baking powder
1 teaspoon salt
1 teaspoon ground cinnamon
½ teaspoon ground nutmeg
1 cup butter or margarine
2 cups sugar
4 large eggs
2 cups ripe bananas (about 4), mashed
2 cups coarsely chopped fresh cranberries
1 cup chopped pecans or walnuts

Preheat oven to 350°. Brush a 9x5x3" loaf pan and 5x7x3" pan with melted butter or coat with vegetable spray.

Combine the flour, baking powder, salt, cinnamon and nutmeg either by sifting or stirring together in a bowl. Set aside. In the large bowl of an electric mixer cream the butter and sugar until light and creamy. Add the eggs one at a time, beating well after each addition. Stir in the bananas, then slowly add the dry ingredients, beating constantly until well moistened. Fold in the cranberries and nuts. (Chop cranberries in a food processor or use a curve chopping blade in a wooden bowl.) Transfer the batter to the two prepared pans smoothing with a rubber spatula — each pan should be about two-thirds full. Bake the smaller loaf 45 to 50 minutes, the larger one for one hour. Test both for doneness. If frozen cranberries are used cooking time may take 10 minutes longer. Remove the loaves from the oven and cool in the pans on a wire rack 10 minutes. Turn breads out on the rack to finish cooling.

MARGUERITE'S ZUCCHINI BREAD

A superb cook and friend of many years has provided me with the recipe for the original Zucchini Bread, which should now be considered a classic for its moistness, ease of preparation and flexibility. If the bread is too sweet, reduce sugar to 1½ cups and for variety substitute one cup of whole wheat flour for one cup of white.

3 cups sifted all purpose flour
1 teaspoon baking powder
1 teaspoon baking soda
½ teaspoon salt
1 teaspoon ground cinnamon
3 medium eggs
2 cups sugar
1 cup light oil
1 teaspoon vanilla extract
2 cups grated zucchini
1 cup chopped pecans

Preheat oven to 350°. Brush two 8x4x3" loaf pans with melted butter or coat with vegetable spray.

Resift the flour with the baking powder, baking soda, salt and cinnamon. Set aside. In a large mixing bowl beat the eggs until foamy. Add the sugar, blending well. Stir in the oil and vanilla. Gradually add the dry ingredients until thoroughly incorporated. Fold in the zucchini and nuts. Divide the batter equally between the two pans. Bake one hour and test for doneness. Remove breads from the oven and cool in the pans on a wire rack for 15 minutes. Remove breads to the rack to finish cooling.

IRISH SODA BREAD

This classic bread is a must for your table on St. Patrick's day. The solid peasant loaf blends well with corned beef and cabbage but is also excellent with a variety of cheeses. My most memorable loaf was one that I watched the mistress of Ballymaloe, Ireland prepare for luncheon. Warm and crusty, it was all I had hoped for.

2 cups whole wheat flour
1½ cups all purpose flour
½ cup rolled oats
3 teaspoons baking powder
1 teaspoon baking soda
¼ cup sugar
¼ cup margarine, melted
1 egg, beaten
1¾ cups buttermilk
2 cups currants (optional)

Preheat oven to 375°. Lightly coat a baking sheet with vegetable spray or brush with melted shortening. In a large mixing bowl combine the whole wheat flour, white flour, oats, baking powder, baking soda and sugar. Stir until well mixed. Combine the margarine, egg and buttermilk. Stir the milk mixture into the dry ingredients and mix with a rubber spatula until well blended. (The mixing may be done in a heavy mixer using the flat beater.) Fold in the currants if you are using them. Turn the dough out on a surface lightly dusted with white flour and knead about two minutes to gather the dough into a smooth ball. Divide in two equal portions and round each into a ball. Place on a prepared baking sheet spaced well apart and press down each lightly. Slash a cross atop each loaf with a razor. Bake about 40 to 45 minutes until brown and crusty. Serve hot or at room temperature.

VARIATION: You may choose to use 3½cups white flour, eliminating the whole wheat. Currants are excellent in the white loaves. Proceed as directed.

New England Maple Bread

One memorable trip took me through Quebec, New Brunswick, Nova Scotia and then south into New England following the fall colors. It was a breathtaking seven weeks. In Vermont I purchased grade C maple syrup for cooking — a bit darker and thicker but just as delicious as the top grade.

2 cups all purpose flour
4 teaspoons baking powder
½ teaspoon salt
⅓ cup butter or margarine, melted
¾ cup milk
¾ cup maple syrup
1 large egg
1 cup golden raisins, scalded and dried
1 cup chopped pecans

Preheat oven to 350°. Brush a 9x5x3" loaf pan with melted butter or coat with vegetable spray.

In a mixing bowl combine the flour, baking powder and salt and blend well. Set aside. In a separate bowl stir together the butter, milk, maple syrup and egg. Beat well and with a rubber spatula add to the dry ingredients, stirring quickly until well moistened. Fold in the raisins and nuts. Pour the batter into the prepared pan, spreading evenly. Bake one hour and test for doneness. Remove bread from the oven and cool in the pan on a wire rack 15 minutes. Turn the bread out on the rack to finish cooling. A delightfully simple bread with a charming, light flavor of maple syrup.

WHOLE WHEAT PRUNE BREAD

The availability of moist pitted prunes makes this lovely bread easy to prepare. Whole wheat pastry flour is available in health food stores.

1¾ cups whole wheat pastry flour
½ cup all purpose flour
1 teaspoon baking soda
1 teaspoon baking powder
½ teaspoon salt
¾ teaspoon ground cinnamon
⅓ cup butter or margarine
¾ cup brown sugar, packed
2 large eggs
1 cup buttermilk
12 ounces pitted prunes, snipped into bits with kitchen scissors
¾ cup chopped walnuts

Preheat oven to 350°. Brush a 9x5x3" loaf pan with melted butter or coat with vegetable spray.

Combine the whole wheat flour, white flour, baking soda, baking powder, salt and cinnamon in a mixing bowl and blend well. In the bowl of an electric mixer beat the butter and brown sugar until creamy. Stir in the eggs one at a time until mixture is smooth. Add the flour mixture and buttermilk alternately to the creamed butter and sugar, beginning and ending with the dry ingredients. Fold in the prunes and nuts until well distributed. Spoon the mixture into the prepared pan and spread evenly. Bake about 70 minutes or until the bread tests done. Remove from oven and cool bread in the pan on a wire rack 15 minutes. Remove the bread and finish cooling on the rack.

WHOLE WHEAT FRUIT AND NUT BREAD

One thick slice for lunch will last until dinnertime for this is a bread filled with flavor and nourishment. Whole wheat flour lends a sturdy, rough texture, making this a dense, satisfying bread to enjoy for its contents.

½ cup raisins
½ cup chopped dried apricots
½ cup pitted and chopped dates
½ cup chopped candied orange peel
⅔ cup chopped pecans or walnuts
1½ cups sifted all purpose flour
3 teaspoons baking powder
¼ teaspoon baking soda
½ teaspoon salt
1½ cups whole wheat flour
2 large eggs
¾ cup brown sugar
1¼ cups milk
⅓ cup butter or margarine, melted
Grated rind of 1 large orange

Preheat oven to 350°. Brush a 9x5x3" loaf pan with melted butter or coat with vegetable spray.

Combine the raisins, apricots, dates, orange peel and nuts in a mixing bowl. Mix thoroughly with two tablespoons of the white flour and set aside. Sift remaining white flour with the baking powder, baking soda and salt. Combine the flour mixture with the whole wheat flour, blending thoroughly. In a mixing bowl combine the brown sugar and eggs and beat well. Add the milk, butter and orange rind. Quickly stir the liquid mixture into the flour mixture, blending until just absorbed. Fold in the fruit and nuts. Transfer the mixture into prepared pan and spread evenly. Bake for one hour and test for doneness. Cool the bread in the pan on a wire rack for 15 minutes. Remove the bread and finish cooling on the rack.

FOUR-GRAIN QUICK BREAD

Stone ground flours and an unbleached white flour will definitely enhance the flavor of this hearty, nourishing bread. Excellent accompanied with cheese and a crisp apple.

2 cups whole wheat flour
¾ cup unbleached white flour
¼ cup wheat germ
¼ cup millet or soy flour
1 cup brown sugar, packed
4 teaspoon baking powder
¼ teaspoon baking soda
½ teaspoon salt
2 large eggs
1¼ cups buttermilk
⅓ cup butter or margarine, melted
1 cup pecans, chopped

Preheat oven to 350°. Brush a 9x5x3" loaf pan with melted butter or coat with vegetable spray.

In a large mixing bowl combine the whole wheat and unbleached flour with the wheat germ, millet or soy, brown sugar, baking powder, baking soda and salt. Blend very well. In a separate bowl whisk together the eggs, buttermilk and butter. Make a well in the dry ingredients and stir in the liquid mixture until well moistened. Fold in the nuts. Pour batter into prepared pan and bake one hour, testing for doneness. Remove bread from the oven and cool in the pan on a wire rack. Remove bread to the rack to finish cooling.

OAT BRAN MUFFIN BREAD

Ellen Fly, an expert on natural foods and a knowledgeable writer, transformed her wheat bran muffin into an oat bran bread. This recipe makes a savory loaf plus twelve delicious muffins.

1 cup boiling water
1 cup oat bran
¼ cup light oil
¼ cup butter or margarine, melted
¾ cup honey
2 large eggs
2 cups buttermilk
2½ cups whole wheat pastry flour
2½ teaspoons baking soda
2 cups oat bran cereal*
1½ cups raisins, scalded and dried

Preheat oven to 325° for the bread, 400° for the muffins. Brush an 8x4x3" loaf pan with melted butter or coat with vegetable spray. Brush twelve 2" muffins cups with melted butter or a vegetable spray. Combine the water and oat bran, stirring well, and set aside. In a mixing bowl or a four-cup measure blend the oil, butter, honey, eggs and buttermilk. Separately combine the flour, baking soda, bran cereal and raisins in a mixing bowl. Add liquid ingredients and the oat bran mixture to the dry ingredients, beating quickly with a rubber spatula or an electric mixer. Beat very well as the bran-water mixture may have thickened and should be mixed smoothly into the batter. Pour batter into the prepared pan until it is just over half full. Spread evenly. Bake about 55 minutes and test for doneness. Cool in the pan on a wire rack for 10 minutes, then turn out onto the rack to finish cooling. The remaining batter may be placed in prepared muffin cups, each filled almost full. Bake approximately 20 minutes. Serve hot or cool, or wrap and freeze.

*Any of the flaked oat bran cereals such as those made by Kelloggs or General Foods will work well.

BOSTON BROWN BREAD

Steaming Boston Brown Bread involves several hours and special equipment not available to everyone. To my delight the idea of simply baking the breads worked out beautifully. Relax and relish a nostalgic evening that recalls early America with Boston baked beans or a steaming bowl of bean soup and warm Boston Brown Bread.

> 2 cups buttermilk
> ¾ cup molasses
> 1 cup all purpose flour
> 1 cup whole wheat flour
> 1 cup yellow cornmeal
> 2 teaspoons baking soda
> ½ teaspoon salt
> 1 cup currants or raisins

Preheat oven to 350°. Brush two 8x4x3" loaf pans or two one-pound coffee cans with melted butter or coat with vegetable spray. In a large mixing bowl whisk together the buttermilk and molasses. Separately combine the flours, cornmeal, baking soda and salt. Using an electric mixer gradually add the dry ingredients to the buttermilk mixture. Fold in the currants or raisins until thoroughly distributed. Divide the batter evenly between the two prepared containers. Bake approximately 40 minutes if using loaf pans and 50 minutes if using coffee cans. Test for doneness. Turn the breads out on a wire rack to cool. Serve hot or at room temperature.

The choices in cooking methods available to today's cooks are truly extraordinary. Housewives of the 17th century had neither clocks nor thermometers. They sometimes calculated cooking times by observing the progession of the sun with the aid of a crude sundial painted on the kitchen floor. As late as 1842, the city of Boston still did not have running water, and Boston Brown Bread would usually have been steamed over water drawn from an outdoor pump.

SESAME WHOLE WHEAT BREAD

This substantial and nutritious all-whole wheat bread crunchy with
flavorful sesame seeds is an excellent choice for a quick satisfying breakfast.

1½ cups buttermilk
3 eggs whites, lightly beaten
3 tablespoons light oil
2 cups whole wheat flour
3 tablespoons wheat germ
1 cup brown sugar, packed
2 teaspoons baking soda
⅓ cup millet flour
1 teaspoon salt
½ cup sesame seeds

Preheat oven to 350°. Brush an 8x4x3" loaf pan with melted butter or coat with
vegetable spray.

In a small mixing bowl combine the buttermilk, egg whites and oil, beating with
a fork or whisking until well mixed. In a large bowl combine the flour, wheat
germ, sugar, baking soda, millet flour, salt and seeds. Stir well with a rubber
spatula. If the brown sugar sticks together in lumps, break them with your hands
to make a smoother mixture. Make a well in the center of the dry ingredients
and pour in the liquid mixture, stirring quickly but thoroughly. When batter is
smooth pour into prepared pan and spread evenly. Bake about 50 minutes and
test for doneness. Remove bread from the oven and cool in the pan on a wire
rack 15 minutes. Remove the bread and finish cooling on the wire rack.

93

POPPY SEED BREAD

A really superb poppy seed bread had eluded me until I met Louise Allis whose reipe is the basis for this absolutely perfect cake-like bread.

3 cups all purpose flour
2 cups sugar
5 teaspoons baking powder
1½ teaspoons salt
1½ tablespoons poppy seeds
3 large eggs
1⅛ cups light oil
1½ teaspoons vanilla extract
1½ teaspoons almond extract
1½ teaspoons butter flavoring
1½ cups milk
  GLAZE:
¼ cup orange juice
½ cup sugar
½ teaspoon vanilla extract
½ teaspoon almond extract
½ teaspoon butter flavoring

Preheat oven to 325°. Coat two 8x4x3" loaf pans with vegetable spray thoroughly. In the large bowl of an electric mixer measure in the flour, sugar, baking powder, salt and poppy seeds. With a heavy mixer use the flat beater. Beat the dry ingredients until mixed. Add the eggs, oil, vanilla, almond extract and butter flavoring and the milk. Start beating slowly to mix all ingredients and then at medium high speed beat for two minutes. Divide the batter between the two pans and bake for one hour. Test for doneness and if necessary bake 10 minutes more. Remove from the oven and let cool for 10 minutes while the glaze is made. Combine the orange juice, sugar and the flavorings. Beat with a fork until the ingredients are well mixed and the sugar has dissolved. Turn the breads out on wire racks and punch holes in the tops of the loaves with a toothpick or cake tester. Spoon the glaze over the two breads, dividing evenly.

Coffee Cakes: Quick & Delicious

A hot, fresh, melt-in-your mouth coffee cake served with an exotic blend of coffee or aromatic herbal tea is perfection for a special breakfast. All quick coffee cakes freeze beautifully. With a variety of cakes tucked in your freezer, you are ready for an impromptu luncheon, an afternoon tea, or to make a quick gift on any occasion.

There are two basic preparations for quick coffee cakes. The first method is similar to that used for most cakes. Butter and sugar are creamed together in the bowl of an electric mixer until light and fluffy. Remaining ingredients are added as directed and the batter is poured into a prepared pan. Serve hot from the oven or at room temperature. The second method of preparation is similar to that used for muffins. Dry ingredients are combined in one bowl and liquids in another. The two are mixed with quick strokes and the batter is ready to be baked. Most quick coffee cakes are made with all purpose flour. If the flour is unsifted, loosen it before measuring — do not pack it into a cup. Dip a cup into the flour, scrape off the top with a knife and do not shake the cup to make it full. For whole wheat coffee cakes use a good stone ground flour or pastry flour — the quality of the flour does make a difference in the flavor of the cake.

To some, coffee cakes are synonomous with confectionery, but versions of these favorite quick breads made with fruits and nuts will appeal to health food devotees as well as to those with a sweet tooth.

FOR THE BEST CAKES

Always plump raisins by placing them in a sieve and running very hot or boiling water over them. Spread them on paper towels to dry.

Combine dry ingredients by stirring them vigorously in a large bowl.

If there is time, have ingredients at room temperature.

COCONUT-BROWN SUGAR COFFEE CAKE

"We literally inhaled that recipe you had me test and I want a copy as soon as possible!" That was the opinion of my youngest daughter-in-law Laura about this cake!

CAKE:

1¾ cups all purpose flour
2½ teaspoons baking powder
¼ teaspoon salt
⅓ cup butter or margarine
⅔ cup sugar
1 egg
1 cup milk
1 teaspoon vanilla extract

TOPPING:

½ cup plus 1 tablespoon
 brown sugar, packed
5 tablespoons butter or margarine,
 melted
¼ cup light cream
½ cup moist coconut

Preheat oven to 350°F. Brush a 7x11" cake pan with melted butter.

To make the cake, mix the flour, baking powder and salt together in a small bowl and set aside. In the large bowl of an electric mixer cream the butter and sugar until light and fluffy. Add the egg and beat thoroughly. Add the dry ingredients alternately with the milk, beginning and ending with the dry mixture. Beat well after each addition. Stir in the vanilla. Pour batter into the prepared pan and spread evenly. Bake about 25 minutes or until the cake tests done.

While the cake is baking, prepare the topping. Combine all the ingredients in a bowl and stir until well mixed. Turn the temperature to broil and place a rack about six inches from the broiling element. Remove the finished cake from the oven. Spread the topping over the hot cake. Place under the broiler for about four minutes, until the top becomes light brown and bubbly. Serve hot, although the cake is also excellent at room temperature. Serves 6.

Cottage Cheese Fruit Coffee Cake

My note beside this recipe after testing was "exceptionally good," and so it is. It is filled with delicious fruit, easy to slice and excellent right out of the oven or served cool the following day.

1 cup dried apricots, chopped
1 cup pitted dates, chopped
2½ cups all purpose flour
3 teaspoons baking powder
1 teaspoon baking soda
½ cup butter or margarine
¾ cup brown sugar, packed
Grated rind of 1 large orange
Grated rind of 1 large lemon
2 large eggs
1½ cup creamy small curd cottage cheese

Preheat oven to 350°F. Brush a bundt pan with melted butter or coat with vegetable spray. The apricots can be chopped easily in a food processor or by hand. The dates should be cut with a sharp knife or scissors. Combine the flour, baking powder, baking soda and salt in a mixing bowl, blending well. Add the fruit and stir, preferably by hand, to cover the fruit well and break up the dates in pieces.

Cream the butter, sugar and grated rinds in the large bowl of an electric mixer. Add the eggs and beat until the batter is smooth. Blend in the cottage cheese, scraping down the sides of the bowl as necessary. Stir in the flour mixture and beat until smooth — if you are using a heavy duty mixer, this can be done with the flat beater. The batter will be a bit stiff. Spoon the batter into a prepared bundt pan and spread evenly. Bake 45 minutes and test for doneness. Remove cake from the oven and let stand in the pan on a wire rack 10 minutes. Remove the cake from the pan and place on a wire rack for cooling. The cake will slice into 12 to 14 ample slices.

BLUEBERRY BUCKLE

A whiff of grated lemon rind and fresh lemon juice blend with fresh blueberries in this favorite coffee cake of my youngest grandchildren.

TOPPING:	CAKE:
½ cup sugar	½ cup butter or margarine
½ cup all purpose flour	½ cup sugar
½ teaspoon ground cinnamon	2 large eggs
½ teaspoon ground nutmeg	2 cups all purpose flour
¼ cup cold butter, cut in pieces	¼ teaspoon salt
Grated rind of 1 large lemon	2 teaspoons baking powder
	½ cup milk
	2 tablespoons fresh lemon juice
	2 cups fresh or frozen blueberries

To make the topping, combine all the ingredients in a food processor, using the steel blade, until the mixture resembles coarse cornmeal. When a food processor is not available, cut the butter into the dry ingredients with a pastry blender. The butter should be a bit soft with this method. Set the topping aside. Preheat oven to 350°F. Brush a 10" cake pan or springform cheesecake pan with melted butter or coat with vegetable spray.

To make the cake, combine the butter and sugar in the bowl of an electric mixer and cream until smooth. Add the eggs one at a time, beating well after each addition. Scrape down the sides of the bowl. In a separate bowl mix the flour, salt and baking powder — or sieve the mixture. Add the dry ingredients to the butter mixture alternately with the milk, beginning and ending with the flour mixture. Beat in the lemon juice until mixture is smooth and creamy. Pour the batter into the prepared pan and sprinkle the berries over the top evenly. Spread the topping over the berries, smoothing lightly by hand. Bake approximately one hour (allow an extra 15 minutes if the berries were frozen) and test for doneness. Remove the cake from the oven and cool on a wire rack for 20 minutes before removing from the pan. Serves 8 to 10.

CRANBERRY BUCKLE

Cranberry Buckle is similar to Blueberry Buckle but has an entrancing tart sweetness that is perfect for Thanksgiving and Christmas holidays.

TOPPING:	CAKE:
½ cup sugar	½ cup butter or margarine
½ cup all purpose flour	½ cup sugar
1 teaspoon ground cinnamon	2 large eggs
½ teaspoon ground nutmeg	2 cups all purpose flour
½ cup cold butter, cut in pieces	½ teaspoon salt
Grated rind of 1 large orange	2 teaspoons baking powder
	½ cup milk
	2 cups fresh cranberries, chopped

To make the topping, combine all ingredients in a mixing bowl and blend with a pastry blender or fingertips until the mixture has the consistency of coarse cornmeal. (A food processor fitted with a steel blade does the job well.). Be certain the butter is cold. Set aside. Preheat oven to 350°. Brush a 10" cake pan or springform cheesecake pan with melted butter or vegetable spray.

Cream the butter and sugar together in the bowl of an electric mixer until fluffy. Add the eggs one at a time, stirring well after each addition. Combine the flour, salt and baking powder either by sifting or by stirring together in a small bowl. Beat in the flour mixture alternately with the milk until light and creamy, scraping down the sides when necessary. Pour into a prepared baking pan and spread evenly. Chop the cranberries coarsely with a sharp knife or whirl them in a food processor. Sprinkle the berries over the batter evenly. Spread the topping over the berries evenly. Bake the cake 50 to 60 minutes and test for doneness. Remove from the oven and cool the cake in the pan on a wire rack (or serve while hot). If using a cake pan with removable sides, let the cake stand for 15 minutes before removing the sides. The recipe doubles easily — one to eat and one for the freezer. Serves 10 easily.

SOUR CREAM COFFEE CAKE

Sour Cream Coffee Cake has been a delight for bakers both at home and in commercial establishments long enough to give it classical status. Lighter sour cream with less fat content works just as well as regular sour cream. Following is my version of this luscious cake with several variations.

FILLING:

½ cup brown sugar, packed
⅓ cup all purpose flour
2 teaspoons ground cinnamon
¼ cup cold butter, cut in pieces
1 cup walnuts or pecans,
coarsely chopped

CAKE:

2 cups all purpose flour
1½ teaspoons baking powder
1 teaspoon baking soda
½ teaspoon salt
½ cup butter or margarine
1 cup sugar
2 large eggs
1 cup sour cream
1 teaspoon vanilla extract

To make the filling, combine the brown sugar, flour and cinnamon in a food processor. With the steel blade in place pulse several times to mix ingredients. Add the cold butter, whirling until the mixture resembles coarse cornmeal. Transfer to a small bowl, stir in the nuts and set aside. Preheat oven to 350°. Brush a bundt pan with melted butter or coat with vegetable spray.

To make the cake, sift the flour, baking powder, baking soda and salt together and set aside. In the large bowl of an electric mixer, cream the butter and sugar together until light and fluffy. Add the eggs one at a time, beating well after each addition. Alternately add the dry ingredients and the sour cream to the butter mixture, beginning and ending with the flour mixture. Scrape down the sides and beat until creamy. Stir in the vanilla and mix well. Pour half the batter into the prepared bundt pan, spreading evenly. Sprinkle the filling over the batter. Spread remaining batter over the filling. Bake approximately 40 minutes, test for doneness and if necessary bake 10 minutes longer. Remove the cake to a wire rack and cool 10 minutes before turning out of the pan. Serves 10 to 12.

Five Delicious Versions of Sour Cream Coffee Cake

Each starts with the batter for Sour Cream Coffee Cake at left.

~ With Almonds ~

½ cup sugar
⅓ cup all purpose flour
¼ cup almond paste, chopped
¼ cup cold butter
1 cup blanched almonds, sliced
¾ teaspoon almond extract or 1 tablespoon Amaretto

Combine the sugar, flour and almond paste in the bowl of a food processor. With the steel blade in place, pulse several times to break up the almond paste. Cut the cold butter in small pieces and add it to the sugar mixture. Whirl several times until the mixture resembles coarse cornmeal. Preheat oven to 350°. Brush a bundt pan with melted butter or coat with vegetable spray. Sprinkle 1 cup of sliced almonds in the bottom of the pan. Prepare the batter as directed for Sour Cream Coffee Cake deleting the vanilla and substituting the almond extract or Amaretto.   Pour half the batter into the prepared pan over the sliced almonds. Sprinkle the filling over the batter. Top with remaining H cup of almonds. Carefully spoon remaining batter over the filling, spreading evenly. Bake 40 minutes and test for doneness. Baking time is longer in a kugelhopf pan because it is deeper than a bundt pan. Remove from the oven and cool in the pan on a wire rack 10 minutes. Turn the cake out on a wire rack to cool and serve immediately. Serves 10 to 12.

~ With Blueberries ~

½ cup sugar
⅓ cup all purpose flour
1 teaspoon ground cinnamon
Grated rind of 1 large lemon
¼ cup cold butter
1 cup fresh or frozen blueberries

Combine the sugar, flour, cinnamon and grated rind in the bowl of a food processor. With the steel blade in place pulse several times to mix the ingredients. Cut the cold butter into pieces and add to the mixture. Whirl several times until the mixture resembles coarse cornmeal. Set aside. Preheat oven to 350°F. Brush a bundt pan with melted butter or coat with vegetable spray. Prepare the batter for Sour Cream Coffee Cake. Spread half the cake batter in the prepared bundt pan. Sprinkle the filling over the batter and top with the blueberries. Spoon the remaining batter over the berries, spreading to cover the fruit. Bake 40 minutes. If using frozen berries, the baking time will be about 10 minutes longer. Test for doneness and bake longer if necessary. Remove from the oven and place on a wire rack for 10 minutes. Turn out on a serving tray if serving immediately. Serves 10 to 12.

- With Raspberries -

1/3 cup sliced or slivered unblanched almonds
One 10-ounce package frozen raspberries,
    thawed and drained
Grated rind of 1 large lemon

Preheat oven to 350°F. Brush a bundt pan with melted butter or coat with vegetable spray. Sprinkle the almonds on bottom of the bundt pan and set aside. Thaw the raspberries, draining the juice (save for ice cream or yogurt). There should be about three-fourths cup of raspberries. Prepare the batter for Sour Cream Coffee Cake, adding the grated rind of one lemon to the dry ingredients. Add the raspberries to the batter and gently stir just to swirl the berries through the batter. Pour the batter into the prepared bundt pan, spreading evenly. Bake 50 to 60 minutes. Remove to a wire rack and cool 10 minutes. Serves 12.

~ With Fresh Apples ~

1 cup chopped pecans or walnuts
1/2 cup brown sugar, packed
2 teaspoons ground cinnamon
1 large or 2 tart small fresh apples (Granny Smith)

Combine the nuts, brown sugar and cinnamon in a small bowl, mixing well. Set aside. Preheat oven to 350°F. Brush a bundt pan with melted butter or coat with a vegetable spray. Mix the batter for Sour Cream Coffee Cake. Peel, core and thinly slice the apples, then cut the slices in half. (Do not prepare apples until batter is finished.) Place half the batter in the prepared pan. Arrange the apples on top the batter. Sprinkle the brown sugar mixture evenly over the apples. Spread the remaining batter over the filling and smooth evenly. Bake 50 minutes and test for doneness. Remove from oven and let stand on a wire rack 10 minutes. Remove cake to rack or serving tray. Serves 10 to 12

~ With Chocolate ~

1 cup coarsely chopped pecans
1/2 cup semi-sweet chocolate chips, melted
2 tablespoons water
1/4 teaspoon baking soda

Preheat the oven to 350°F and prepare the bundt pan and the batter for the Sour Cream Coffee Cake. Add the nuts to the batter, stirring well. Remove one-third of the batter to another mixing bowl. Combine the water and baking soda and mix until the soda is dissolved. Add to the melted chocolate and stir until smooth. Beat the chocolate into the one-third portion of the batter. Spoon half the remaining batter into the prepared bundt pan. Spread the chocolate batter on top. Spoon the last of the plain batter on top the chocolate. With a knife make pointed oval shapes like petals through the cake. Bake 40 minutes. The cake may be served immediately or cooled on a wire rack. Serves 10 to 12.

WHOLE WHEAT SOUR CREAM COFFEE CAKE

Whole wheat pastry flour is available in health food stores as well as many supermarkets. Even though it is finely ground, it retains the nutrition and robust flavor of whole grain flour, giving this coffee cake a hearty flavor.

FILLING:	CAKE:
½ cup brown sugar, packed	2 cups whole wheat pastry flour
½ cup all purpose flour	1½ teaspoons baking powder
1 teaspoon ground cinnamon	1 teaspoon baking soda
Grated rind of 1 orange	½ teaspoon salt
¼ cup cold butter, cut in pieces	½ cup butter or margarine
1 cup walnuts, coarsely chopped	1 cup sugar
	2 large eggs
	1 cup sour cream
	1 teaspoon vanilla extract
	Grated rind of 1 large orange

To make the filling, combine the brown sugar, flour, cinnamon and orange rind in the bowl of a food processor. With the steel blade in place pulse several times to mix well and add the cold butter. Whirl until the mixture resembles coarse cornmeal. The process may also be done with a pastry blender. Set the mixture aside. Preheat oven to 350°. Brush a bundt pan with melted butter or coat with vegetable spray. To make the cake, combine the pastry flour, baking powder, baking soda and salt in a small bowl, mixing well. In the large mixing bowl of an electric mixer cream the butter and sugar until light and fluffy. Add the eggs one at a time, beating well after each addition. Add the dry ingredients alternately with the sour cream to the butter mixture, beginning and ending with the flour mixture. Beat well until creamy and stir in the vanilla and orange rind. Pour one-half the batter into the prepared pan and spread the brown sugar filling on top. Sprinkle the walnuts atop the filling. Carefully spoon the remaining batter over the filling. Bake 40 minutes, then check for doneness. Remove from the oven and cool on a wire rack for 10 minutes. Loosen the cake with a knife and turn out on a tray or cool on a wire rack. Serves 12 to 14.

ALMOND COFFEE CAKE

This delectable coffee cake may be served for breakfast, brunch, lunch, afternoon tea or even dessert. As the volume of batter is not large, it is easy to prepare two cakes at once so that you will have one to freeze.

TOPPING:	CAKE:
1 cup brown sugar, packed	1¾ cups all purpose flour, sifted
1 teaspoon ground cinnamon	3 teaspoons baking powder
¼ teaspoon ground nutmeg	½ teaspoons salt
1 cup coarsely chopped blanched almonds or pecans	½ cup butter or margarine
½ cup butter or margarine, melted	1 cup sugar
	2 large eggs
	1 cup milk
	1 teaspoon vanilla extract

To make the topping, combine the brown sugar, cinnamon, nutmeg and almonds in a small bowl, mixing well. Melt the butter in a small saucepan and set aside. Preheat oven to 350°. Brush a bundt pan with melted butter or coat with vegetable spray. Resift the flour with the baking powder and salt. Set aside. In the bowl of an electric mixer cream the butter and one cup of sugar until light and fluffy. Add the eggs one at a time, beating well after each addition. Add the dry ingredients to the batter alternately with the milk, beginning and ending with the flour mixture. Stir in the vanilla and continue to beat until the batter is light and creamy, scraping down the sides when necessary. Pour the batter into the prepared bundt pan and spread evenly. Sprinkle the brown sugar topping over the batter. Spoon the melted butter over the topping, distributing evenly. Bake about 50 minutes and test for doneness. Remove cake from the oven and allow to set on a wire rack in the baking pan for 5 minutes. Invert the cake on a serving plate or on a wire rack to cool, topping side, and gently lift the pan off the cake. There will probably be topping left in the pan; scoop it out with a spoon and scatter it over the cake where needed. If this is done immediately while hot from the oven the topping will hold beautifully. Serves 10.

GINGERBREAD

In spite of its name I class gingerbread with coffee cakes. This fragrant treat appeals to every age and can be served at any temperature and at any time of day.

> 2 cups all purpose flour, sifted
> 2 teaspoons baking powder
> ¼ teaspoon baking soda
> 2 teaspoons ground ginger
> 1 teaspoon ground cinnamon
> ¼ teaspoon ground cloves
> ½ teaspoon salt
> ⅓ cup butter or margarine
> ½ cup sugar
> 1 egg, beaten
> ⅔ cup molasses
> ¾ cup buttermilk

Preheat oven to 350°. Brush an 8x8x2" baking pan with melted butter or coat with vegetable spray.

Resift flour with the baking powder, baking soda, ginger, cinnamon, cloves and salt. Set aside. In the large bowl of an electric mixer cream the butter and sugar together until light and fluffy. Blend in the egg and molasses. Add the flour mixture alternately with the buttermilk, beginning and ending with the dry ingredients. Beat well after each addition. Bake in prepared pan approximately 50 minutes. Serves 6 to 8.

NOTE: Serve Gingerbread with whipped cream and a touch of cinnamon, sweetened yogurt (molasses makes a delicious sweetener) or honey butter — or just plain!

GINGERBREAD APPLE UPSIDE DOWN CAKE

> 2 tablespoons butter or margarine
> ½ cup molasses
> ⅓ cup dark or golden raisins
> 1 large Granny Smith apple, peeled, cored and sliced
> Batter for Gingerbread, previous page

Preheat oven to 325°. Coat a deep glass pie plate with vegetable spray. In a small saucepan, combine the butter and molasses. Heat until the butter is melted, stir well and add the raisins. Pour the mixture into the pie plate. Place the slices of apple over the molasses mixture. If needed add another half apple.

Pour the Gingerbread batter over the topping and spread evenly. Bake about 60 minutes and test for doneness. Turn the cake out on a serving tray upside down and the apples will be on top.

Confectioners' Icing

There are as many variations for confectioners' icing as there are flavorings in your cabinet. Start with one cup of confectioners' sugar. Add 2 teaspoons of lemon juice. Beat with a whisk, adding water or more lemon juice a little at a time, until the icing is the proper thickness for spreading on coffee cake or bread. Try adding ¼ teaspoon of vanilla, a tablespoon of liqueur, a tablespoon of strong coffee, a little melted chocolate, almond flavoring, rum, fresh orange juice or grated lemon, lime or orange rind. The recipe may be doubled or tripled for whatever amount is needed. Unless you are going to freeze a coffee cake, frost it immediately after removing it from the oven. The frosting melds into the cake and helps to keep it moist and delicious. But if you plan to freeze the cake, do not frost it until you are ready to serve it.

BANANAS FOSTER KUCHEN

This absolutely superb kuchen would be welcome as a dessert. Bake it in a deep glass pie plate and bring it to the table hot and flaming.

1½ cups all purpose flour
2 teaspoons baking powder
½ teaspoon salt
Grated rind of 1 lemon
½ cup butter or margarine
½ cup sugar
2 medium eggs
¼ cup milk
2 bananas
6 tablespoons brown sugar
1 tablespoon butter or margarine
2 tablespoons rum

Preheat oven to 350°. Brush a large deep cake pan with melted butter or coat with vegetable spray. (If using a glass baking dish set heat at 325° the first 25 minutes and then at 350° the last 30 minutes.)

Combine the flour, baking powder, salt and grated rind in a mixing bowl, blending well. Cream the butter and sugar until fluffy, add the eggs and beat until smooth. Blend in the milk. Stir in the flour mixture until well mixed — the batter will be a bit stiff but easy to spread. Pour batter into prepared pan and spread evenly. Slice the bananas crosswise and arrange them over the batter circling the dish and filling the center. Sprinkle brown sugar over the bananas. Cut the tablespoon of butter in small pieces and dot over the sugar. Bake about 50 minutes. Remove kuchen from the oven. Pour the rum into a small saucepan, heat, and pour over the kuchen. Touch a lit match carefully to the hot rum, causing it to flame up. Serves 8 to 10.

FRESH PEACH KUCHEN

A kuchen topped with fresh or frozen peaches and sprinkled with orange or lemon streusel makes a perfectly luscious breakfast — or dessert!

Batter for Bananas Foster Kuchen (see recipe at left)
One 16-ounce package fresh frozen peaches,
drained, or 2 cups fresh sliced peaches
2 tablespoons lemon juice

STREUSEL:
⅓ cup all purpose flour
⅓ cup sugar
⅓ cup cold butter
Grated rind of 1 large orange or lemon

Preheat oven to 350°. Brush a deep glass 10" pan with melted butter or coat with vegetable spray.

Prepare the batter as described for Bananas Foster Kuchen. Pour the batter into the pie plate, spreading evenly. Drain the peaches and sprinkle with the lemon juice. Arrange the peaches in a circular design on top of the batter. Combine the flour, sugar, cold butter cut in pieces and grated rind in a food processor. With the steel blade in place pulse several times until the mixture resembles coarse cornmeal. Sprinkle the streusel over the peaches, spreading evenly by hand. Bake approximately 45 minutes and test for doneness. Remove and serve. Serves 10.

CURRANT SALLY LUNN

There are several versions of the origin of Sally Lunn Cake but I prefer the one that credits an actual Sally Lunn who owned a bakery in Bath, England during the 18th century.

2½ cups sifted all purpose flour
3 teaspoons baking powder
1 teaspoon salt
⅓ cup sugar
Grated rind of 1 lemon
½ cup cold butter, cut in pieces
4 egg yolks
1 cup milk
1 cup currants, scalded and dried
4 egg whites

Preheat oven to 350°. Brush a bundt pan with melted butter or coat with vegetable spray.

Resift the flour, baking powder, salt and sugar. Transfer to the bowl of a food processor with the steel blade in place. Add the grated lemon rind. Pulse to mix the ingredients and add the butter. Whirl until the butter is well cut into the dry ingredients. Add the egg yolks and milk, whirling until well blended. Transfer to a mixing bowl and stir in the currants. Beat the egg whites until softly stiff and fold into the batter. Spread the batter in prepared bundt pan. Bake 45 to 50 minutes and test for doneness. Remove cake from the oven and turn out on a wire rack to cool or on a serving tray. Serves 12 although after standing for a day the cake can be sliced thinly into twice as many servings.

WHOLE WHEAT COFFEE CAKE

Make this gratifying and nutritious coffee cake with a good stone ground whole wheat flour.

1½ cups whole wheat flour
3 teaspoons baking powder
½ teaspoon salt
⅓ cup honey
⅓ cup light oil
⅔ cup milk
Grated rind of 1 large orange
½ cup orange juice
1 large egg
1 cup raisins, scalded and dried
¾ cup coarsely chopped pecans or walnuts

Preheat oven to 350°. Brush a deep glass pie plate with melted butter or coat with vegetable spray.

Combine the whole wheat flour, baking powder and salt. Stir and set aside. In a large mixing bowl beat together the honey, oil, milk, orange juice and egg. Stir in the flour mixture until the batter is smooth. Fold in the raisins and nuts. Pour into the prepared pie plate, spreading evenly. Bake in a preheated oven 35 to 40 minutes and test for doneness. The cake may be served hot from the oven in the glass plate or cooled on a wire rack.

AN OPTIONAL TOPPING: Combine ¼ cup honey with ¼ cup melted butter and 1 teaspoon cinnamon. Stir until well mixed. Spread this over the cake immediately after removing from the oven.

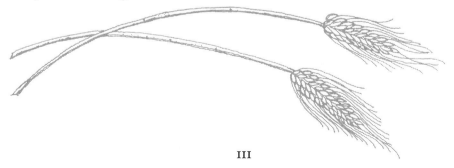

A QUICKIE COFFEE CAKE

One of Webster's definitions of quick is "manifesting a characteristic activity or quality suggestive of life." Here is a lively coffee cake that is extremely quick to make, but has a fine flavor and texture. Two adaptations follow the main recipe.

1½ cups all purpose flour
2 teaspoons baking powder
½ teaspoon salt
½ cup sugar
1 egg
½ cup milk
¼ cup butter or margarine, melted
　 STREUSEL:
¼ cup all purpose flour
¼ cup sugar
1 teaspoon ground cinnamon
¼ cup butter or margarine, cut in pieces
½ cup pecans or walnuts, chopped

Preheat oven to 350°. Brush 9x9" baking pan or a 9" cake pan with melted butter or coat with vegetable spray.

In a mixing bowl combine the flour, baking powder, salt and sugar. Blend well. In a separate bowl or four-cup measure beat the egg, milk and butter together. Make a well in the dry ingredients and quickly stir in the liquids until the batter is smooth. Pour the batter into the prepared pan. Spread evenly.

Combine the ¼ cup of flour, sugar, cinnamon and butter in a food processor. Pulse until the mixture resembles coarse cornmeal. Add the nuts and whirl several times until well mixed. Sprinkle the streusel on top of the batter. Bake 25 to 30 minutes. Serves 6.

COCONUT QUICKIE CAKE

This recipe will follow the same principle as the Quickie Coffee Cake but with an entirely different flavor that reminds me of Hawaii.

Batter for Quickie Coffee Cake, previous page
⅓ cup dark or golden raisins, scalded and dried
⅓ cup coarsely chopped pecans or walnuts
   TOPPING:
¼ cup brown sugar, packed
¼ cup moist coconut
2 tablespoons melted butter

Preheat oven to 350°. Brush a deep glass pie plate or a 9" square baking pan with melted butter or coat with a vegetable spray.

Prepare the batter for Quickie Coffee Cake. Fold in the raisins and nuts until well distributed. Spread evenly in prepared pan. In a small bowl combine the sugar, coconut and melted butter. Spread over the top of the batter. Bake the coffee cake for 25 to 30 minutes or until it tests done. Remove from oven and serve while hot. Serves 6.

Cinnamon Sugar

In a jar with a lid, combine 1 cup of granulated sugar with 2 tablespoons cinnamon. Shake to mix well. Double or triple this to keep in a pretty jar in the kitchen. It's perfect for finishing coffee cakes or making cinnamon toast for the children or grandchildren. You can make vanilla sugar by adding one strong, fresh vanilla bean to a jar of sugar instead of the cinnamon.

ORANGE COFFEE CAKE WITH ORANGE STREUSEL

This splendid large cake will serve twelve guests. It is filled with fresh orange juice and topped with crunchy orange streusel.

4 cups all purpose flour, sifted
4 teaspoons baking powder
1 teaspoons salt
⅔ cup butter or margarine
1 cup sugar
Grated rind of 2 large oranges
3 large eggs
1 cup orange juice, freshly squeezed
  or made from frozen concentrate
1 cup milk
½ cup chopped blanched almonds
½ cup golden raisins, scalded and dried
  STREUSEL:
¼ cup all purpose flour
½ cup sugar
Grated rind of 1 large orange
2 tablespoons cold butter, cut in pieces

Preheat oven to 350°. Brush a 10" round mold cake pan (angel food pan) with melted butter or coat with vegetable spray. Resift the flour, baking powder and salt together and set aside. In the large bowl of an electric mixer cream the butter, sugar and orange rind until light and fluffy. Add the eggs one at a time, beating well after each addition. Add one-half the flour mixture and then the orange juice, beating until smooth. Stir in the remaining flour and then the milk and blend until smooth. Mix in the raisins and nuts until well distributed. Pour the batter into the prepared pan, spreading evenly. Combine the streusel ingredients in a food processor. With the steel blade in place pulse until the mixture resembles coarse cornmeal. Sprinkle the streusel on top of the batter. Bake approximately one hour and 20 minutes and test for doneness. Remove the cake to a wire rack for cooling. Serves 12 to 14.

TROPICAL FRUIT COFFEE CAKE

With all the luscious ingredients in this cake, one slice is very satisfying. Accompany with cheese and a crisp green salad for a complete lunch.

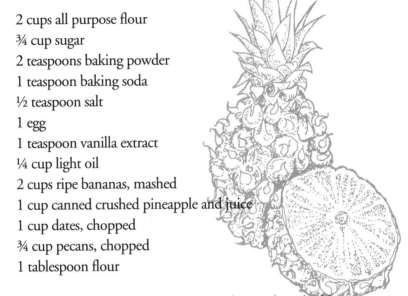

2 cups all purpose flour
¾ cup sugar
2 teaspoons baking powder
1 teaspoon baking soda
½ teaspoon salt
1 egg
1 teaspoon vanilla extract
¼ cup light oil
2 cups ripe bananas, mashed
1 cup canned crushed pineapple and juice
1 cup dates, chopped
¾ cup pecans, chopped
1 tablespoon flour

Preheat oven to 325°. Brush a 10" deep glass cake plate with melted butter or coat with vegetable spray.

Sift the two cups of flour, sugar, baking powder, baking soda and salt in a mixing bowl. Separately combine the egg, vanilla, oil, bananas and pineapple. Chop or snip dates with scissors and combine with the pecans. Sprinkle the tablespoon of flour over the date mixture and mix well with your hands to separate the sticky dates. Stir the banana-pineapple mixture into the dry ingredients quickly until well mixed. Fold in the dates and nuts. Spread the batter in the prepared cake plate. Bake about 40 minutes and test for doneness. Remove the cake and let stand on a wire rack for 10 minutes. Serves 10.

MARGO'S GRANOLA COFFEE CAKE

This nutritious coffee cake was devised by my Aspen daughter-in-law, who loves the outdoor life and my granola. It is perfect for a mountain-top picnic.

1 cup all purpose flour
¾ teaspoon baking powder
¾ teaspoon baking soda
½ teaspoon salt
½ teaspoon ground mace
1 cup granola
½ cup butter or margarine
½ cup sugar
3 medium eggs
1 cup sour cream
   TOPPING:
⅓ cup brown sugar, packed
½ teaspoon cinnamon
⅓ cup pecans, chopped

Preheat oven to 350°. Brush an 8x8" baking pan or a 9" deep pie plate or cake tin with melted butter or coat with vegetable spray.

Combine the flour, baking powder, baking soda, salt, mace and granola in a mixing bowl and blend well. Set aside. Cream the butter and sugar together in the large bowl of an electric mixer until smooth and fluffy. Add the eggs and beat until well mixed. Blend in the sour cream and the granola mixture until well mixed. Spoon the batter into the prepared pan, spreading evenly. Combine the brown sugar, cinnamon and nuts and stir until blended. Sprinkle on top of the batter evenly. Bake 30 minutes and test for doneness. Serve hot or cool on a wire rack. Serves 8.

Mary's Granola

Crunchy granola is versatile and wholesome. I love it on cereal with bananas, on yogurt or ice cream, or just with milk.

6 cups rolled oats
1 cup sesame seeds, untoasted
1 cup sunflower seeds, untoasted
1 cup raw wheat germ
1 cup oat bran
1 cup powdered skim milk
½ cup raw peanuts
½ cup slivered blanched almonds
½ cup whole almonds, blanched or with skin
1¼ cups safflower or corn oil
1¼ cups honey
1½ teaspoons vanilla extract
¾ cup raisins, optional

Preheat oven to 250°. You will need a very large baking sheet or two small ones — do not oil them. In a large mixing bowl combine the oats, sesame seeds, sunflower seeds, wheat germ, oat bran, powdered skim milk, peanuts, slivered and whole almonds. The whole almonds may either be blanched or left in their skins but none of the nuts should be salted. Stir well with a wooden spoon or combine with your hands. In a 4-cup measure combine the oil, honey and vanilla and stir thoroughly. Add the oil mixture to the oat mixture and stir with a wooden spoon or with your hands (easier although messy) until all the dry ingredients are well covered with the oil mixture. Spread the granola on a large baking sheet and place in the oven. Bake about 1½ to 2 hours, stirring every 20 to 25 minutes. If raisins are desired, add when granola is removed from the oven. Place the pan on a wire rack to cool. Return and stir in 10 minutes. Stir again in another 10 minutes. This keeps the mixture from massing together. When cool, place in containers with tight-fitting lids.

CHERRY-FILLED COFFEE CAKE

This, too, is fashioned after the Quickie Coffee Cake, but I have enlarged the recipe. There are hidden cherries and streusel in the center.

> 2 cups all purpose flour
> 3 teaspoons baking powder
> ½ teaspoon salt
> ⅔ cup sugar
> 2 eggs
> ⅔ cup milk
> ⅓ cup butter or margarine, melted
> One 1-pound can unsweetened red cherries, drained
> STREUSEL:
> ⅓ cup all purpose flour
> ⅓ cup sugar
> 1 teaspoon ground cinnamon
> ⅓ cup butter or margarine, cut in pieces
> ½ cup chopped pecans

Preheat oven to 350°. Brush an 8x12" baking pan or a 10" deep glass pie plate with melted butter or coat with vegetable spray. If using glass, lower heat to 325°.

Combine the two cups of flour with the baking powder, salt and sugar, blending well. Separately beat eggs, milk and butter together. With a rubber spatula stir the liquid ingredients into the flour mixture until smooth. Spread half the batter in prepared pan. Sprinkle the cherries over the batter. Combine the streusel ingredients in a food processor. Pulse until well mixed. Sprinkle the streusel atop the cherries. Spoon the remaining batter over the streusel and spread carefully. If there is not enough to cover, don't worry. The cake will puff up beautifully. Bake 40 to 45 minutes. Remove from the oven and cool 10 to 15 minutes on a wire rack. Serve warm. Serves 8 to 10.

FOOD PROCESSOR CARROT COFFEE CAKE

At a wonderful picnic brunch on Easter morning in Chevy Chase, I found this little gem, obtained originally from Judith Baldinger.

> 1 cup carrots, grated (about 3 carrots)
> Grated rind of 1 lemon
> Juice of ½ lemon
> ¾ cup butter or margarine
> 6 tablespoons brown sugar
> 2 medium eggs
> 1¼ cups all purpose flour
> ½ teaspoon salt
> 1 teaspoon baking powder
> ½ teaspoon baking soda

Preheat oven to 350°. Brush a 6-cup round mold with melted butter or coat with vegetable spray.

Grate the carrots in the processor and transfer to a small bowl. Add the grated rind and lemon juice. Combine the butter and sugar in the processor and pulsate several times until creamy. Add the eggs and pulse until well mixed. Return carrot mixture to the processor. In a small bowl combine the flour, salt, baking powder and baking soda and mix well. Add the dry ingredients to the food processor. Pulse until well mixed — the batter will be somewhat sticky. With a rubber spatula transfer the batter to the prepared mold and spread evenly. Bake about 30 minutes and test for doneness. Cool in the mold on a wire rack for 10 minutes. Invert on a round serving plate. Delicious hot or at room temperature. Serves 8.

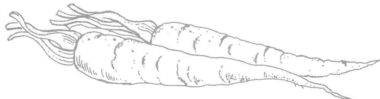

Biscuits &
Scones

I
n most quick breads, soda, baking powder and cream of tartar are
the leavenings that create carbon dioxide, causing the batter or
dough to rise. Before the mid-1800s, when commercial
baking powders first appeared, eggs and much hand beating were used to
raise breads and cakes whose batters were too thin to be affected by yeast. In
the last decade of the 18th century, pearl ash (or potassium carbonate) was
made in the new American Republic by burning wood — not good for the
forests but a boon to bakers. Americans shipped over 8000 tons of pearl ash
to Europe. Later baking powder was made by combining baking soda, an
alkali, with cream of tartar, an acid. In the presence of liquid, the two
create the carbon dioxide that makes tiny bubbles in batter or dough.
When the batter is heated in the oven, the bubbles or air pockets expand
further, and the bread hardens around them.

In ancient Egypt bakers had learned to produce risen breads with beer
foam, wine scum and a form of "sourdough starter" kept over from one baking
to the next. They flavored breads with date syrup, honey, nuts, spices, herbs and
figs. Although their breads were not as high and puffy as ours today, they must
have pleased the Pharaohs, who were buried in their magnificent tombs with
plenty of bread for the long journey to the hereafter. Egyptian bakers learned the
art of shaping breads into animal and bird forms, flowers and even human
figures. With the development of their art, bakers rose high in the strata of
Egyptian society.

In this chapter we venture further into the wide world of quick breads
dependent on baking powder, baking soda and cream of tartar for their lightness.
Both biscuits and scones are delightfully simple and amazingly quick to prepare.
Twenty minutes and they are ready to serve — and that includes the mixing.

TENDER BISCUITS

For tender, flaky biscuits, be careful not to overmix. Mixing time should be a scant half minute.

If too much soda is added, or if the rising agent is not well distributed through the batter, small brown spots will appear on the finished biscuits.

Biscuits may be rolled out or dropped by the spoonful, depending on the consistency of the batter and the desired result.

Mix them in a shallow bowl — you probably have one in your kitchen. I use a heavy china salad bowl, a wedding present of 53 years ago that has withstood the travesty of many moves and the active presence of growing sons. It is my biscuit bowl and nothing else will do. Its shallow shape is perfect for mixing dough with a pastry blender.

In making biscuits and scones, typically the dry ingredients are measured or sifted directly into a bowl and stirred together. Butter or margarine (vegetable shortening if preferred) is cut into the flour mixture with a pastry blender or with two knives or a knife and fork. The mixture is blended quickly until it is crumbly or resembles very coarse cornmeal. The distribution of small fat particles makes a flaky biscuit or scone. Next, a well is made in the dry mixture and the liquid is stirred in rapidly with a rubber spatula until the dough forms a rough ball and pulls away from the sides of the bowl. The dough is turned out onto a floured surface and kneaded lightly for one or two minutes. Overkneading results in tough biscuits. The dough is patted into a flat circle with hands or a rolling pin and cut with a biscuit cutter. Biscuits and scones are baked at 450° in a preheated oven for 12 to 15 minutes. Then they are ready to serve hot from the oven with good butter and favorite jelly or preserves.

I've loved testing these biscuits for they remind me of my childhood when I was given hot biscuits at least four or five times a week. Many have responded well to a little elaboration. Try some experimenting yourself and enjoy biscuits for breakfast or dinner or as a snack with afternoon tea.

BUTTERMILK BISCUITS

"Take two while they're hot and pass the butter around," were my father's words when we had biscuits. So I took two and watched the butter ooze down the sides and sometimes I turned them over so their tops would have plenty of butter melting through.

> 2 cups all purpose flour
> 3 teaspoons baking powder
> ½ teaspoon baking soda
> ¾ teaspoon salt
> ⅓ cup butter, margarine or vegetable shortening
> ¾ cup buttermilk

Preheat oven to 450°. Select an ungreased baking sheet.

In a shallow mixing bowl combine the flour, baking powder, baking soda and salt and mix well with a rubber spatula — or if preferred sift the ingredients into the bowl. Cut the butter into the dry ingredients with a pastry blender or use a knife and fork. Cut into the dry ingredients until the mixture is crumbly or like very coarse cornmeal. Make a well in the mixture and pour in the buttermilk. Stir quickly with a rubber spatula until the dough pulls away from the sides of the bowl. Turn the dough out on a floured surface and knead lightly for about a minute to gather all the little pieces of dough together into a smooth ball. Pat or roll ½" thick. If a thinner biscuit is preferred roll dough ¼" thick. Cut with a 2" biscuit cutter. Gather up all extra pieces of dough, knead together and pat out into a second circle. Cut this into biscuits until you come to the last bit of dough which you can roll in your hands — I always loved that biscuit for it would come out such an odd shape. Place on the ungreased baking sheet. For soft biscuits, place close together and for crispy biscuits, place about one inch apart. Bake 12 to 15 minutes and serve hot. Makes about 20 two-inch biscuits.

SWEET MILK BISCUITS

These are called Sweet Milk Biscuits to distinguish them from biscuits made with buttermilk.

> 2 cups all purpose flour
> 4 teaspoons baking powder
> 2 teaspoons sugar
> ¾ teaspoon salt
> ½ teaspoon cream of tartar
> ⅓ cup butter, margarine or vegetable shortening
> ⅔ cup milk

Preheat oven to 450°. Select an ungreased baking sheet, 9x13".

Combine the flour, baking powder, sugar, salt and cream of tartar in a shallow mixing bowl. Mix the ingredients together well or sieve if preferred. Cut in the butter quickly with a pastry blender. Make a well in the center of the dry ingredients and add the milk. With a rubber spatula stir quickly until the dough leaves the sides of the bowl and all the pieces of dough are brought together. Turn out on a floured surface and knead about one minute into a smooth ball. Roll out with a rolling pin or pat with your hands about ½" thick. Cut with a 2" biscuit cutter and place on ungreased pan. Bake 12 to 15 minutes. Makes 16 biscuits.

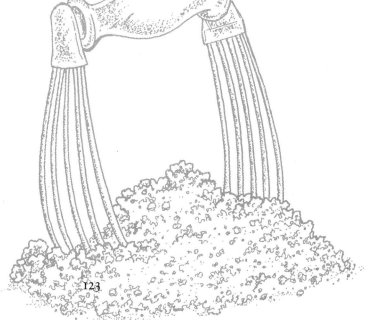

A Feast of Biscuits

Start with Buttermilk Biscuits or Sweet Milk Biscuits.

~ Orange Biscuits ~

Dough for Sweet Milk Biscuits or Buttermilk Biscuits
Grated rind of 1 large orange
Sweet orange marmalade

Combine the dry ingredients for the biscuit recipe and add the grated orange rind, stirring until well mixed. Cut in the butter and proceed as directed. Cut the biscuit dough with a 2" cutter and place on a baking sheet. Make an indentation on top each biscuit with forefinger and thumb. Place one teaspoon of marmalade in each indentation. Bake as directed for Buttermilk Biscuits. Makes 16 biscuits.

~ Christmas Biscuits ~

Dough for Buttermilk Biscuits or Sweet Milk Biscuits
1 cup candied fruits, chopped
(pineapple and red cherries)

When the butter has been cut into the dry mixture, add the fruits. Mix until well distributed. Add the milk as directed. Cut the biscuits and bake as directed for Buttermilk Biscuits.

~ Biscuits with Sausage ~

Dough for Buttermilk Biscuits or Sweet Milk Biscuits
Small smoky sausages, cooked

Make up the biscuit dough as directed and roll out to ¼" thickness. Prepare biscuits with a 2" or 2½" biscuit cutter. Flatten each circle and place one sausage on top the round of dough. Place another circle on top the sausage and pinch around the edges to seal. Place on the ungreased baking sheet. Bake as directed for Buttermilk Biscuits. Makes 11 biscuits.

~ Cheddar Cheese Biscuits ~

Dough for Buttermilk Biscuits or Sweet Milk Biscuits
2 cups sharp Cheddar cheese, finely grated

Combine the dry ingredients as directed in either recipe and cut in the
butter. Add the cheese and stir until well distributed. Proceed as stated
in the recipes, shape the biscuits and bake as directed for Buttermilk
Biscuits. The biscuits will be flecked with gold. Makes about 20 biscuits.

~ Biscuits with Lemon Sugar Cubes ~

*Many years ago when the Shamrock Hotel in Houston, Texas was
in all its glory and infamous reputation, I was served these entrancing
biscuits at the Cork Club for a luncheon. I was intrigued, but I could
never find a recipe. This evolution is a perfect copy.*

Dough for Buttermilk Biscuits
or Sweet Milk Biscuits
Grated rind of 1 lemon
Cubes of sugar
Lemon juice

Preheat oven to 450°. You will need one ungreased baking sheet.

Prepare biscuit dough as described adding the grated lemon rind to the
dry ingredients before the butter is cut in. Proceed as directed. Cut the
dough with a 2" biscuit cutter or a smaller one if desired. The biscuit
should be no more than two bites. Place 10 to 15 sugar cubes on a small
plate. Squeeze a few drops of fresh lemon juice atop each cube of sugar
(Do not allow them to stand or the cubes will disappear into the juice!) Place
a cube on top of each biscuit and press down into the dough. Bake 15
minutes or until golden — the sugar will turn quite golden around the
edges. Allow to cool a little before serving. No butter is needed. Makes
10 to 15 biscuits.

WHEAT GERM BISCUITS

1½ cups all purpose flour
½ cup toasted wheat germ
4 teaspoons baking powder
¾ teaspoon salt
½ teaspoon baking soda
⅓ cup margarine or vegetable shortening
¾ cup buttermilk

Preheat oven to 450°. One ungreased baking sheet will be needed.

Combine the flour, wheat germ, baking powder, salt and baking soda in a shallow mixing bowl, blending ingredients well. Cut in the margarine until the mixture resembles coarse cornmeal. Make a well in the ingredients and add the buttermilk. Stir rapidly with a rubber spatula until the dough leaves the side of the bowl. Turn out on a floured surface and knead about one minute until smooth. Roll out or pat with your hands ½" thick. Cut with a 2" biscuit cutter and place on ungreased baking sheet. Makes 19 biscuits.

WHOLE WHEAT BISCUITS

2 cups whole wheat flour
4 teaspoons baking powder
½ teaspoon baking soda
1 teaspoon salt
⅓ cup butter or margarine
¾ cup buttermilk

Preheat oven to 450°. One ungreased baking sheet will be needed. Combine the flour, baking powder, baking soda and salt together (do not attempt to sift as some of the nutrients in the whole wheat flour will be lost). Blend together well. Cut in the butter with a pastry blender until the mixture resembles coarse corn-meal. Make a well in the dry ingredients and pour in the buttermilk. Stir rapidly with a rubber spatula until the dough leaves the sides of the bowl. Turn out on a lightly floured board and knead about one minute to gather all the little pieces together and make a smooth ball. Roll out with a rolling pin or pat with your hands to ½" thick. Cut with a 2" biscuit cutter and place on the ungreased baking sheet. Bake 12 to 15 minutes. These biscuits will not be as high-rising as white biscuits but they have a wonderful earthy flavor. If a lighter whole wheat biscuit is desired, use one cup of whole wheat flour and one cup of all purpose flour. Makes 20 biscuits.

CREAM BISCUITS

These smooth, lovely biscuits made with cream will melt in your mouth. These are for pure, pleasant indulgence.

>   2 cups sifted all purpose flour
>   3 teaspoons baking powder
>   ¾ teaspoon salt
>   2 teaspoons sugar
>   ⅓ cup butter
>   ¾ cup cream or half and half

Preheat oven to 450°. One ungreased baking sheet will be needed. Combine the flour, baking powder, salt and sugar in a shallow mixing bowl and stir well. Cut in the butter with a pastry blender until the mixture resembles coarse cornmeal. Make a well in the center of the mixture and add the cream. With a rubber spatula stir quickly until the dough leaves the side of the bowl. Turn out on a floured surface and knead lightly for one or two minutes. Roll or pat dough to ½" thickness. Cut with a 2" biscuit cutter and place on the ungreased baking sheet. Bake 12 to 15 minutes. The biscuits will be a lovely golden color. Makes 16 biscuits.

YOGURT PARSLEY BISCUITS

These are extraordinarily delicious and with yogurt and parsley full of good nutrition.

2 cups all purpose flour
3 teaspoons baking powder
¾ teaspoon salt
¼ teaspoon baking soda
4 tablespoons butter or margarine
¾ cup plain yogurt
⅓ cup fresh parsley, finely chopped

Preheat oven to 450°. An ungreased baking sheet will be needed. In a shallow mixing bowl combine the flour, baking powder, salt and baking soda. Cut in the butter until the mixture resembles a coarse cornmeal. Make a well in the center of the mixture and add the yogurt and parsley. Stir quickly with a rubber spatula until the dough leaves the side of the bowl. Turn out on a floured surface and knead lightly until the dough is smooth. Roll out ½" thickness. Cut out biscuits with a 2" biscuit cutter and place on ungreased baking sheet. Bake 12 to 15 minutes. Makes about 16 biscuits.

Parsley

Lovely green parsley is a boon to many, many dishes. The ancient Romans knew five kinds of it, and relished a few leaves with bread as a breakfast dish. Charlemagne ordered it planted in his domains in the year 800, at which time it already flourished in French monastery gardens. It begins to be recorded in colonial United States cooking around the mid-1800s and today, as with the ancient Romans, we have five kinds — though not the same five! For flavor, the flat-leafed, or Italian parsley is superior to the curly-leafed variety.

COCONUT LEMON BISCUITS

These are in honor of my youngest daughter-in-law, Laura, who loves coconut on anything. They are sometimes comical for they tip in different directions.

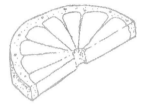

2 cups sifted all purpose flour
2 teaspoons baking powder
½ teaspoon salt
5 tablespoons butter or margarine
Grated rind of 1 lemon
⅔ cup milk
   FILLING:
4 tablespoons sugar
2 teaspoons lemon juice
2 tablespoons coconut
Melted butter

Preheat oven to 450°. Brush 20 muffin cups with melted butter or coat with vegetable spray. Sift together the flour, baking powder and salt into a shallow mixing bowl. Cut in the butter with a pastry blender until the ingredients resemble coarse cornmeal. Add the lemon rind and stir until well distributed. Make a well in the center of the dry mixture and stir in the milk quickly with a rubber spatula until the dough leaves the sides of the bowl. Turn out on a floured surface and knead lightly until smooth — about 1 minute. Cover with a cloth while mixing the filling.

Combine the sugar, lemon juice and coconut in a small bowl and stir to mix well. Roll the biscuit dough ¼" thick. Cut biscuits with a 1½" cutter. Place one in each muffin cup and brush with melted butter. Place ¼ teaspoon coconut filling atop the biscuit and cover with a second round of dough pressing lightly to adhere. Repeat with remaining ingredients until all the biscuits are made. Bake 12 to 15 minutes. Some may topple a bit like the tower of Pisa but don't worry — they are fun to look at and delicious to consume. Makes approximately 20 double biscuits.

SELF-RISING BISCUITS

With a well-chosen flour the self-rising biscuit can be remarkably good and is certainly delightfully easy to make. Biscuit variations may be made with this recipe.

2 cups self rising flour*
6 tablespoons butter, margarine or vegetable shortening
⅔ cup milk or buttermilk

Preheat oven to 450°. Use an ungreased baking sheet for baking. Measure flour into a shallow mixing bowl. Cut in the butter with a pastry blender until the mixture resembles coarse cornmeal. Make a well in the center of the mixture and add the milk. Stir quickly with a rubber spatula until the contents gather together and leave sides of the bowl. Turn out on a floured surface and knead about 1 minute until the dough is smooth. Roll or pat ½" thick. Cut with a 2" biscuit cutter and place on ungreased baking sheet. Bake 12 to 15 minutes. Makes 16 biscuits.

*Self-rising flour already contains a rising agent and salt.

LAURA'S BISCUIT SHORTCAKE

This is the perfect shortcake one remembers mother or grandmother preparing. Load it with fresh summer strawberries and heap with whipped cream. This recipe comes from my youngest daughter-in-law who has a never-ceasing sweet tooth.

2 cups all purpose flour
½ teaspoon salt
4 teaspoons baking powder
½ teaspoon baking soda
¼ cup sugar
7 tablespoons vegetable shortening
1 cup buttermilk

Preheat oven to 450°. Brush a baking sheet lightly with melted butter or coat with vegetable spray.

Combine the flour, salt, baking powder, baking soda and sugar in a shallow mixing bowl. Add the vegetable shortening and cut in with a pastry blender until mixture resembles coarse cornmeal. Make a well in the center and add the buttermilk. With a rubber spatula quickly stir together until dry ingredients are moistened. Turn out on a floured surface and knead lightly until the dough melds together. Pat or roll dough out ¼" thick. With a 3" biscuit cutter, cut out 8 rounds. As the dough is cut, gather the leftover pieces, knead together, and cut rounds until the dough is completely used. You may end up with a small shortcake at the end. Place biscuits on the baking sheet and bake 12 minutes or until puffed and golden. Remove and cool. Split the cakes when ready to serve. If desired, split while hot from the oven and brush each side with melted butter — richer still but delicious. Prepare the berries and sprinkle with sugar. Pile berries on one half a split biscuit, top with another and add more berries. Serve plain or with whipped cream or ice cream. Makes 11 large shortcakes.

BISCUIT TEA RING

2 cups all purpose flour
4 teaspoons baking powder
½ teaspoon baking soda
½ teaspoon salt
5 tablespoons butter or margarine
1 cup buttermilk

FILLING:
Melted butter
½ cup Cinnamon Sugar (page 113)
FROSTING:
1 cup confectioners' sugar
2 teaspoons strong coffee

Preheat oven to 425°. Brush a baking sheet with melted butter or coat with vegetable spray. Combine the flour, baking powder, baking soda and salt in a shallow mixing bowl. Mix thoroughly. Cut in the butter with a pastry blender until the mixture resembles coarse cornmeal. Make a well in the center and add the buttermilk. Combine quickly with a rubber spatula and turn the dough out on a well-floured surface. Knead dough until smooth, about 1 minute. Gently roll the dough into a 9x16" rectangle. Brush with melted butter leaving ¼" edge free around the dough. Sprinkle with the cinnamon sugar and smooth with your hand. Roll from the long side using a dough scraper to assist if the dough sticks to the counter surface. The dough cannot be easily pinched together but can be pressed together lightly. Pick up the roll and turn seam side down on the baking sheet. Form into a circle inserting the ends together. With scissors cut deep slashes into the dough 1" apart. Turn each finger on its side and press the cake lightly. Brush the ring with melted butter. Bake 20 to 25 minutes or until lightly golden. Remove to a serving tray. Whisk the confectioners' sugar and coffee together until smooth. Drizzle over the biscuit ring while hot. Serves 6 to 8.

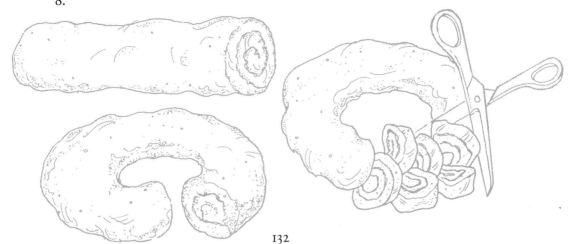

SCOTTISH OATMEAL SCONES

On a journey from Edinborough up the east coast of Scotland, I was awestruck by the high waves of the Northern Sea dashing on wicked looking rocks. Further north, on the shores of Loch Ness we watched hoping for the monster to appear and enjoyed daily afternoon tea with hot buttered scones. My maiden name was Douglass and my father had assured me that an Egyptian princess brought the Stone of Scone to the Black Douglass whom she married and that I could trace my lineage back to Adam and Eve. Well, I believed anything my father told me!

> 1½ cups all purpose flour
> ½ cup rolled oats
> 1 teaspoon baking soda
> 2 teaspoons cream of tartar
> 6 tablespoons butter or margarine
> ½ cup raisins
> ½ cup milk

Combine the flour, oats, baking soda and cream of tartar in a shallow mixing bowl. Salt isn't really necessary for scones, but for these you may wish to add ½ teaspoonful. Cut in the butter until the mixture is crumbly. Add the raisins, mix well and stir in the milk with a rubber spatula until the dough is gathered into a ball. Remove to a floured surface and knead lightly approximately one minute until smooth. Roll into a circle ½" deep. Cut in triangles with a sharp knife or dough scraper. Place on a baking sheet and bake 12 to 15 minutes or until golden and crisp on the outside. Makes 14 scones.

Scones are usually cut into triangles but they can be made into rounds with a biscuit cutter. Rapidity is important in the preparation. Serve scones hot from the oven or split, brushed with melted butter, and toasted until they are crisp and crunchy.

WHOLE WHEAT SCONES

½ cup all purpose flour
½ cup whole wheat flour
1 teaspoon baking soda
2 teaspoons cream of tartar
7 tablespoons butter or margarine
½ cup milk

Preheat oven to 450°. An ungreased baking sheet will be needed. In a shallow mixing bowl combine the two flours, baking soda and cream of tartar. Cut in the butter until the mixture is crumbly. Make a well in the center and add the milk. Stir with a rubber spatula until the dough comes together. If the mixture seems too dry add a bit more milk. Turn out on a surface dusted with white flour and knead lightly until a smooth ball, about one minute. Roll into a circle ½" deep and cut into triangles using a sharp knife or dough scraper. Bake the triangles on the ungreased baking sheet until lightly browned and crisp, about 12 minutes. The dough may be cut in rounds as with biscuits if desired. Makes 10 scones.

ENGLISH CURRANT SCONES

1½ cups all purpose flour
2½ teaspoons baking powder
½ teaspoon salt
¼ cup butter or margarine
⅓ cup currants
1 tablespoon sugar
½ cup milk or cream
1 egg, lightly beaten

134

Preheat oven to 375°. Use an ungreased baking sheet. Sift together the flour, baking powder and salt into a shallow mixing bowl. Cut in the butter with a pastry blender until the mixture resembles coarse cornmeal. Add the currants and sugar and mix well. Gradually stir in the milk or cream until a soft dough is formed. Round the dough into a ball and place on a floured surface. Knead lightly one minute. Roll ½" thick. Cut scones with a 2½" biscuit cutter and place on baking sheet. Brush tops of scones with beaten egg. Bake approximately 20 minutes. Split with a fork and brush each side with soft butter. Serve hot. Makes 14 scones.

NOTE: Raisins may be used instead of currants. For a change of flavor, add the grated rind of one orange to the dry ingredients. Or you may marinate the currants in Grand Marnier or Curaçao 30 minutes. Add to the mixture after the butter has been cut in. Proceed as directed.

CHEESE SCONES

> 2 cups all purpose flour
> 2 teaspoons cream of tartar
> 1 teaspoon baking soda
> 1 teaspoon sugar
> 6 tablespoons butter or margarine
> 1 cup sharp Cheddar cheese, grated
> 1 medium egg
> ½ cup milk

Preheat oven to 450°. Use an ungreased baking sheet. Combine the flour, cream of tartar, baking soda and sugar in a shallow mixing bowl. Cut in the butter with a pastry blender until the mixture is crumbly. Stir in the grated cheese. Combine the egg and milk, mixing well, and add to the flour mixture. With a rubber spatula quickly stir the two mixtures until they come together in a ball. Turn the dough out on a floured surface and knead one minute or until smooth. Roll into a circle ½" in depth. Cut in 1½ or 2" rounds with a biscuit cutter. Place on a baking sheet and bake 12 to 14 minutes. Makes 35 scones with the smaller biscuit cutter.

BLUEBERRY SCONES

Frozen berries are better in this dough than fresh. Do not let the berries thaw. Use them frozen right from the package.

> 2 cups all purpose flour
> 2 teaspoons cream of tartar
> 1 teaspoon baking soda
> ½ teaspoon salt
> 1 teaspoon sugar
> 6 tablespoons butter or margarine
> ¾ cup fresh or frozen blueberries
> 1 egg
> ½ cup milk

Preheat oven to 450°. Brush a baking sheet lightly with melted butter or coat with vegetable spray.

Sift the flour, cream of tartar, baking soda, salt and sugar into a shallow mixing bowl. Cut the butter into the dry ingredients with a pastry blender. Add the blueberries to the dry mixture and stir quickly to distribute evenly. Combine the egg and milk together, mixing well. Add to the blueberry mixture and stir with a rubber spatula until the dough comes away from sides of the bowl. Turn out on a lightly floured surface and knead quickly. Press or roll the dough ½" thick. Cut into triangles and place on the baking sheet. Bake 12 to 15 minutes or slightly longer. Makes 14 scones.

Pancakes & Waffles

There are as many different kinds of pancakes in the United States as there are minestrone soups in Italy — from orange pancakes in Florida to sourdough griddle cakes in Alaska. Home cooks often have their own versions of this "Sunday morning specialty." Pancake restaurants serve myriads of cakes topped with fruit, nuts, whipped cream or sour cream or stuffed with sausage or crumbled bacon. All this abundance began when the Indians taught America's first European settlers to make corn cakes, saving many lives in their first hard winter. When commercial baking powder and baking soda became available pancakes became lighter, puffier and certainly easier to prepare.

Inventive Shakers constantly experimented with foods, seeds, furniture and celibacy. They were the first to combine dry ingredients in a mix similar to Aunt Jemima's for they ate communally and those in the kitchen worked consistently to make preparation of foods easier and faster. I have spent several enjoyable nights at the Shaker Inn in Kentucky, in a room furnished with simple, functional objects, including a handsome railing built around the room at just the right height for hanging coats, hats and umbrellas. The buffet breakfast offered many choices but my favorite was a plate of light, delicious pancakes with sautéed apples.

The earliest pancakes were probably made by ancient people who learned to grind seeds and grains into a rough paste, mix it with a little water, and slap it on a hot rock. Evidence of such cakes has been found in the Lake Dwellings in Switzerland which date to 12,000 years ago. Now we are blessed with huge, thick pancakes for camping, elegant crepes wrapped around fresh fruits, cakes bursting with whole grains, and high-rising cakes invented by the old sourdoughs of Alaska mining fame. So much can be done with a simple pancake by adding nuts, coconut, fresh fruits, sausages, poached eggs — or even caviar!

Pancakes and waffles are prepared by combining dry ingredients and quickly stirring in the liquids. Egg whites are whipped until softly stiff and folded into the final batter to give lightness and wonderful texture. Frequently I allow the batter to rest for 10 to 15 minutes and then quickly beat again just before baking.

This chapter includes one waffle and one pancake made with yeast. The Belgian waffle is thicker and crisper than a regular waffle — with all the proper adornments it will fill anyone for breakfast. The Belgians serve these with whipped cream but Americans often prefer sour cream. Both pancakes and waffles should be made quickly, and not beaten too much or a tough pancake will result. Through all the recipes I have used a one-fourth cup measure to ladle batter onto the griddle — it makes a perfect medium-sized pancake. But plate-sized or dollar-sized cakes are certainly easy to make as well. The griddle should be heated over medium high heat until a drop of water sizzles on it — then it is ready. Serve the cakes or waffles as quickly as possible. If there is a delay, place the cooked pancakes on an ovenproof plate in an oven preheated to approximately 200°. Waffles can be recrisped in a toaster oven.

Buttermilk Pancake Variations

~ With Blueberries ~

Follow the directions for Buttermilk Pancakes, adding 1 cup of fresh blueberries. Berries should be dry. Pick over carefully and use right from the container or wash and spread on paper towels to dry. When the batter is finished, fold in the berries and bake as directed.

~ With Pecans ~

Prepare batter for Buttermilk Pancakes, then fold in 1½ cups coarsely chopped pecans until well distributed. If desired, add 1 teaspoon cinnamon and ½ teaspoon nutmeg to the batter. Bake as directed.

BUTTERMILK PANCAKES

This light and airy pancake whose delicate flavor can survive being smothered in butter and swathed in syrup relies on the combination of buttermilk and eggs. The recipe is easy and adaptable to many variations.

> 2 cups sifted all purpose flour
> 1 teaspoon baking soda
> ¾ teaspoon salt
> 2 tablespoons sugar
> 2 large eggs, beaten
> 2 cups buttermilk
> 2 tablespoons butter or margarine, melted

In a medium sized mixing bowl, combine the flour, baking soda, salt and sugar and mix very well. In a separate bowl (I use a two-cup measure), blend the eggs, buttermilk and butter. Make a well in the dry ingredients and pour in the buttermilk mixture. With a rubber spatula mix quickly to moisten the dry ingredients and *stop*. Don't beat the batter too much. If it is lumpy, allow it to rest for 10 minutes and stir quickly once or twice. Brush a griddle lightly with a light oil or coat with vegetable spray. Place over moderately high heat. Dip out the batter with a fourth-cup measure, and pour pancakes one at a time onto the griddle. Cook the pancakes on one side until bubbles appear and begin to break. If the cakes brown too quickly, lower the heat. Turn the pancakes and bake until a light brown. Want the fun of flipping? Go right ahead. If you miss one, your dog will love you for it. Makes 16 pancakes about 4" in diameter.

NOTE: For an even lighter pancake, separate the eggs. Add the beaten egg yolk to the buttermilk and follow directions as given. Beat the egg whites until softly stiff and fold into the batter.

COTTAGE CHEESE PANCAKES

These have a special, tender texture. Serve with confectioners' sugar or fruit preserves for breakfast, or for dessert after a light supper.

3 large eggs
¾ cup cottage cheese
½ teaspoon salt
⅓ cup all purpose flour
1 teaspoon sugar
2 tablespoons butter, melted
Grated rind of 1 lemon

Add the eggs and cottage cheese to a blender and whirl to mix. Measure in the salt, flour, sugar, butter and grated rind. Blend on medium high until well mixed, then whirl a few seconds on high speed until the batter is smooth. Heat a griddle to medium high heat and brush lightly with corn oil or coat with vegetable spray. Drop the batter by tablespoons onto the hot griddle. Cook cakes on one side until golden, then flip to bake the other side. This will take only a few minutes with small pancakes. Makes approximately 22 cakes, 2¼" in diameter.

YOGURT PANCAKES

Delicious, healthful and light. Try them with blueberry syrup.

1 cup whole wheat flour
¼ cup toasted wheat germ
2 tablespoons brown sugar
¼ teaspoon baking soda
1 teaspoon baking powder
¾ cup low-fat plain yogurt
1 egg, beaten
1 tablespoon fresh lemon juice
½ cup skim milk

In a mixing bowl combine the whole wheat flour, wheat germ, sugar, baking soda and baking powder. Blend well. In a separate container stir together the yogurt, egg, lemon juice and skim milk. Stir the yogurt mixture into the dry ingredients with quick strokes. Set aside for 20 minutes while preparing the rest of breakfast. Spray a griddle with vegetable spray and place over medium high heat. Cook the pancakes using ⅓ cup batter for each cake. Makes 8 cakes.

Delicious Sweet Butters

~ Maple Butter ~

Combine ½ cup maple syrup, ½ cup softened butter or margarine, and 1 cup confectioner's sugar in the small bowl of an electric mixer and blend until creamy, or whisk the mixture together vigrorously with a whisk.

~ Honey Butter ~

Combine equal amounts of honey with soft butter or margarine and whip with a wire whip until fluffy and smooth.

~ Orange Macaroon Butter ~

Cream 1 cup of butter or margarine with 1 cup of granulated sugar in a small bowl of an electric mixer. Crumble 6 small macaroons and add to the butter mixture with the grated rind of 1 large orange, 3 tablespoons finely chopped almonds and 3 tablespoons Grand Marnier.

~ Sweet Citrus Butter ~

Combine ½ cup soft butter or margarine, 1 cup confectioner's sugar, and the grated rind of 1 large orange or lemon with the juice from the fruit in the small bowl of an electric mixer. Beat until the mixture is smooth and creamy.

MIXED GRAIN PANCAKES

Satisfying whole grain pancakes flavored with honey or brown sugar could please any health food devotee. Serve with a light margarine, honey or natural maple syrup. For an added nutrient, add ¼ cup sesame or sunflower seeds to the finished batter.

1½ cups stone ground whole wheat flour
¼ cup oat bran
¼ cup millet or soy flour
1 teaspoon baking powder
1 teaspoon baking soda
1 teaspoon salt
2 tablespoons honey or brown sugar
2 large eggs
2½ cups buttermilk
¼ cup butter, margarine or a light oil, melted

In a mixing bowl combine the whole wheat flour, oat bran, millet or soy, baking powder, baking soda, salt and brown sugar (if used). Mix well. Separately blend the honey (if used), eggs, buttermilk and butter. Add the liquids to the dry ingredients, stirring until well mixed. Heat a griddle over medium high heat and brush with light oil or coat with vegetable spray. When the griddle is ready, pour batter from a fourth-cup measure, wait until bubbles appear and then flip the pancakes to finish baking on the other side. Makes 17 pancakes, 4½ to 5" in diameter.

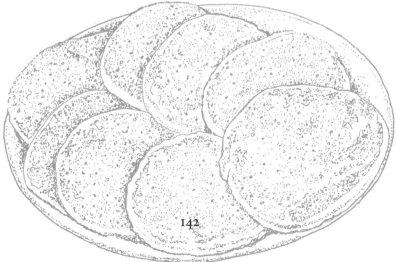

JONNYCAKES

These colonial cakes should be made with a finely ground Rhode Island cornmeal but I have found that stone ground white cornmeal also works beautifully. The spelling of "Jonnycake" comes directly from the Association for the Preservation of Jonnycakes located in the state of Rhode Island, which traces the name from "journeycake" to "jarney cake" to "jonnycake." As with all very old breads, the ingredients are simple.

> 2 cups stone ground cornmeal (See Sources of Supply, page 276)
> ½ teaspoon salt
> 2 cups boiling water
> 6 tablespoons milk, approximately

Measure the cornmeal into a mixing bowl with the salt. Pour in the boiling water and whisk quickly until smooth. The batter will be stiff. Add sufficient milk to obtain the consistency desired — some like it thick, some like it thin. Heat a griddle over medium high heat or use an electric skillet. Brush heavily with light oil. Drop the batter onto the griddle by tablespoons. Cook until crisp on one side, then flip over and cook crisp on the other side. Makes 11 cakes, 3" in diameter.

Traveler's Food

Westbound settlers of the late 1800s had to be provident about food. Reay Tannahill records that some women even learned to make butter on the trail, using the regular lurching of the wagon as a sort of dasher to churn the butter, and to time the rising of bread in the warmth of the wagon so that it was ready to bake when the wagon train stopped for the night. But the commonest traveler's foods of the time were dried corn, jerky or other dried meats, little blocks of "pocket soup" (a forerunner to today's bouillon cubes), and jonnycake.

WHOLE WHEAT-WHEAT GERM PANCAKES

This recipe follows the precept of Buttermilk Pancakes but results in a totally different flavor due to the combination of whole wheat flour, toasted wheat germ and brown sugar.

> 1 cup whole wheat flour
> 1 cup all purpose flour
> ⅓ cup toasted wheat germ
> 2 tablespoons brown sugar
> 1 teaspoon baking soda
> ¾ teaspoon salt
> 2 large eggs, beaten
> 2 cups buttermilk
> 2 tablespoons butter or margarine, melted, or light oil

Combine the whole wheat flour, white flour, wheat germ, brown sugar, baking soda and salt. Stir until mixed thoroughly. Do not attempt to sieve this mixture for part of the nutrients will be lost. In a separate bowl combine the eggs, buttermilk and butter. Make a well in the dry mixture and add the liquids, stirring until well moistened. If the batter seems too stiff, add ¼ cup more of the buttermilk to obtain the correct consistency. The kind of whole wheat flour used will affect the thickness of the batter. For example, a coarsely ground whole wheat sometimes will require more liquid. Brush a griddle lightly with oil or coat with vegetable spray. Heat the griddle over moderately high heat. Using a fourth-cup measure, dip out the batter onto the griddle. Bake cakes until bubbles appear on top, flip and cook on the other side until golden. If the heat seems too high, turn temperature down. Makes 18-20 pancakes, 4" in diameter.

NOTE: 1 cup of coarsely ground pecans or walnuts or chopped golden raisins may be added to the batter. Fold into the finished batter until well distributed.

GRIDDLE CAKES

This quick and easy pancake has many interesting variations. Add fresh or frozen blueberries or nuts to the finished batter if desired.

2 cups all purpose flour
4 teaspoons baking powder
¾ teaspoon salt
2 tablespoons butter or margarine, melted
2 cups milk
2 egg yolks
2 egg whites, beaten lightly stiff

Measure the flour, baking powder and salt together in a bowl, stirring well to mix, or sift the ingredients directly into a mixing bowl. Separately combine the butter, milk and egg yolks and whisk until smooth. Make a well in the dry ingredients and add the liquid mixture, beating rapidly with a rubber spatula until dry mixture is well moistened. Fold in the egg whites. Brush a griddle with light oil or coat with vegetable spray and heat over medium high heat. Test with a drop of water. If it sizzles, the griddle is ready. Using a fourth-cup measure pour out batter onto the griddle. Bake the pancakes on one side until bubbles appear then flip over. Cook on the other side until golden brown. Makes 18 pancakes, 3" in diameter.

NOTE: Whole, low fat or reconstituted powdered skim milk may be used.

VARIATION: Peel 2 ripe bananas and slice each down the center — the long way. Then slice across, making small bite-size pieces. Fold into the finished batter for Griddle Cakes until well distributed. Proceed with recipe as directed.

CORNMEAL PANCAKES

Follow the directions for Golden Corn Muffins (page 35). Add ¼ to ½ cup additional buttermilk to the batter until it is easy to pour. Brush a griddle with light oil or coat with vegetable spray. Place on medium high heat. When the griddle is ready, pour batter onto it using a fourth-cup measure. Bake on one side until bubbles appear on top, flip, and bake on the other side until golden. Serve hot off the griddle. Marvelous with Vermont maple syrup. Makes approximately 16 to 18 pancakes.

OATMEAL OAT BRAN PANCAKES

Needless to say, these are healthful and they are delectable to eat.

1½ cups quick rolled oats
½ cup oat bran
2 cups buttermilk
¾ cup all purpose flour
2 teaspoons sugar
1 teaspoon baking soda
1 teaspoon salt
3 large eggs, beaten
2 tablespoons margarine, melted, or light oil

Measure the oats and oat bran into a mixing bowl and stir in the buttermilk until thoroughly blended. Set aside for 10 minutes. In a separate mixing bowl combine the flour, sugar, baking soda and salt. Stir well. Add the oatmeal mixture to the dry ingredients, stirring just until well moistened. Blend in the eggs and margarine. Brush a griddle with light oil or coat with vegetable spray. Heat until hot but not smoking — test with a drop of water until it sizzles. Use a fourth-cup measure to dip out the batter. Cook pancakes until bubbles appear and flip to the other side. If the cakes brown too quickly, lower heat under the griddle. Makes twelve pancakes, 4" in diameter.

ORANGE PANCAKES

Light, delicate, fragrant with essence of orange, these are perfect morning pancakes. Top with warm marmalade or hot Fruit Syrup.

2 cups cake flour
2½ teaspoons baking powder
1 teaspoon salt
¼ cup sugar
1¼ cups orange juice
2 large eggs
¼ cup butter or margarine, melted
Grated rind of 1 large orange

In a mixing bowl combine the cake flour, baking powder, salt and sugar, stirring until well mixed. Separately blend together the orange juice, eggs, butter and grated rind. Make a well in the dry ingredients and with a rubber spatula beat in the liquid mixture until thoroughly mixed. Heat a griddle and brush with light oil or coat with vegetable spray. Ladle the batter onto the griddle with a fourth-cup measure. Cook until bubbles appear in the pancakes, then flip over and cook on the other side. Makes 14 pancakes.

A Few Syrups for Gilding the Lily

~ Fruit Syrup ~

Select 3 cups of flavorful fresh fruit – peaches, cherries, or berries. Place the fruit in a food processor with steel blade in place. Add ½ cup lemon juice. Pulse off and on until the fruit is fairly smooth. Transfer to a saucepan. Mix 3 tablespoons cornstarch with ½ cup cool water and stir until smooth. Bring the fruit to a boil over medium heat and add the cornstarch mixture. Lower heat to simmer and cook until smooth and thick. Add ½ cup light corn syrup, 1 cup water and 1 cup sugar. Let simmer, stirring occasionally, until the sugar is dissolved. Refrigerate, covered, if not used immediately.

~ Buttered Lyle's Golden Syrup ~

Lyle's Golden Syrup, a pure cane sugar syrup with a deliciously distinctive flavor, is available in specialty and gourmet stores. It is wonderful for baking in place of honey or molasses. For buttered Golden Syrup, combine one cup of syrup with ⅔ cup butter in a saucepan. Heat until mixture simmers and the butter melts. Remove from heat and add 1-2 tablespoons rum or orange liqueur if desired.

~ Blueberry Syrup ~

Mix 2 teaspoons cornstarch with 2 tablespoons water in a saucepan, stirring until smooth. Add 6 more tablespoons of water, ¾ cup fresh or frozen blueberries and 2 teaspoons honey. Mix, crushing some of the berries with the back of a spoon. Bring to a boil over medium heat, stirring constantly. Cook until thickened. Remove from heat and stir in 2 teaspoons lemon juice. Makes approximately one cup.

~ Maple Syrup, Molasses and Sorghum ~

Real maple syrup goes a long way. Check Sources of Supply if none is available in your shops. There are various grades of maple syrup and the one for cooking to me is just as good as the top grade. When I was a small child growing up in small towns of southern Oklahoma no maple syrup was available, but my mother could buy a small bottle of a concentrate called Mapeline (see Sources of Supply). She added drops of it to hot sugar water and to me it was absolutely the tops. The hot syrup melted the butter right into the pancakes. Heat the real maple syrup, pour gently and just don't squander the lovely liquid. An alternate idea comes from my father who loved molasses and sorghum. He mixed soft butter with either of those syrups in a small bowl and slathered my toast or topped my pancakes with it. When there were neither of those syrups we used my mother's homemade strawberry preserves. She made "pink tea" for me with preserves, hot water and condensed milk. I loved it all – most anything placed in front of me – except my father's turnip greens splashed with peppersauce!

BUCKWHEAT BLINIS

Tiny buckwheat pancakes wrapped around luscious Russian caviar make a seductive appetizer. One episode during my last journey to Russia centered around caviar. My husband and I decided one evening to leave our group and dine in Stavinsky's Bazaar, a private restaurant offering excellent food and a chance to watch the upper Bureaucracy at play. Since the cafe was close to our hotel, we walked, first descending into a tunnel to cross expansive streets bordering on Red Square. When we arose out of the depths, we saw two young Russian women standing close to the exit with semi-wilted flowers and the inevitable commodious handbags carried by Russians, who must be always ready to join a line and buy whatever is available. They spotted the Polaroid camera around my husband's neck and begged in broken English for photographs. With great pleasure we took several, they insisted I take the flowers, and we waved goodbye and walked on to our cafe.

When we were seated at our table a waitress took my flowers, installed them in a vase and placed them in front of me. Then we were immediately served vodka, champagne and light rye bread lavished with butter and caviar. I even was able to obtain ice and bottled sparkling water. An excellent steak and salad followed and just as dessert was served we were astonished to look up and see the two young girls standing by the table and greeting us happily. Without being asked, they sat down and ordered another round of champagne, vodka and caviar. More pictures were taken and then people at every table around us asked for photos. A lively party ensued, with a big American style band playing dance music. But the time had come for us to depart — we were satiated with caviar and had used all our film. I gave the girls lipsticks, miniature bottles of perfume and chewing gum. One of the girls reached deep into her cavernous bag and pulled out a tin of caviar, offering it to me with a happy, shy smile. We knew the girls had stood outside for a long wait just to get into the restaurant and must have paid dearly for the caviar. I left them with tears in my eyes and with a glowing feeling about young Russians.

⅓ cup water water
1 package active dry yeast
1 cup warm milk
1 cup buckwheat flour
2 cups warm milk
2 cups buckwheat flour
3 egg yolks
½ teaspoon salt
½ teaspoon sugar
½ cup butter or margarine, melted
3 egg whites

In a small bowl, stir the warm water and yeast together with a fork until the yeast has dissolved. In a large mixing bowl combine the one cup of warm milk, buckwheat flour and yeast mixture. Beat until smooth, cover with plastic wrap and let proof to make a bubbly sponge, about 45 minutes.

To this mixture stir in the two cups of warm milk and two cups of buckwheat flour. Blend the egg yolks, salt, sugar and butter together in a separate bowl, then beat into the buckwheat mixture. Cover again and set aside for 30 minutes. Beat the egg whites until softly stiff and fold into the batter. Heat a griddle over medium high heat and coat with vegetable spray. Drop the batter with a tablespoon, bake until bubbles appear, flip and brown on the other side. Makes 35 small pancakes plus 16 pancakes 4" in diameter.

NOTE: Place a full teaspoon of caviar on each small pancake and top with a spot of sour cream. Roll and enjoy!

ALMOND CRUSTED OVEN PANCAKES

Oven pancakes make a spectacular breakfast and for all their puffed glory they are amazingly easy to prepare. Ingredients are measured into a blender or food processor and whirled to mix well. The sides should then be scraped down with a rubber spatula and the blender run at high speed until the mixture is creamy and well mixed. The cooking dish is coated with butter, heated in the oven, then filled with batter while still piping hot. The pancake is baked at high heat for a short time until puffed high on the sides. Its concave center can be filled with fresh fruits or simply sprinkled with sugar and lemon juice. The pancake in its various forms will bring exclamations of admiration for your prowess in the kitchen.

3 large eggs
½ cup milk
½ cup all purpose flour
½ teaspoon salt
1 teaspoon sugar
Pinch of nutmeg (optional)
2 tablespoons butter
½ cup blanched slivered almonds

Preheat oven to 425°. Select a round skillet or a quiche pan.

Combine eggs, milk, flour, salt and sugar and whirl in a blender or beat with a wire whip. If using a blender, scrape down its sides to be certain all the flour is in the batter and whirl again until creamy. If you are baking the pancake in a skillet, place it over a burner, add butter and almonds and sauté the almonds for two minutes. If a quiche pan is used, place in the oven with the butter until melted, add the almonds and let cook about 2 to 3 minutes. Carefully pour in the batter and bake 20 minutes. The pancake will rise with the sides encrusted with almonds. Serve filled with fresh fruit if desired, or with cooked apples on the side. Serves four amply.

OVEN APPLE PANCAKE

The following two pancakes are both prepared with apples but in entirely different ways. The Oven Apple Pancake wraps sliced apples in a light airy batter which is then baked. For German Apple Pancake, apples are sautéed and batter is poured over them in a hot pan. Both are delectable and no syrup or other adornment is necessary.

> 1 tablespoon butter or margarine, melted
> 2 eggs, separated
> 3 tablespoons milk
> 3 tablespoons flour
> ½ teaspoon baking powder
> 1 cup Granny Smith apples, peeled, cored and diced
> 1 tablespoon lemon juice
> 6 tablespoons sugar
> ½ teaspoon cinnamon

Preheat oven to 400°. Brush an ovenproof 10" skillet with one tablespoon of butter.

In a small bowl whisk the egg yolks until light and creamy. Stir in the milk, blending well. Combine the flour and baking powder. Whisk the dry ingredients into the liquids, mixing until smooth. Set the batter aside. Place the apples in a small bowl and add the lemon juice. Stir until thoroughly coated. Place the prepared skillet in the oven.

Beat the egg whites until softly stiff. Slowly add 3 tablespoons of the sugar and beat until texture is similar to that of meringue. Combine the batter with the apples, then fold in the beaten egg whites. Turn the mixture into the hot skillet. Combine the remaining sugar and cinnamon and sprinkle over the top of the pancake. Place in the oven. Bake about 12 to 15 minutes or until puffed and a light golden color. Serves four.

GERMAN APPLE PANCAKE

Bake this pancake in a fairly large receptacle — either an ovenproof glass dish or perhaps a large oval ovenproof pottery bowl. The pancake will not puff as high as other oven pancakes, but its flavor is superb and its texture is light and delicate.

2 Granny Smith apples, peeled, cored and thinly sliced
2 tablespoons butter or margarine
⅓ cup brown sugar
1 teaspoon cinnamon
2 large eggs
1¼ cups milk
¾ cup all purpose flour
½ teaspoon salt
Pinch of nutmeg

Preheat oven to 400°. Select a glass or pottery baking dish approximately 12 x 19".

Sauté the apples in the butter. (If you have a large enough skillet with sloping sides, use it both to sauté the apples and to bake the pancake. Otherwise cook the apples in a skillet and transfer them to a baking dish.) Combine the brown sugar and cinnamon and sprinkle it over the apples in the skillet. Continue sautéeing, stirring occasionally, until the apples are tender and transparent. While the fruit is cooking, combine the eggs, milk, flour, salt and nutmeg in a blender. Blend on medium high, then stop and scrape down the sides to be certain all the flour is in the batter. Turn to high speed and blend until smooth. Spray the selected baking dish with vegetable spray and place in the oven until it is hot. Remove from the oven and fill with the apples. The dish and the apples should be very hot. If not place back into the oven for a few minutes until the apples are bubbling. Pour the batter over the apples. Return to the oven and bake 25 minutes. Serve immediately. Serves six.

DUTCH BABY

2 large eggs
½ cup milk
½ cup all purpose flour
⅛ teaspoon nutmeg
¼ teaspoon salt
2 tablespoons butter or margarine
Sugar
Lemon juice

Preheat oven to 400°. Select an 8x8" baking pan or a quiche pan.

Combine the eggs, milk, flour, nutmeg and salt in a blender. If no blender is available, beat the mixture with a wire whip. With a blender, be certain to scrape the sides down after the first blending, then whirl until batter is smooth. Place butter in the pan, then put the pan in the oven to melt the butter. When the pan is hot, remove it from the oven and pour in the batter. Return immediately to the oven and bake 15 to 20 minutes. The pancake will puff high on the sides. It is especially attractive baked in a quiche pan for as the cake rises it will be scalloped around the edges. Sprinkle a little sugar — one or two tablespoons — over the pancake and add a few drops of lemon juice. Serve plain or with fresh fruit such as strawberries cut and lightly sugared. A little whipped cream or sour cream flavored with brown sugar makes an even more delightful picture. Serves two generously. The recipe can easily be doubled in a larger pan.

Pannekoeken

The Dutch brought pancakes and waffles to the United States. Their word for pancakes, "pannekoeken," is still sometimes used to refer to the beautiful oven-baked version of pancakes, although the usual modern method for making pancakes employs a hot griddle or skillet.

A BASIC WAFFLE

I tested these first, then turned the recipe over to Laura, my young daughter-in-law, who had a waffle iron different from mine and a smashing idea for a variant on this theme.

> 2 cups all purpose flour
> 3 teaspoons baking powder
> ¾ teaspoon salt
> 1½ cups milk
> 2 egg yolks
> 6 tablespoons butter or margarine, melted
> 2 egg whites, beaten softly stiff

Combine the flour, baking powder and salt in a mixing bowl. Separately mix the milk, egg yolks and butter until well blended. Make a well in the dry ingredients and pour in the liquids, stirring rapidly until well mixed. Fold in the egg whites. Bake on a waffle iron according to the manufacturer's directions. Makes 6 large golden crisp waffles that can be divided into fourths.

Waffle Variations

Buttermilk Waffles

Follow directions as given for A Basic Waffle but substitute buttermilk for the milk and 1/4 teaspoon baking soda to the dry ingredients.

Note: 3/4 cup of coarsely chopped pecans or walnuts may be folded into the batter just before baking.

Laura's Italian Cream Waffles

Use either the Basic Waffle or Buttermilk Waffle and add to the batter ½ cup chopped pecans and ½ cup coconut. These are smashing!

GINGERBREAD WAFFLES

A spicy, slightly soft waffle with optional crystalized ginger. I will be frank with you about the ginger — I liked it but my youngest grandchildren thought it made the waffles taste like flowers. You can take their judgment or mine!

⅔ cup molasses
⅓ cup butter or margarine, melted
2 egg yolks
1 cup buttermilk
2 cups all purpose flour
½ teaspoon baking soda
2 teaspoons baking powder
2 teaspoons cinnamon
1 teaspoon ginger
½ teaspoon nutmeg
¼ teaspoon cloves
½ teaspoon salt
½ cup chopped crystalized ginger (optional)
2 egg whites, beaten softly stiff

Combine the molasses, butter and egg yolks and beat with a whisk or fork until smooth. Blend in the buttermilk.

Sift together the flour, baking soda, baking powder, cinnamon, ginger, nutmeg, cloves and salt into a mixing bowl. Stir in the crystalized ginger if desired. Make a well in the center of the dry mixture and add the molasses mixture, beating quickly until smooth. Fold in the egg whites. If the batter seems too thick, add an additional ¼ cup buttermilk. Bake according to directions for your waffle iron until a dark golden brown. Yields 4 thick quadruple waffles.

CORNMEAL WAFFLES

These are a favorite of all my family for we are all exceptionally fond of the cornmeal flavor. They are a lovely golden color and are delightfully crisp — they deserve your best syrup served warm.

1½ cups stone ground cornmeal
½ cup all purpose flour
2 teaspoons baking powder
½ teaspoon baking soda
1 teaspoon salt
2 tablespoons sugar
2 egg yolks
1½ cups buttermilk
4 tablespoons butter, melted or light oil
2 egg whites, beaten softly stiff

In a mixing bowl combine the cornmeal, flour, baking powder, baking soda, salt and sugar. Blend well. In a smaller bowl whip together the egg yolks, buttermilk and butter. Make a well in the dry ingredients and pour in the liquids, stirring until very well mixed — the batter may be a bit stiff. Fold in the egg whites. Bake according to directions for your waffle iron. Makes 4 quadruple waffles.

BELGIAN WAFFLES

Flying from Tulsa to southwestern Oklahoma in a private plane, I was fascinated to watch the topography change from the rolling green prairie around my city to flat prairie of red dirt and rich grass excellent for raising Hereford and Angus cattle. My cooking partner and I had been invited for Sunday brunch with Ginny and Ned Shelton. The big Belgian waffle iron was hot and soon we were consuming huge, deep, crisp waffles with sautéed apples and sour cream flavored with raspberry liqueur. Naturally I begged for the recipe and our hostess was most gracious. I learned from a young friend born in Belgium that the waffles in her country are served only with whipped cream — take your choice.

1 package active dry yeast

¼ cup warm water

2 cups warm milk

½ cup melted butter

2 tablespoons sugar

1 teaspoon salt

2 eggs

2 egg yolks

3½ cups all purpose flour

1½ teaspoons vanilla extract

2 egg whites, beaten softly stiff

TOPPING:

1½ teaspoons brown sugar

1 cup sour cream

2 tablespoons Chambord liqueur

Sautéed apples or fresh blueberries or strawberries

Sprinkle yeast into water in a small bowl and stir with a fork until yeast is dissolved. Set aside. Combine the milk with the butter, sugar and salt, blending well. Beat the eggs and egg yolks together and add to the milk mixture. Stir in the yeast mixture. With a wire whip beat in the flour and vanilla extract. Cover the bowl with plastic wrap and a towel. The batter can proof for 45 minutes and then be ready to bake but is much better if refrigerated overnight. The next morning remove batter from refrigerator, beat the egg whites and fold them thoroughly into the batter. Bake according to directions given for your Belgian waffle iron. Makes 5 large waffles.

To make the topping, combine the sugar and sour cream — this can be done the night before. Next morning add the liqueur and transfer to a serving compote. Serve with the waffles and fruit.

Popovers & Crepes

One story about the origin of crepes begins once upon a time with two kings who loved a good time more than attending to their kingly duties. Together they spotted a flower girl in tattered clothes and decided to transform her into a gay Parisienne. They had her bathed, coiffured and dressed in the most beautiful clothes they could find, then they took her to dinner. At their request, the chef prepared a new dessert for the waif, using very thin pancakes. The little flower girl was thrilled and cried out that the pancakes were as thin as curtains, or crepes in French. Since her name was Suzette, the dessert became known as Crepes Suzette. That is the story I was told.

No leavening is needed for crepes. Eggs give the needed body, and plenty of liquid is used as the batter must be thin. The batter can be made several hours ahead. A crepe pan is wonderful to have for it is just the right size, 7". However, a skillet of similar size will also do very well. One of the nicest things about crepes is that they freeze beautifully. The batter is quickly made, the baking of the crepes takes very little time and then stacks can be frozen. Let cool, wrap thoroughly, then label and freeze. Frequently I place small sheets of oiled paper between the crepes to be certain they do not stick. Another method of freezing is to prepare the crepes with a chicken or fish filling, place them in an ovenproof dish, cover with sauce of your choice, cool, wrap, label and freeze. An elegant dinner is all in place awaiting the perfect moment.

Like crepes, popovers require no leavening. Instead they depend on thorough beating of the eggs, milk and flour, plus high heat that causes steam within the batter to puff and blow into a shell. A perfectly prepared popover is like a shell of tender, crusty pastry wrapped around a sphere of fragrant air. Lovely.

POPOVERS

Light oil for coating pan
1 cup all purpose flour
3 large eggs
2 tablespoons butter or margarine, melted or light oil
1 cup milk

Preheat oven to 450°. I use antique heavy iron popover pans given me by my mother-in-law, but you may wish to obtain some of the new, well-shaped popover pans, which work very successfully. Brush each popover cup with oil. I like to pour a little oil in a custard cup and use a one-inch pastry brush to brush it in each cup. Place the pan in the oven while mixing the batter so that it will be piping hot. Combine all the ingredients in a blender and whirl on high speed until mixed. Stop and scrape down the sides of the blender and whirl again until the batter is creamy and smooth. If no blender is available use a sturdy wire whip to beat the ingredients. Remove the popover pan from the oven and close the door so no heat is lost. Fill each cup one-half to two-thirds full of batter. Leftover batter may be poured into oiled custard cups. Bake the popovers at 450° for 20 minutes. Lower temperature to 350° and bake 15 to 20 minutes longer. Makes 12 popovers.

LIME-PISTACHIO POPOVERS

Follow directions for Popovers, adding the grated rind of 1 lime, 1 tablespoon of fresh lime juice and ½ cup pistachios. Blend thoroughly twice to be certain the nuts are well incorporated into the batter. Bake as directed. Excellent with lime or lemon marmalade or Lemon or Lime Butter.

160

WHOLE WHEAT POPOVERS

Light oil for coating pan
½ cup all purpose flour
½ cup whole wheat flour
3 large eggs
2 tablespoons butter or margarine, melted or light oil
1 cup milk

Preheat oven to 450°. Brush the cups of a popover pan with oil. Combine all ingredients in a blender, whirl on high speed, stop and scrape down sides of the blender and whirl again. Bake as directed for Popovers.

Fruit Butters

~ *Tangy Lemon Butter* ~

Combine ½ cup soft butter or margarine, 4 teaspoons lemon juice or lime juice, and the grated rind of the lemon or lime in a small mixing bowl and whisk until it is smooth. Add ½ teaspoon lemon thyme if desired.

~ *Sweet Cranberry Butter* ~

Place 1 cup fresh or frozen cranberries, 1¾ cups powdered sugar, ⅔ cup soft butter or margarine, 1 teaspoon ginger or the grated rind of 1 orange, and 1 tablespoon lemon juice in a food processor with the steel blade in place. Pulse to blend, scraping the sides of the bowl as necessary. Excellent with corn pancakes and corn muffins.

Savory Butters

Delicious savory butters are quickly made and keep well. Store them in the refrigerator in a covered container but serve them at room temperature for the best flavor. Butters may be frozen for longer keeping.

~ Basic Garlic Butter ~

Peel and slice 4 large cloves of garlic. Place in a saucepan with ½ cup of butter or margarine. Turn burner to medium heat and slowly heat the mixture until it begins to bubble. Let it simmer for one minute. Remove and spread on desired bread.

~ Garlic Butter with Parsley ~

Place 8 peeled garlic cloves in a small saucepan and cover with boiling water. Allow to set 10 minutes. Drain the water off and dry the garlic. Place in a small bowl of an electric mixer and add ½ cup soft butter and 3 tablespoons snipped parsley. Salt to taste. Stir until ingredients are well blended.

~ Herb Butter ~

Place ½ cup soft butter, ½ teaspoon prepared mustard, ½ teaspoon basil, ¼ teaspoon Worcestershire sauce, 1 teaspoon lemon juice, and ⅛ teaspoon garlic salt in the small bowl of an electric mixer. Blend at medium speed until the mixture is smooth.

~ Herb Butter with Parsley ~

Place ½ cup soft butter, 1 tablespoon chopped parsley, 1 tablespoon oregano or tarragon, 1 teaspoon Dijon mustard and a few grindings of white pepper in the small bowl of an electric mixer. Stir at medium speed until creamy. Salt to taste.

CHEESE POPOVERS

Crisp and a lovely dark golden color, these popovers make a delightful change from the usual breads served with barbecue.

> Light oil for coating pan
> 4 large eggs
> 1 cup milk
> 1 cup all purpose flour
> ½ teaspoon salt
> 1 cup grated sharp Cheddar cheese
> (do not pack cheese into the cup)

Preheat over to 450°. Brush popover cups with oil. Place the popover pan in the oven to get piping hot while mixing the batter. Combine all the ingredients in a blender. Blend on medium, stop and scrape down the sides of the blender jar. Blend again at high speed until the batter is well mixed. Remove the popover pan from the oven, close the oven door and pour batter into the cups filling each about two-thirds full. Return to the oven and bake 20 minutes. Reduce heat to 350° and bake another 20 minutes. If the popovers seem to be browning too deeply, bake only 15 minutes. Makes 12.

PARSLEY PARMESAN POPOVERS

These enticing popovers are speckled with light green parsley. They are unusually delicious with luncheon or a light supper.

> Light oil for coating pan
> 4 large eggs
> 2 tablespoons light oil
> 1 cup milk
> 1 cup all purpose flour
> ⅓ cup Parmesan cheese
> ½ cup chopped fresh parsley

Preheat oven to 450°. Brush the cups of a popover pan with oil. Place the prepared pan in the oven to become piping hot while making the batter. Combine all the ingredients in a blender in the order given. Whirl at medium speed, stop and scrape down the sides of the blender. Whirl at high speed until the batter is smooth. Remove the popover pan from the oven and close the door. Pour batter into each cup until it is one-half to two-thirds full. If any batter is left, brush a custard cup with oil and fill with remaining batter. Return pan to oven and bake 20 minutes. Reduce heat to 350° and bake 15 more minutes. Serve immediately.

ORANGE POPOVERS

Luxurious and fragrant with orange and almonds, these deep golden popovers are an elegant treat for guests. I started out with the idea of making orange popovers but once in a hurry I accidently threw in a half cup of almonds intended for another dish — the result was serendipity!

> Light oil for coating pan
> 3 large eggs
> ½ cup milk
> Grated rind of 1 orange
> ½ cup orange juice
> 1 cup all purpose flour
> ¼ teaspoon salt
> 1 teaspoon sugar
> ½ cup untoasted slivered almonds (optional)

Preheat oven to 450°. Brush popover cups with oil. Assemble all ingredients, then place the popover pan in the oven to preheat. Combine the eggs, milk, orange rind and juice in a blender. Add the flour, salt, sugar and almonds if desired. Whirl in the blender, stop and scrape down the sides of the blender bowl. Blend again at high speed until the mixture is perfectly smooth. Remove the popover pan from the oven, close the door and pour the cups one-half to two-thirds full of batter. Return to the oven and bake at 450° for 20 minutes. Lower heat to 350° and bake 15 more minutes. Serve while hot with butter and, for a marvelous contrast, raspberry jam.

YORKSHIRE PUDDING

No prime roast of beef would be quite complete without Yorkshire Pudding — at least my family feels that way. For many years our Christmas dinner has centered around an aged prime beef and Yorkshire Pudding baked in antique popover pans brushed with beef drippings before heating. I prefer the pudding in individual servings but it can be baked in any pan at least 2" deep. Yorkshire Pudding begins to droop soon after leaving the oven, so pop it in the oven as guests are seated at the table. Keep the gravy simmering until the plates are served and then pass the gravy boat and the Yorkshire Pudding. There is nothing worse than congealing gravy over soggy Yorkshire Pudding!

1 cup sifted flour
1 teaspoon salt
1 cup milk
½ cup water
4 large eggs
Beef drippings

Measure the flour, salt, milk, water and eggs into a blender. Whirl at a low speed, stop and scrape down the sides. Turn to high speed and blend until the batter is smooth. Keep the lid on the blender and let the batter stand for 30 minutes. When the roast is done and waiting to be carved, turn the oven temperature to 475°. Pour 1 teaspoon of beef drippings into each of 12 popover or muffin cups. If using a baking pan, spoon in enough drippings to cover the bottom of the pan. Place pan in the oven to become piping hot. Fill cups half full of batter. Return to the oven and bake 20 to 25 minutes or until the pudding is brown and crisp.

Cooking With Crepes

Breakfast Crepes

With Poached Eggs: Place a poached egg in the center of a crepe and fold over. Top with grated cheese and place in the broiler to melt cheese. Or top with Hollandaise sauce. Serve with Canadian bacon.

With Scrambled Eggs: Fill crepes with eggs scrambled in butter with bits of cooked sausage or bacon. Or scramble eggs with sautéed chopped red and green bell pepper, mushrooms, and green onion. Top with melted sharp Cheddar cheese. Or use blue corn crepes and top with Mexican salsa.

Entree Crepes

With Seafood: Fill crepes with sautéed seafood (shrimp, scallops, lobster, crab) in brandy sauce. Roll the crepes and arrange them in an ovenproof dish, cover with extra sauce and place in the oven to heat through.

With Spinach: Fill crepes with cooked, well-drained spinach mixed with cream and cheese (Parmesan, cream cheese, ricotta, feta, or other cheese).

With Chicken and Broccoli: Combine leftover cooked chicken or turkey with a light cream sauce and crisp-tender broccoli for a delicious crepe filling. Top with melted Cheddar.

Other fillings: Try ratatouille, caponata, creamed chicken and mushrooms, even beef stroganoff. When you are inventing a filling using materials on hand, don't forget the nuts. Almonds, walnuts and pine nuts are delicious.

Dessert Crepes

With Fruit: Prepare fresh strawberries, raspberries, peaches, blueberries or a combination of fruits, sprinkle with sugar or liqueur and allow to stand for 30 minutes. Spoon onto sweet crepes, roll up, and serve with whipped cream or ice cream. Peaches may be simmered briefly in a little wine, then rolled into crepes. Granny Smith apples sautéed in a skillet with butter, brown sugar, cinnamon, and nutmeg make a delicious filling. Or fill sweet crepes with plain yogurt, roll up and top with jam or preserves.

CHRISTI'S CREPES

One morning I descended the stairs of my Number Two son's home in Chevy Chase to find Number Two granddaughter, Christi, flipping crepes. Christi was twelve and loved crepes. Her mother was busy and suggested she prepare them herself. Christi and her sister Sasha were devouring these lovely crepes sprinkled with a little sugar and a few drops of lemon juice and rolled quickly while still hot. As I joined them for a crepe I recalled a day twelve years earlier and a shopping excursion with their mother, Annie, in Paris. Annie, who was very pregnant with Christi, was living in Amman, Jordan, where there was little to buy for the city was too crowded with refugees. After shopping, we settled into a tiny place for lunch and ordered crepes and a green salad. The crepe was huge and thin and folded around a poached egg. With the salad, it was perfect.

3 large eggs
1 cup milk
½ cup water
1 cup sifted flour
2 tablespoons butter or margarine, melted or light oil
½ teaspoon salt

Combine all the ingredients in a blender. Blend at low speed to mix, stop, and scrape down the sides of the blender with a rubber spatula. Turn to high speed and blend until the batter is smooth. Set aside or leave in the blender for one hour. Pour light oil, butter or margarine into a small bowl such as a custard cup. Heat the crepe pan (7" in diameter) over medium high heat. Brush with the oil. Each crepe takes 4 tablespoons of batter. For convenience use a fourth-cup measure. Pour batter into the crepe pan swirling it around quickly to cover the bottom. Use a pancake turner or spatula to turn the crepe, which takes only a minute or two to bake. Turn to the other side, cook until lightly brown and place on a cool counter or bread board. Brush the crepe pan with oil as necessary between crepes. With each crepe the technique becomes easier and soon you will be quite an expert. Makes 14 crepes.

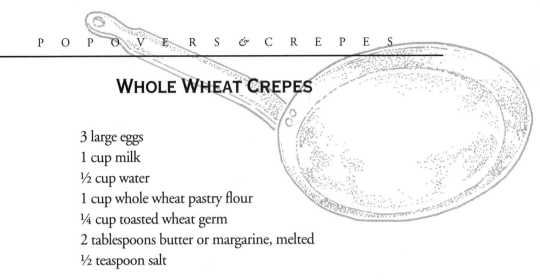

WHOLE WHEAT CREPES

3 large eggs
1 cup milk
½ cup water
1 cup whole wheat pastry flour
¼ cup toasted wheat germ
2 tablespoons butter or margarine, melted
½ teaspoon salt

Combine the ingredients as described in Christie's Crepes. Follow directions as given for making the batter and baking the crepes. Makes fourteen 7" crepes.

BLUE CORN CREPES

Blue corn flour is available in specialty shops by order (see Sources of Supply, page 276). Try these with a Mexican menu instead of tortillas.

2 large eggs
1 tablespoon light oil
4 tablespoons all purpose flour
¾ cup milk
½ cup blue corn flour
¼ teaspoon salt

Combine all the ingredients in a blender and whirl at low speed to mix. Stop, scrape down the sides of the blender and whirl at high speed until batter is smooth. (Alternatively, ingredients may be mixed in a bowl using a wire whip.) Set aside for 30 to 60 minutes. Pour the oil into a small bowl and use some to brush the crepe pan. Heat over medium high heat. The pan will take four tablespoons of batter. Use a one-fourth cup measure to pour the batter into the crepe pan. Bake each crepe until light brown, flip and cook the other side. Brush the crepe pan with oil between crepes as necessary. Place crepes on a cool counter when cooked. Makes 8 crepes. When cooled the crepes may be wrapped securely, labeled and frozen.

SWEET CREPES

Sweet crepes freeze just as well as plain ones, providing a charming spur-of-the-moment dessert. When summer fruits come in season, fill a crepe with strawberries, blueberries or peaches lightly sweetened and topped with whipped or ice cream.

3 large eggs
¾ cup milk
¾ cup water
1 cup sifted all purpose flour
1 tablespoon butter, melted or light oil
2 tablespoons sugar
1 teaspoon vanilla extract or 1 tablespoon cognac

Combine all the ingredients in a blender. Blend at low speed, stop and scrape down sides of the blender. Turn to high speed and whirl until the batter is smooth. If there is no blender, combine ingredients in a mixing bowl and use a wire whip to blend. Set aside for one hour. Pour the butter or oil into a custard cup and have a pastry brush ready. Select a 7" crepe pan. Brush the crepe pan with oil and place over medium high heat until quite hot. Use a one-fourth cup measure to pour four tablespoons of batter into the pan for each crepe. Pour the batter into the crepe pan and swirl immediately to cover the bottom. Cook until lightly brown, flip to the other side and bake until brown. Brush pan with oil between crepes as necessary. Place the cooked crepes on a cool counter. Makes 14 to 16 crepes.

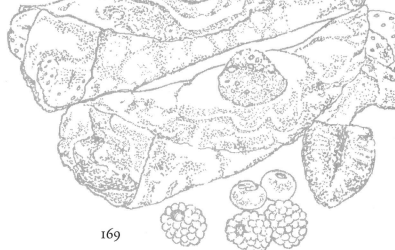

Quick Yeast Breads

I will never forget the first loaves of bread I struggled to make, knowing nothing of techniques, and then my great joy and excitement at pulling those golden and fragrant loaves from the oven. The aroma had tantalized us during the baking but I had no idea what was happening inside the oven. The time was many years ago and the stove was second-hand with no window for peeking. Holding my breath I gently opened the door and gasped at the size of those beautiful swollen loaves. The realization came suddenly that I had actually created bread through the glorious process of bringing yeast to life. The boys and I immediately consumed one gorgeous loaf with homemade butter — it was indeed a soul-satisfying moment.

Our ancestors of long ago ground wild grains, splashed a bit of water on the resulting meal and slapped the pancake on a hot rock. The first woman who discovered such breadmaking while the men were off hunting must have vented a good-natured grunt of

USING THE PROCESSOR

1. Lock the bowl of the food processor onto its base and put the steel blade in place.

2. Measure dry ingredients into the bowl of the processor.

3. Sprinkle yeast over warm water in a small bowl; stir to dissolve.

4. In a separate bowl, combine liquid ingredients, first melting the butter if used.

5. Pulse the food processor several times to mix the dry ingredients.

6. Allowing the machine to run, pour the dissolved yeast into the processor through the feed tube.

7. Still allowing the machine to run, pour liquid ingredients through the feed tube. Process until the dough pulls away from the sides of the work bowl and forms a ball, about 20 seconds.

8. Remove dough from processor, knead lightly a few times, place in a buttered bowl in a warm place to rise.

satisfaction. The man returned to the cave, was pleased with the hot rock bread and perhaps built his mate a crude rock oven to house a little fire of twigs and possibly mammoth dung — who knows? Bread continued to be flat and rough until the Assyrians and then the Egyptians began to refine the process about 3000 B.C. with the discovery that yeast spores made bread a bit lighter. In Egypt I was shown a bread that was 2000 years old, grey with age and not high and puffy as ours but still a great progression from the primitive cakes. From the Egyptian era bread was on the upswing with improvements made next by the Romans. During the Middle Ages bread was made in huge wooden troughs and baked in ovens not much better than those of Egyptians. With the discovery of the New World quick breads became important and immigrants brought their sourdough starters on the long journey across the sea. Then it was back to hot rocks and buffalo chips. Not until the 20th century was an electric mixer modified for home use. Finally came the heavy duty mixer equipped with a dough hook which proved a wonderful convenience for the art of breadmaking. Now the exciting food processor mixes and kneads the dough in minutes. Although the processor is limited to one or two loaves of bread, this innovative machine provides a chance for those with more desire than time to make delicious home-made yeast bread.

FROM A HOT ROCK TO A FOOD PROCESSOR

Breadmaking with a food processor is completely different from the way great-grandmother did it, and it is even different from using a heavy duty mixer with a dough hook. Combining ingredients is easy and it is fascinating to just stand there, push a lever and watch the dough come together.

Kneading Bread in a Food Processor

Measure the dry ingredients into the processor bowl with the steel blade in place. The yeast may be dissolved in warm water (called "proofing" because it proves that the yeast is active) or added directly to the dry ingredients. Butter may be melted and combined with egg and milk or chilled and cut in pieces and added to the dry ingredients. In the latter case the machine is pulsed several times to meld the butter into the flour mixture. Yeast mixture, the egg, melted butter and other liquid ingredients can be added using the feed tube. Liquid is added in a steady slow stream as the machine whirls until a ball of dough forms. As you run the machine, the dough will pull away from the sides of the processor bowl and mass around the center. Knead by machine an additional 30 to 60 seconds. Then turn the dough out on a lightly floured surface and knead 1 to 2 minutes by hand to create a smooth resilient ball. The dough still must go through a rising period but that is shortened with quick rising yeast. Poof, and it is ready to bake. Quick yeast breads take longer to prepare than quick breads made with leavenings other than yeast but there is nothing more relaxing and satisfying in the world of cuisine.

Certain cautions must be observed with a food processor for it is a powerful machine. First, do not overknead the dough. After a mass of dough forms around the center or blade and pulls away from the sides of the bowl, let it knead no more than 60 seconds more. The recipes that follow state the kneading time. Second, flour your hands when removing the dough for the blade is quite sharp and can easily slip if not handled carefully. Pick up the bowl by the handle and turn it over so that the dough and blade fall on the floured spot you have arranged. The dough pulls off easily and the blade can be set aside. If the dough is sticky, sprinkle a little flour over both the dough and your hands and remove the dough from the blade and bowl. Third, consider the capacity of your processor.

The machine I have used for testing is a Cuisinart DLC-7. The size is perfect for one large or two small loaves. Fourth, it is important to remember that a food processor blends, mixes and kneads extremely quickly. If the machine is over-loaded, a burning aroma will emanate from the motor. The action slows and may stop altogether. This is a safety mechanism designed into the machine. If this happens, wait until the motor cools, then proceed with the bread. If there is too much dough, some of it may have to be removed and kneaded by hand. Standard machines will hold no more than four cups of flour comfortably. Most of the recipes that follow contain 3 to 3½ cups of flour.

Kneading by Hand

When the processor finishes the short kneading period, the dough is removed and finished by hand for one or two minutes. If you wish to knead a little by hand, do so. Place the dough on a floured surface, pick up the top edge and fold it toward the center, then push the heels of your hands hard into the middle of the dough, dragging it forward a little. Give the dough a quarter turn, and repeat. Keep giving quarter turns, folding the dough over and pressing down with the heels of your hands and soon you will acquire a delightful rhythm that is the "therapy" part of breadmaking. You can slam the dough on the table and it will be quite happy — it doesn't mind at all. The kneading process activates the gluten that begins stretching the elastic bubbles that in turn makes the dough rise. When the kneading is finished, place the dough in a bowl — plastic, glass, pottery — that has been warmed with hot water, dried and then either brushed with melted butter or coated with vegetable spray. Place the dough in the bowl, swirl it around and turn it over so that its top is coated with the oil. This keeps the dough from forming a "skin" or becoming dry. Cover loosely with plastic wrap so that some air will filter inside and then cover with a towel. Put the bowl in a cozy corner free of drafts and set a timer for the approximate time of rising. Test the dough by pressing a finger into it. If the indentation remains, the dough is ready for the next step. If the indentation pulls back, cover the dough again and let it continue to rise.

Forming the Loaf

Molding a loaf of bread can be accomplished through several methods. When the dough has properly risen, punch your fist into the center while it is in the bowl and then transfer it to a kneading surface. Knead lightly, form into a ball, cover and let rest 10 minutes. A loaf can be made simply by shaping the dough with your hands and placing it in a prepared pan. Press it down and tuck in the corners. A second method is to roll the dough into a rectangle the width of the baking pan and about 12 to 14 inches long. Fold as with a pocketbook, one-third of the dough downward and

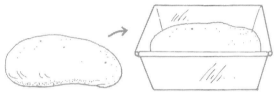

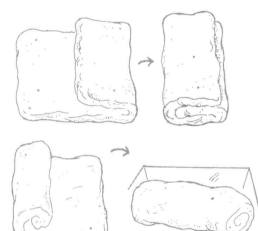

towards you from the top and one-third upwards from the bottom. Fold the second third over the first so that all three thirds are stacked and pinch the sides and ends to seal. Turn seal side down and place in a baking pan. A third method is to roll the dough into a rectangle and then to roll it up jelly roll style from the short ends, pinching the sides and ends. Plump the loaf and turn it seam down in a loaf pan.

Baking the Loaf

The dough will rise to the top of the pan or mound up above it and then it is ready to be baked. During its first 15 minutes in the oven the bread will rise a third time and then all those bubbles inside will be set by the heat and trapped in the stiffening dough and the bread will finish baking with no more rising. To check a bread at the end of the baking period, take it out and turn it over with a towel or hot pad. If the bottom is brown and the loaf makes a hollow sound when thumped, it is finished. A recipe will state whether the bread is to be removed from the pan immediately to a wire rack to cool.

Pots and Pans

The primary loaf pans that will be used are 8 x 4 x 3" and 9 x 5 x 3" in size. The best coating is vegetable spray, particularly when preparing a cinnamon loaf that can present a sticky problem. If the loaf pan has been sprayed, the bread will slide right out. There are also free form breads and coffee cakes that require baking sheets. Traveling in European countries one seldom sees a pan loaf — most are free form loaves. American bakers use thousands of loaf pans. I noticed in my trips to Russia and other countries of the Soviet Union that they also use bread pans — the commercial baking industry has followed that of the United States. And the bread was tasteless; there was no good black bread. Baking temperatures are given for regular bread pans. When a glass pan is used, lower the temperature 25°.

Ingredients

All Purpose White Flour: All my recipes have been tested with commercial all purpose flour because of its wide availability. The flour is composed of both soft and hard wheat, providing sufficient protein and gluten to make a fine loaf of bread. Through fast milling processes the wheat germ and bran have been removed. Chemicals have been added as supplements.

Unbleached White Flour: Available in health food stores and special departments of supermarkets, this flour has no added chemicals, is usually higher in protein and makes excellent breads but still has no wheat germ.

Bread Flour: Bread flour is high in protein and gluten and produces an extremely puffy bread. If a high rising bread is desired, use one-half bread flour and one-half all purpose flour so the dough can be kept under better control.

Whole Wheat Flour: The wheat berry is composed of three parts. It includes a skin, which is the bran; an endosperm, or main portion of the berry; and the germ, which contains most of the vitamins and minerals. The oil-rich germ can become rancid and this is one of the reasons millers began refining flour to remove it. By adding chemicals even to whole wheat flour the shelf life of bread has been lengthened. Fast milling introduced from Hungary casts off both the bran and the germ and leaves white flour. Whole wheat flour contains all three parts of the wheat berry. It makes a heavier loaf of bread than does white but its flavor is superb. In making whole wheat bread, measure flour quantities carefully as whole wheat flour is slower to absorb liquid and suddenly the dough can become quite dry. Mixing unbleached white flour with stone ground whole wheat flour results in a lighter and easier-to-handle dough.

Stone Ground Flour: Stone ground flour is wheat ground slowly using milling stones, a process that leaves all the nutrients, especially the germ, in the flour. Such good flour may be obtained in small mills across the country and in health food stores. See Sources of Supply. For long-term storage, keep these flours in the freezer as the oil-rich wheat germ can become rancid.

Rye Flour: One of the best flours to provide the fiber so vitally needed for good health, rye flour has less gluten than whole wheat. A bread made of rye alone will be dense and heavy — this is the bread of the European peasant during the Middle Ages. Mixing white and whole wheat flour provides the gluten necessary while rye gives the flavor. Originally rye grew as a weed with wheat and the two grains were cut and milled together. The discovery that rye withstood the damp and cold climate in northern Europe and Russian made it the pre-dominate grain used for hundreds of years.

Soy, Millet, Buckwheat, Barley, Oats: These are the ancient grains used by primitive man before wheat was discovered. Breads made with them are heavy and coarse. All are high in protein but each makes a compact, thick bread. Today these flours are added in small quantities to breads to enhance their protein and vitamins. Millet is used in third world countries, particularly in

Africa, where the bread is a small loaf rather like a brick. I have experimented with soy and millet breads for people who are allergic to gluten. To create a palatable soy or millet loaf, egg whites or extra yeast are added.

Self-Rising Flour: "Self-rising" flour contains baking powder and salt. Because of these additions the flour is best for biscuits, pancakes, waffles, scones, but not for the quick breads that require yeast.

Confusing Terms: *Graham flour* is whole wheat flour. The Reverend Sylvester Graham was an early modern exponent of the use of whole wheat and other whole grain products. Apparently he was a colorful figure during the 19th century and through the press had a great deal of influence on the American public. Many companies use his name for whole wheat flour. *Pumpernickel* is not a grain; it is a mixture of flours, primarily rye, whole wheat, cornmeal and white flours. The name presumably stems from a gentleman in Germany who first mixed these flours together and made a wonderful bread. *Durum wheat* is a hard wheat grown to make semolina for the macaroni market. The name *water ground flour* originates from the old mills where the wheel that powered the mill was turned by a stream of water. The milling has no special effect on the flour itself. *Buhr* is the name of a French stone that millers preferred for its hardness. It produced the finest grist mill stones. You may use flour sacks printed with the term "buhr ground flour" which has now become meaningless for buhr stones are no longer brought to the United States. The term *bolted flour* recalls an early process in which a round drum inside the mechanism of the grist mill was covered with fine silk. The flour was sifted through this silk to create a white flour desired by many people. Now grist mills use a fine nylon similar to the silk used for the sifting process. "Bolted flour" refers to flour whose germ and bran have been sifted out.

Yeast: The first yeast was similar to our sourdough starter or made from beer and wine foam. A piece of each day's dough was saved for the next day's baking. Centuries passed before housewives learned to make their own yeast, which required time and labor. Commercial yeast was finally introduced in the 19th century, primarily through beer companies. The 20th century brought packaged dry yeast which dominated the market after World War II. The most recent development was quick-rising yeast which cuts proofing time for breads in half. *(Note: All the breads for this chapter have been tested with quick-rising yeast but they may be made with regular yeast – just roughly double the rising time.)* To bring yeast to life, the water must be a cozy warmth, between 108-112.° Let water run from the faucet over your hand until it feels pleasantly warm. To be certain, test with a candy thermometer. Water that is too hot can kill the yeast and water too cool makes it sluggish. When in doubt about the age of yeast (expiration date is always on a packet) test by adding 1 teaspoon sugar and ¼ teaspoon ginger to the yeast and water. Stir until dissolved and allow to set for 10 minutes. If the mixture is not bubbling and foamy, buy fresh yeast.

Yeasts are tiny forms of plant life called micro-organisms, made up of cells so tiny they can only be seen through a microscope. It requires twenty billion of them to make one gram of compressed yeast. The yeasts digest food such as sugar, producing carbon dioxide which cannot escape when it is caught within an elastic dough. As a result the dough stretches and rises. This is a process of fermentation and in breadmaking the yeast actually ferments the sugars available from flour and sugar. When the bread is baked the heat stops the fermentation. Yeast loves all the sugars including the natural sugar in flour. It is not necessary to add sugar. For example, French bread by law is made only with white flour, water, yeast and salt. When bread recipes do call for sugar, honey may be substituted if you prefer or sugar can be cut in half if desired. Sugar is for taste and to entice the yeast to its best efforts.

Salt: Salt in bread is purely for flavor. Yeast does not need salt to work. I have experimented with breads made with neither salt nor sugar. The breads had excellent texture. They were a bit blank in flavor but with a little light margarine or special jams were quite good.

Eggs: Eggs provide color, flavor and texture and are used in abundance in many sweet doughs. Any dough with eggs has beautiful texture for braiding and molding. If eggs are off your diet, use an egg substitute or just egg whites. I make one bread whose recipe calls for 10 eggs and when I prepared it using an egg substitute no one could tell the difference.

BASIC WHITE BREAD

An excellent crusty bread that is wonderful for making cinnamon toast. It is very adaptable to variations of your own devising or two of mine at the end of the recipe. If a puffier loaf is desired, use half all purpose flour and half bread flour.

3 cups all purpose flour
1 teaspoon salt
¾ cup warm milk
2 tablespoons honey
2 tablespoons butter or margarine, melted
1 package quick-rising dry yeast
¼ cup warm water

Measure the flour and salt in the bowl of a food processor with the steel blade in place. In a small mixing bowl combine the milk, honey and butter, mixing well. Sprinkle the yeast over the warm water in a separate bowl and stir with a fork until dissolved. Pulse several times to mix the flour and salt. Allowing the processor to run, pour the yeast mixture into the feed tube and follow with milk mixture. The dough will pull away from the sides of the bowl and form a ball around the center. Allow 20 seconds for kneading. Remove the dough from the bowl to a lightly floured surface and knead by hand one minute. Round into a ball and place on a clean board, cover with plastic wrap and a heavy towel. Let proof 30 minutes. Knead down for one or two minutes, cover and let rest 10 minutes.

Preheat oven to 400°. Coat an 8x4" loaf pan with vegetable spray. Form the dough into a loaf and place in the prepared pan. Bake 30 to 35 minutes. A handsome crust will form. Remove from the oven and turn bread out onto a wire rack to cool slightly before slicing. Remember that hot bread can be difficult to slice well so use a sharp bread knife or an electric knife.

White Bread Variations

Carrot-Raisin Bread:

Eliminate 1 cup of white flour and substitute 1 cup of whole wheat flour. Grate enough carrots to make 1½ cups – 1 to 2 carrots – using the food processor if desired. If using the processor, remove the grater disc but leave the grated carrots in the bowl of the food processor. Put the steel blade in place. Add the dry ingredients and pulse several times to blend. Follow recipe as directed. When the dough is finished, remove to a lightly floured surface and knead in the raisins until well distributed. Allow to proof, mold into a loaf and bake at 350° for 35 to 40 minutes.

Cinnamon Bubble Loaf:

When the basic white bread has completed the bowl rising, remove to a lightly floured surface and knead down quickly. Cut the dough into strips about ¾" wide using a dough scraper. Snip the strips into pieces the size of a walnut or smaller. Combine 2 tablespoons brown sugar with 3 teaspoons cinnamon, or to taste, in a small bowl. Place the melted butter in a separate small bowl. Roll each piece of dough quickly (they do not have to be smooth as the rising will eliminate lumps) and dip one side first into the melted butter and then into the sugar mixture. Place sugar side up in a 9x5x3" loaf pan coated heavily with a vegetable spray. Pile the balls on top each other and then cover the pan and let rise until about ½ to 1 inch from the top. Preheat oven to 350°. Bake 35 minutes and check for doneness. If necessary, bake five more minutes. Place the pan on a wire rack and allow to cool 20 minutes. Turn out on the rack to finish cooling. The bread freezes very well.

A Variation on the Variation:

For Christmas, prepare Cinnamon-Bubble Loaf but add sliced red candied cherries between the "bubbles" and decorate the top with red and green candied cherries. An easy Christmas breakfast or a delightful gift. Two loaves can be made by using 7" loaf pans.

FRENCH BREAD

When my eldest granddaughter was eighteen months old, she and her parents were living in crowded Amman, Jordan just at the beginning of the civil war in Beirut. All three needed a totally different vacation and luckily were able to rent an apartment in Paris for the month of August. My husband and I joined them for one week and what fun it was to shop with a baby each day from market to market. The very first item on our list was always French bread. The top was torn off and given to Sasha, who happily munched away as we purchased cheeses, eggs in gelatin and beautifully baked chicken. French bread is the easiest of breads to make; the baking can be a bit tricky but all is well as long as you do not expect a loaf exactly like those bought in Paris.

> 4 cups all purpose flour
> 1 teaspoon salt
> 1½ cups warm water
> 1 package quick-rising dry yeast

Combine the flour and salt in the bowl of a food processor. Measure the water into a small bowl and sprinkle in the yeast, stirring with a fork until dissolved. Pulse the dry ingredients to mix. While the processor is running, pour the yeast mixture into the feed tube and process until a ball of dough forms and pulls away from the sides of the bowl. Remove the dough to a lightly floured surface and knead by hand for 1 or 2 minutes. Round the dough into a ball and place in a warm buttered bowl. Cover loosely with plastic wrap and a towel. Set aside in a warm spot and let it rise for at least an hour, preferably longer. Punch the dough down, knead lightly, cover and let rest 10 to 15 minutes.

Divide the dough in half. Cover one half while working with the first one. Spray a baking sheet with vegetable spray. Roll one portion of dough into a rectangle about 12 by 8". Roll from the long side jelly roll style into a tight roll. Pinch the sides and taper the ends. Place the loaf on a prepared baking sheet. Form the remaining dough as described. Cover with a light teacloth and set aside to proof until doubled, 30 to 35 minutes. Preheat the oven to 450°. With a razor make 3 diagonal slashes into the loaves. When you are ready to bake the bread, spray the inside of oven with water and lightly mist the loaves. Place the bread in the center of oven, close the door and then in 3 minutes spray again. Close door and again in 3 minutes spray the loaves. Then let the loaves finish baking. The total time will be about 25 minutes. Let breads cool on a wire rack. These loaves can be frozen. When perfectly cooled, wrap carefully and tightly with aluminum foil. Label and freeze. When ready to use, place wrapped breads in a 375° oven for about 15 minutes. Remove the bread, unwrap, turn off the oven and place bread back in the oven to crisp for about 5 minutes. Leave the door ajar. Tear off the top and enjoy!

PIDEH

This delightful Armenian bread is made in the morning, molded, refrigerated and baked six hours later for dinner. A frustrating search in Yerevan, Armenia for any kind of real local bread finally led me to a huge building that turned out to be the black market. There were magnificent fruits of all kinds, spices, huge bunches of basil with piles of ripe tomatoes, but no bread. Finally I was pushed up to the balcony and there sat several women beside huge piles of something all swathed in big sheets. One raised the sheet and underneath was a pile of thin soft Lavosch. I pulled a piece out of the pile — it must have been two feet long and over a foot wide — and offered money. She grinned and shook her head so I pulled out a packet of chewing gum. We both parted happy.

> 1 package quick-rising dry yeast
> 2 tablespoons warm water
> 3 cups all purpose flour
> 1½ tablespoons sugar
> 1 teaspoon salt
> ⅓ cup dry powdered skim milk
> 1½ tablespoons light oil
> 1 cup warm water
> 1 egg white, beaten with 1 teaspoon water
> 2 tablespoons sesame seeds

Sprinkle yeast over the warm water in a small bowl, stirring with a fork, until dissolved. Set aside. Into the bowl of a food processor with steel blade in place put the flour, sugar, salt and dry milk. Pulse a few times until well mixed. Add the oil to the yeast mixture and pour into the processor through the feed tube as the machine runs. Slowly pour in the water until the dough forms a ball around the blade. Let knead about 30 seconds. Remove the dough to a lightly floured surface and knead at least one minute into a smooth ball. Place the dough in a warm buttered bowl, turning to coat the top. Cover loosely with plastic wrap and a towel. Set aside to proof until doubled, about 45 minutes.

Coat a large round baking sheet such as a pizza pan or a regular baking sheet with vegetable spray. Knead the dough down, cover and let rest 10 minutes. With a dough scraper cut off one-fourth of the dough and set aside. Shape the large piece into a round and place on the baking sheet. Flatten the dough with your hands and make a 3" hole in the center by pulling the dough back with your fingers. Make a smooth bun out of the small portion of dough. Place in the center in the hole. Cover with plastic wrap and refrigerate six hours or overnight.

Preheat oven to 350°. Remove bread from refrigerator and take off the plastic wrap. Let bread stand at room temperature 15 minutes. Brush with egg white wash and sprinkle with the sesame seeds. Bake 30 minutes or until a lovely golden color. Cool on a wire rack or serve hot.

ENGLISH CRUMPET BREAD

No bread is quite as enticing for breakfast as an English muffin or a crumpet. Baking crumpets individually can be a bit of trouble for the batter must be confined in rings. But a loaf of English Crumpet Bread is equally good and easier to make. The baking time will be longer than for most breads because the batter is very moist. The resulting bread has lots of holes to fill with melted butter and for toasting it is absolutely superb. The recipe will make 2 loaves, one for breakfast right away and the other for the freezer.

> 1 package, quick-rising dry yeast
> 1 cup warm water
> 3 cups all purpose flour
> 1 teaspoon salt
> 1 tablespoon sugar
> ½ cup milk
> 1 large egg

Sprinkle yeast over the water in a small bowl, stirring with a fork until dissolved. In the bowl of a food processor with steel blade in place add the flour, salt and sugar and pulse two or three times to blend. Combine the milk and egg, beating well. Turn the machine on and pour the yeast mixture and then the milk mixture into the feed tube, continuing to whirl until the batter is smooth and thick. Transfer the batter to a mixing bowl and cover. Allow the batter to proof 45 minutes, stirring thoroughly with a rubber spatula every 15 minutes. Coat two one pound coffee cans completely with vegetable spray. Divide the batter evenly between the two cans. Cover with plastic wrap or the tops to the cans. Let rise to within one inch of the top, which will take about 40 minutes. During the last ten minutes preheat the oven to 375°. Bake the breads 1 hour. Remove one loaf and check by feeling the sides. If too soft, return to the oven for another ten minutes. Remove from the cans and cool on wire racks. Slice, toast and serve with butter and an assortment of preserves and marmalade.

QUICK DINNER ROLLS

Here is a delightfully simple and rapid way to prepare dinner rolls. There are two ways to proof the rolls that cut down the time so that within an hour there will be hot rolls for dinner.

1 package quick-rising dry yeast
¼ cup warm water
4 tablespoons butter or margarine, melted
½ cup warm milk
2½ cups all purpose flour
2 tablespoons sugar
½ teaspoon salt
Butter or margarine, melted

Sprinkle yeast over the water in a small bowl, stirring with a fork until dissolved. Set aside. Separately combine the butter and milk. To the bowl of a food processor with steel blade in place add the flour, sugar and salt. Pulse three times to blend. Keep the machine running and add the yeast mixture and then the milk mixture through the feed tube. Let continue to run until the dough forms a ball around the blade. Knead 30 seconds more. Remove the dough to a lightly floured surface and knead until smooth, about 1 minute. Divide the dough into three portions, cutting with a dough scraper. Cut off pieces of dough about the size of a walnut or larger (whatever size you decide to cut, remember that it will be more than double in size.) Roll by cupping one hand over a piece of dough and rotating the dough gently until it is a smooth ball. Place in a buttered baking pan, either cake pans or an oblong pan of about 9x12". Brush the top with melted butter.

For quick rising, place the pan on top of toaster oven and turn the oven to low. Or pour boiling water in a large pan one inch deep and place in a cold oven. Place the pan of shaped rolls on the rack above the water. Cover rolls and close the oven door. Let rise 30 minutes. Uncover and remove hot water. Turn oven to 375° and bake 25 minutes. If you use the first method, the oven must be pre-heated to 375° while the rolls are proofing. Makes 26 rolls when dough is shaped the size of a large walnut.

PEPPERY CHEESE BREAD

When spices and pepper began to slowly filter into the Middle East and into Rome, intrepid adventurers constantly sought ways to find their sources. The Romans would pay anything for spices and even the Visigoths wanted pepper, not gold. Arabs attempted to hide the land routes but undaunted sailors rounded Africa and found Indonesia, rich in spices, as well as India. Well do I remember that no pepper was available during the years of World War II. Fortunately, for some reason, I had purchased a very large box of pepper that with careful conserving lasted my family through that period of history.

> 1 package quick-rising yeast
> ¼ cup warm water
> 3 cups all purpose flour
> 1 tablespoon sugar
> 1 teaspoon salt
> 1 teaspoon coarsely ground black pepper
> ½ cup warm milk
> 2 tablespoons butter or margarine, melted
> 1 large egg
> ⅔ cup sharp Cheddar cheese, grated

Combine the yeast and water in a small bowl, stirring with a fork until dissolved. Measure the flour into the bowl of a food processor with steel blade in place. Add the sugar, salt and pepper. Combine the milk, butter and egg, stirring well. Pulse the processor several times to mix the dry ingredients. Continuing to run the processor, pour first the yeast mixture and then the milk mixture through the feed tube. When the dough has formed a ball around the center, stop and add the cheese. Pulse again 15 seconds until the cheese is mixed into the dough. Turn the dough out on a lightly floured surface and knead until smooth, about 1 minute. Place dough in a warm, buttered bowl, turning to coat the top. Cover loosely with plastic wrap and a towel. Let rise 30 minutes. Knead down, form into a loaf and place in an 8x4" pan – or make a free-form loaf and place it on a greased baking sheet. Cover and let rise 30 minutes. During the last 10 minutes preheat the oven to 350°. Bake 30 to 35 minutes. Remove the bread to a wire rack to cool.

FRENCH WALNUT BREAD

Many years ago when my eldest son, then 17, was traveling the world with a pack on his back, I met a charming young Parisienne, Denise Minard, in Tulsa. She gave me the name of her father-in-law in Paris and suggested that if Nick had difficulties her husband's family might help him. When Nick arrived in Paris via bicycle he found an international automobile show in progress and no rooms to be had. He finally located the Minard's elegant apartment and the marvelous French family took in the wet, hungry young American. Two years later they helped my second son find a job in southern France and when the youngest, Mike, arrived in Paris they kept him too. Now Denise, a superb cook, exchanges recipes with me from Paris. This is her bread, obtained from her mother-in-law, Germaine. To the Minard family I say, "Viva la France."

1 package quick-rising dry yeast
¼ cup warm water
3 cups all purpose flour
½ cup walnuts
¼ cup toasted wheat germ
½ teaspoon salt
½ cup warm milk
2 tablespoons honey
2 tablespoons butter or margarine, melted
1 large egg
½ cup whole walnuts
1 egg yolk mixed with 1 teaspoon water
3 whole walnuts

Combine yeast and warm water in a small bowl, stirring with a fork until dissolved. Place the flour and ½ cup of walnuts in the bowl of a food processor with the steel blade in place. Pulse several times to chop the nuts coarsely. Add the wheat germ and salt. Whirl twice. Blend the milk, honey, butter and egg together. While continuing to run the machine add first the yeast mixture and then the milk mixture through the feed tube and knead until the dough pulls away from the sides of the bowl and forms into a ball. Knead 20 seconds more. Remove the dough to a lightly floured surface and knead 1 minute.

Place in a warm, buttered bowl turning to coat the top. Cover loosely with plastic wrap and a towel. Place in a warm spot and let rise until doubled, about 45 minutes. Turn the dough out and press into a circle. Place the ½ cup of whole walnuts in circles on top of the round of dough. Roll as for a jelly roll, tucking in the ends and sealing the side by pinching the dough together. Place the loaf seam side down on a baking sheet coated with vegetable spray. Cover and let rise 30 minutes. During the last 15 minutes of the rising preheat the oven to 350°. Bake 35 minutes,then brush heavily with egg wash. Place the three walnuts in a row on top of the bread. Return to oven and bake 10 more minutes.

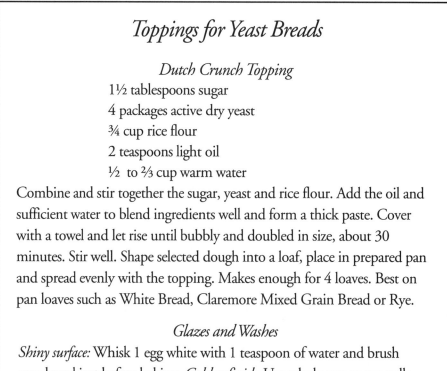

Toppings for Yeast Breads

Dutch Crunch Topping
1½ tablespoons sugar
4 packages active dry yeast
¾ cup rice flour
2 teaspoons light oil
½ to ⅔ cup warm water

Combine and stir together the sugar, yeast and rice flour. Add the oil and sufficient water to blend ingredients well and form a thick paste. Cover with a towel and let rise until bubbly and doubled in size, about 30 minutes. Stir well. Shape selected dough into a loaf, place in prepared pan and spread evenly with the topping. Makes enough for 4 loaves. Best on pan loaves such as White Bread, Claremore Mixed Grain Bread or Rye.

Glazes and Washes

Shiny surface: Whisk 1 egg white with 1 teaspoon of water and brush over bread just before baking. *Golden finish:* Use whole egg or egg yolk plus 1 tablespoon water. Egg wash also helps bind sesame or poppy seeds. *Rich dark finish:* Use instant coffee or postum mixed with a small amount of water. *Soft, glossy finish:* Mix 1 teaspoon of cornstarch with ½ cup water in a small saucepan. Boil 3 minutes, stirring constantly. Brush on bread 5 minutes before removing it from the oven.

PUMPERNICKEL WITH RAISINS

There is no pumpernickel flour unless some purveyor blends together several flours and calls it "pumpernickel." The name refers to bread made usually of rye, whole wheat flour and cornmeal. It resembles the heavy dark breads eaten by peasants through the centuries and has a marvelous flavor.

¼ cup cornmeal
1 cup rye flour
1 cup whole wheat flour
1 cup white flour
1½ teaspoons salt
½ cup instant mashed potato flakes
1 cup warm water
2 tablespoons butter or margarine, melted
⅓ cup dark molasses
¼ cup warm water
1 package quick-rising dry yeast
2 teaspoons caraway seeds or ½ cup dark raisins

In the bowl of a food processor with steel blade in place combine the cornmeal, rye flour, whole wheat and white flours, the salt and potatoes. Pulse a few times to mix the ingredients. Combine in a bowl the 1 cup of water, butter and molasses. In a small bowl sprinkle the yeast into the ¼ cup of water and stir with a fork to dissolve. Turn the processor on and add the yeast mixture through the feed tube, then stir the molasses mixture well and slowly add it also. Continue to process, adding the caraway seeds if desired, until the dough forms a ball. Add the raisins if desired and whirl two or three seconds more. Remove the dough to a lightly floured surface (use white flour) and knead 2 minutes to smooth the dough and distribute the raisins. Round the dough into a ball and place in a warm, buttered bowl covering loosely with plastic wrap and a towel. Let double in bulk, about 1 hour. Knead the dough down and shape into a loaf. Place in an 8x4" loaf pan coated with vegetable spray. If preferred make a free form loaf and place on a small baking sheet coated with vegetable spray. Cover and let rise 40 minutes. Preheat the oven the last 15 minutes of the proofing period to 350°. Bake 40 to 45 minutes. Turn out on a wire rack to cool.

CLAREMORE MIXED GRAIN BREAD

What a marvelous time I had in the small city of Claremore twenty miles north of Tulsa performing a bread demonstration before an enthusiastic stand-ing-room-only crowd. Lee Good, the director of the J. M. Davis Gun Museum, had requested my services — which intrigued me for although I have performed in everything from a country school to a country club, a gun museum was a new experience. The museum displays guns from the year 1320 to the present, plus many other artifacts. The only item lacking was a stove but that was quickly solved through use of one at the supermarket across the street. During the demonstration I made up a white buttermilk bread to show how it could be changed. I began throwing in oat bran, wheat germ and whatever was at hand and the crowd loved it. I announced right there that this would be entitled "Claremore Bread" and be in my next book.

> 1 package quick-rising dry yeast
> ¼ cup warm water
> 1 cup warm buttermilk
> ¼ cup butter or margarine, melted
> 3 tablespoons honey
> 1½ cups all purpose flour
> 1 cup whole wheat flour
> ¼ cup oat bran
> ¼ cup wheat germ
> ½ cup rolled oats
> 1 teaspoon salt

Sprinkle the yeast over the warm water in a small bowl and stir with a fork until it dissolves. Separately combine the buttermilk, butter and honey, blending well. With the steel blade in place, add the remaining ingredients to the food processor bowl. Pulse several times to mix the dry ingredients. While the processor is running, add the yeast mixture and then the buttermilk mixture through the feed tube. Whirl continuously until the dough pulls away from the sides of the bowl and forms a ball around the center. Allow to knead 60 seconds. Remove the dough to a lightly floured surface (use white flour) and knead by hand 1 minute until smooth. Place the dough in a warmed, buttered bowl, turning to coat the top. Cover loosely with plastic wrap and a towel. Let rise for 50 minutes. Punch the dough down, knead lightly, form into a loaf and place in an 8x4" loaf pan coated with vegetable spray. Cover and let rise until it reaches the top of the pan, about 40 minutes. Preheat oven to 375° the last ten minutes of the proofing. Bake the loaf 30 to 35 minutes. Turn the bread out on a wire rack to cool or serve hot with fresh butter.

CHALLAH

When the Israelites left Egypt, they were told to bring only unleavened bread for there was just time to gather their possessions and leave immediately. The journey to the Promised Land was a long trek through the desert and soon there was no bread. Each morning Jehovah provided "manna" but on Friday they had to gather a double portion for on the Sabbath no one was permitted to gather bread. Challah (pronounced "hah-lah") means "bread" and in the Jewish Sabbath ceremony each Friday evening there is a cover over the challah which recalls the dew that covered the manna each morning. Through the centuries the Jews ate ordinary roughly milled bread but on the Sabbath only white bread was served. The covered loaf is brought in after the wine is drunk. Over the years, challah has become a magnificent braided loaf with simple ingredients of flour, oil, water, salt, yeast and eggs. As a bread baker, I consider challah the most perfect bread for braiding. I love the flavor and for me it makes the best of toast.

3 cups all purpose flour
2 tablespoons sugar
1 teaspoon salt
2 tablespoons warm water
1 package quick-rising dry yeast
2 large eggs, beaten
2 tablespoons light oil
½ cup warm water
1 egg beaten with 1 tablespoon water
Poppy seeds

To the bowl of a food processor with steel blade in place add the flour, sugar and salt. Measure the 2 tablespoons of water in a small bowl and sprinkle in the yeast, stirring with a fork until it dissolves. Set aside. Blend the eggs and oil together. Pulse the food processor three times to mix the dry ingredients. Through the feed tube add the yeast mixture and then the egg mixture. With the motor running add the ½ cup of water until the dough masses into a ball around the blade. Let knead 30 seconds. If the dough is too dry, add a teaspoon more of water. If the dough is too wet, add a tablespoon of flour until it makes a soft dough. Turn the dough out on a lightly floured surface and knead 2 minutes. Round into a ball and place in a warm bowl coated with vegetable spray. Turn the dough to coat the top. Cover loosely with plastic wrap and a towel. Let proof until doubled, about 45 minutes. Punch the dough down, turn out and divide in 4 equal portions. Roll into strips 12 to 14 inches long, making them fatter in the center and tapered toward the ends.

Braid in the following manner: Place the strips of dough in the form of a cross overlapping at the center. Take the ends opposite each other and cross over. Take the opposite ends and cross over the center. Continue crossing to the tapered ends which can be tucked under. Plump the braid — do not stretch. Place the braid on a baking sheet coated with vegetable spray. Cover and let double, about 30 minutes. Preheat the oven to 350°. Brush the braid thoroughly with the egg wash and sprinkle heavily with poppy seeds. Bake about 35 minutes or until a deep golden brown. Remove the bread and cool on a wire rack.

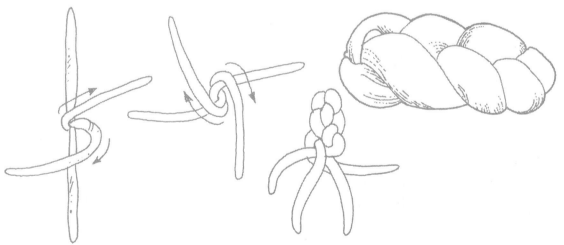

TRITICALE SNACK LOAF

Derived from wheat (triticum) and rye (secale), triticale is a manmade grain only about 100 years old. Triticale (which rhymes with "daily") is hardier than wheat but its gluten content is quite fragile. Because of the high protein count and excellent amino acid balance it is hoped that ultimately triticale will be grown in third world countries. Triticale must be handled gently and not kneaded too strongly nor allowed too many risings.

1½ cups triticale flour
1½ cups all purpose flour
1 cup toasted wheat germ
2 tablespoons brown sugar
1½ teaspoons salt
1 package quick-rising dry yeast
2 teaspoons caraway seeds
    or ½ cup salted and toasted sunflower seeds
1¼ cups warm water
2 tablespoons light oil
1 egg beaten with 1 tablespoon water

Combine the two flours, wheat germ, brown sugar, salt and yeast in bowl of a food processor with steel blade in place. If using caraway seeds, add to the dry ingredients. If sunflower seeds are preferred, knead those into the dough when removed from the processor. Pulse 5 seconds to mix ingredients. Combine the water and oil, stirring to blend. Continuing to run the machine, pour in the water mixture through the feed tube until a ball forms around the blade. Stop. Remove the dough to a lightly floured surface (use white flour) and knead in the sunflower seeds if desired. Otherwise, knead a few times to round the dough into a smooth ball. Cover with a slightly damp cloth and allow to rest for 20 minutes. Coat a baking sheet with vegetable spray. Divide the dough in two equal portions. Shape in round loaves. Press each down to six or seven inches in diameter. Place on the baking sheet. Cover and let rise 1 hour. With a handle of a round wooden spoon or large cooking chopsticks, make 4 or 5 indentations across each round of dough. Preheat the oven to 375° the last ten minutes of proofing. Brush the loaves with egg glaze and bake for 40 to 45 minutes. Remove and cool on wire rack.

WHOLE WHEAT CASSEROLE BREAD WITH SHERRY

The idea for this handsome bread came to me in Taos, New Mexico on a visit to my good friend, Rosalie Talbott, R. C. Gorman's personal secretary. I met Mr. Gorman at a dinner party and was fascinated by this colorful and charming Indian artist. He loves good food and wine and enjoys dabbling in the kitchen but leaves the cuisine to Rose Roybal, his housekeeper, who prepared superb meals. I toyed with the idea of adding Mumm's champagne (Gorman's favorite) to the recipe but settled instead on practical sherry.

1 cup mixed dried fruit, chopped apricots, peaches, prunes
3 tablespoons dry sherry
2 packages quick-rising yeast
½ cup warm water
1¾ cup warm milk
1 large egg
3 tablespoons butter or margarine
1½ cups stone ground whole wheat flour
1½ cups all purpose flour
⅓ cup toasted wheat germ
Grated rind of 1 orange
¼ cup brown sugar, packed

Chop the dried fruits (I prefer slicing by hand), place in a bowl and add the sherry. Allow to marinate while preparing the remaining ingredients. In a small bowl sprinkle the yeast over the water and stir with a fork until it dissolves. Separately combine the milk, egg and butter, blending well. In the bowl of a food processor with steel blade in place measure the flours, wheat germ, grated rind and brown sugar. Pulse several times until dry ingredients are mixed. With the motor running, add the yeast and milk mixtures through the feed tube. Beat the batter 30 seconds, until it is thick and smooth. Add the fruits and whirl few seconds until well distributed. Prepare a 2-quart souffle bowl by coating with vegetable spray. Pour in the batter. Cover with plastic wrap and let rise to within one inch of the top of the bowl. Preheat the oven to 350°. Bake 45 minutes. Cool on a wire rack 15 minutes, then remove from casserole and continue cooling on the rack. Best hot and fresh.

FAST RYE BREAD

Through the assistance of the Kansas Wheat Commission I have permission to use this marvelous recipe for a food processor rye bread. It can be made into a round slashed loaf that slices easily for sandwiches or may be formed into buns for hamburgers or corned beef and cheese. Rye flour will make any dough a bit sticky; rub flour on your hands and there will be little trouble.

> 1½ cups all purpose flour
> 1½ cups rye four
> 2 teaspoons sugar
> 1½ teaspoons salt
> 1 package quick-rising yeast
> 1 tablespoon margarine
> 2 teaspoons caraway or fennel seeds
> 1 cup warm water
> 1 tablespoon honey

In the bowl of a food processor with steel blade in place, combine the two flours, sugar, salt, margarine, choice of seeds, and yeast. Process 10 seconds. Combine the water and honey, blending until honey is dissolved. With the motor running, pour the water mixture through the feed tube until the dough forms a ball. All the water may not be necessary. Continue processing 60 seconds. Remove dough from the processor to a lightly floured surface using white flour and knead one minute or until the dough is smooth and resilient. Round into a ball and cover with a slightly damp cloth. Let rest 20 minutes. Coat a small baking sheet with vegetable spray or sprinkle with cornmeal. Round the dough into a smooth ball and place on the baking sheet. Cover with a slightly damp cloth and let double in bulk, about 40 minutes. Slash a cross in the center. Preheat oven to 375° the last 10 minutes of the rising period. Bake 35 to 40 minutes. Remove bread from the oven and cool on a wire rack.

FOR BUNS: After the short resting period divide the dough into 8 or 9 pieces. Shape into round buns and place on a baking sheet sprinkled with cornmeal. Flatten slightly. Cover with a damp cloth and let double, 40 minutes. Preheat oven to 400°. Bake 15 to 20 minutes. Cool on wire rack.

Mouhamara: Spicy Armenian Spread for Bread

This recipe was given to me by Helen Yeni-Komshian, my son Peter's mother-in-law. On my last visit to Beirut, she drove me into the mountains. As we entered a cave there we saw a sloping wall aglow with the reflection of fire burning deep in a nearby pit. The baker had rolled out a whole-wheat Arabic bread thin as paper. He placed the dough on a huge black pillow, then slung both pillow and bread against the hot wall, where the dough stuck. In just a few moments he peeled the bread off the wall, folded it into a triangle and handed it to me. I had just seen a breadmaking technique thousands of years old.

On another occasion my husband and I were in the Georgian province of the Soviet Union watching shish-ka-bob cooked in a special pit oven that held the meat on the sides (they seem to keep using walls for everything) Beside a baker's table was a bucket of sourdough bubbling away. Soon three men with native instruments began playing exotic tunes and before I knew it I was being whirled around at a fierce speed. Although I did not see bread slapped on the side of the oven I've never had such a great time. Bread is the language of the western world.

1 cup walnuts	¼ cup olive oil (no substitutions)
4 ounce jar pimento, drained	1 teaspoon salt or to taste
½ cup dry bread crumbs	2 teaspoons paprika
½ cup lemon juice	2 tablespoons ground red pepper
1 tablespoon cumin	Dash cayenne
1 tablespoon sugar	

Place the nuts in a food processor with the steel blade in place. Pulse several times to coarsely chop. Add the remaining ingredients and whirl, stopping to scrape down the sides. The mixture should not be blended in a blender as this makes it too smooth. Remove to a glass or plastic container and spoon a light coating of olive oil over the top, cap and the mouhamara will keep indefinitely.

A CORNBREAD LOAF WITH PECANS

One of the joys of recipe testing is combining a group of ingredients that prove to be a bit different with a flavor that stays. Some breads I simply toss to the birds and go on to the next idea. This particular corn loaf was a success. It has an excellent texture and good crust and it toasts to perfection. Try melting cheese atop a crusty slice. Also, do use stone ground cornmeal if you can — the flavor is much richer.

> 2 cups all purpose flour
> ¾ cup stone ground cornmeal
> 3 tablespoons sugar
> ¾ teaspoon salt
> 1 package quick-rising yeast
> ¼ cup warm water
> ¼ cup butter or margarine, melted
> 1 large egg
> ½ cup pecans (optional)
> ½ cup warm milk

In a food processor with the steel blade in place combine the flour, cornmeal, sugar and salt. Sprinkle the yeast over the water in a small bowl and stir with a fork until it dissolves. Separately stir together the melted butter and egg. Pulse the dry ingredients until mixed. With the machine running add the yeast mixture, the butter mixture and the pecans. Slowly add the milk until the dough forms a ball around the center and pulls away from sides of the bowl. Knead for 20 seconds. Remove the dough to a lightly floured surface and knead 1 minute. Round the dough into a ball and place in a warm, buttered bowl. Cover loosely with plastic wrap and towel. Let rise until doubled, about 1 to 1½ hours. Punch the dough down and form into a loaf. Coat an 8x4" loaf pan with vegetable shortening. Place the loaf in the pan and cover; let rise to top, about 1 hour. The last 15 minutes of the rising preheat the oven to 375°. Bake the bread 30 to 35 minutes. Remove from pan and cool on a wire rack.

CHEDDAR SESAME BUBBLE LOAF

This large, handsome loaf is great for a barbecue. Place it in the center of the table so that guests can just reach over and pull off crunchy bubbles as they nibble on juicy barbequed ribs. I assure you the evening will be a great success.

1 package quick-rising dry yeast
¼ cup warm water
3 cups all purpose flour
¾ cup sharp Cheddar cheese, grated (¼ pound)
1 teaspoon salt
2 tablespoons cold butter or margarine
¾ cup warm milk
½ cup butter or margarine
2 cloves garlic, peeled and sliced in half
⅔ cup sesame seeds, approximately

Sprinkle the yeast over the water in a small bowl and stir with a fork until dissolved. Combine the flour, cheese, salt and butter in the bowl of a food processor with steel blade in place. (The cheese may be grated in the processor, either with the grater or the steel blade. If so, leave in the bowl and measure the flour on top.) Pulse to mix the ingredients and cut up the butter into the mixture. Continue to run the machine and pour in the yeast mixture and then the milk. Use just enough milk to form a soft ball of dough that pulls away from sides of the bowl. Remove the dough to a lightly floured surface and knead one minute. Cover loosely with plastic wrap and a towel. Allow to double, about 45 minutes.

Melt the ½ cup of butter in a small saucepan and add the garlic. Let the butter come just to a simmer and remove. Place the sesame seeds in a small bowl. Now you are ready for quick action. With a dough scraper, slice the dough into strips and then into small pieces about the size of a walnut. These do not have to be evenly matched. Round quickly into rough balls. Dip one side of the ball first into the butter mixture and then into sesame seeds. Have a ten inch mold (an angel food cake pan) coated with vegetable spray. Place the balls in the pan, sesame seed side up. The rising of the bubbles will take out any lumps or bumps — the balls do not have to be perfect. It will be most interesting if they are a bit uneven, then guests have a dreadful time deciding which bubble to pursue! Cover with a towel and let rise about 45 minutes. Preheat oven to 350° and bake the bubble loaf 45 to 50 minutes. The bubbles should be lightly brown and golden — and crisp on the outside. Remove the pan to a wire rack and cool 15 minutes. (Do not attempt to turn the bread out directly from the oven or the bubbles will fall apart; give it a chance to meld together.) Then turn the bread out on a serving tray. The bread may be frozen. Sesame seeds will fall off on the table when it is transferred from pan to tray. Just scoop all those good seeds up with a dough scraper and throw them on your next salad!

PERFUMED FRUIT-NUT BREAD

Orange blossom and rose water have been used for centuries in the Middle East, particularly in Persia and then around the Mediterranean. Exotic pine nuts and pistachios, together with candied fruit, make this bread right for any holiday. The dough is whirled in the food processor and all the wonderful fruits and nuts are kneaded into it by hand. That may sound difficult, but the dough is soft and easily handled. During one testing I was fortunate in having home-made candied orange rind given to me by my sister-in-law, who has brought the art to perfection. Try to find a friend who prepares this delicacy or make it yourself — orange, lemon or grapefruit rind gives a very special flavor you will not forget.

3 cups all purpose flour
⅓ cup sugar
½ teaspoon salt
Grated rind of 1 orange
1 package quick-rising yeast
¼ cup cold butter or margarine
2 tablespoons pine nuts
¼ cup pistachios

2 tablespoons candied lemon,
orange or grapefruit rind, chopped
2 tablespoons candied pineapple, chopped
¾ cup golden raisins
¾ cup warm milk
2 tablespoons Marsala wine
2 tablespoons orange flower water
Butter, melted

In the bowl of a food processor combine the flour, sugar, salt, grated rind, yeast and cold butter cut in pieces. In a separate bowl combine the nuts, candied fruits and raisins, mixing well. Add about one tablespoon flour to the fruits to avoid their massing together. Measure the milk into a cup and add the wine and Orange Flower Water. Pulse the flour mixture until it is well mixed and the butter is melded into the dry ingredients. With the machine running, add the milk mixture and knead until a ball of dough forms around the blade. Let knead one minute more. Remove the dough to a lightly floured surface and press out with your hands. Place all the fruits and nuts on top the dough and pull dough over the fruits. Begin kneading slowly and don't worry about fruit and nuts falling on the table. Just pick them up and stick them back into the dough. Keep kneading until the fruit and nuts are well distributed — this will take several minutes. Round the dough into a ball and place in a warm, buttered bowl, turning to coat the top. Cover loosely with plastic wrap and a towel. Set in a cozy corner and allow to double, about 1½ hours. The proofing process will take a bit longer than most doughs because of all the fruit.

Remove the dough to a lightly floured surface and knead about 30 seconds. Round into a ball and place on a baking sheet coated with vegetable spray. Shape into a smooth ball and cover with a towel. Let rise about 60 minutes. The last 10 minutes preheat the oven to 350°. Make three slashes on top the loaf to form a triangle. Brush with melted butter. Bake the loaf 1 hour. Cover the last 20 minutes if the bread becomes too brown. Remove bread and cool on a wire rack. The bread freezes well.

BASIC SWEET DOUGH

A sweet dough with butter, sugar, eggs and milk will often take longer to rise than a plain white dough. But I am pleased with this basic dough for it has risen quickly with all the coffee cakes I have tested. The dough may be made up at night, stored in a plastic bag, refrigerated and then baked the next day at a time that suits you best. The dough can be made into cinnamon rolls or coffee cakes.

1 package quick-rising dry yeast
3 tablespoons warm water
3½ cups all purpose flour
1 teaspoon salt
⅓ cup sugar
¼ cup butter or margarine, melted
1 large egg
1 teaspoon vanilla
¾ cup warm milk

Sprinkle the yeast over the water in a small bowl and stir with a fork until dissolved. Combine the flour, salt and sugar in bowl of food processor with steel blade in place. Blend the butter, egg and vanilla together. Pulse the dry ingredients a few seconds to mix well. With the motor running add the yeast and butter mixtures. Slowly pour in the milk until a moist dough is formed into a ball around the center. All the milk may not be necessary. Remove the dough to a lightly floured surface and knead one minute. Round into a ball and place in a warm buttered bowl, turning to coat the top. Cover with plastic wrap and a towel. Let double in bulk, about 1 hour. Turn out on a clean surface (use a little flour if necessary) knead down, cover and let rest. The dough is now ready to mold into any of the following coffee cakes and cinnamon rolls.

NOTE: The vanilla flavoring may be eliminated. Grated rind of 1 large lemon or orange may be added, if desired.

Variations for Basic Sweet Dough

Cinnamon Coffee Cake

Basic Sweet Dough, page 203
Butter or margarine, melted
Cinnamon-Sugar
Confectioners' Icing

Roll the finished dough into a rectangle 11x16". Brush with melted butter and sprinkle heavily with Cinnamon Sugar. Starting at each end (the short ends) fold the dough over about 1" toward the center. Repeat two more times from each side until they meet in the center. Seal by pinching where the folded portions meet. Place on a baking sheet coated with vegetable spray. Make 6 slashes on each side about 1½" wide and cut at least ½" into center. It is best to do the cutting with kitchen shears. Turn adjoining slices of dough in opposite directions — if they do not turn easily, snip a little deeper into the cut. There will be one at the end and it should turn in an opposite direction from the one next to it. Flatten gently with your hands. Cover and let rise until doubled, about 45 minutes. Preheat the oven the last 10 minutes of the proofing to 350°. Bake the cake 30 minutes or until a golden color. When cool, brush with Confectioners' Icing.

NOTE: At holiday time, candied fruit may be added to the filling and candied cherries tucked into each cut. Drizzle with Confectioners' Icing and decorate with red cherries sliced in half.

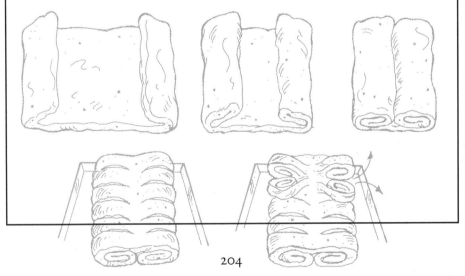

Cinnamon Rolls

Basic Sweet Dough (half the recipe), page 203
Butter, melted
Cinnamon-Sugar
½ cup dark raisins (optional)
Confectioners' Icing

Roll the dough into a rectangle 8x15". Brush with melted butter to within ¼" of edges. Sprinkle with Cinnamon-Sugar, smoothing out with your hand. Sprinkle the raisins on top of the sugar mixture, if desired. Roll from the long side jelly roll style pinching the sides and ends to seal. With a sharp knife (a good bread knife is fine) slice rolls ¾" wide. I like to cut off the ends first and bake those for my grandchildren and of course always adding a bit more cinnamon-sugar. Place the rolls on a baking sheet or cake tins sprayed with vegetable spray. Cover and let rise until doubled, about 45 minutes. Preheat oven to 350° the last ten minutes of proofing. Bake the rolls 25 minutes. Remove from pan, turn out on a serving tray, drizzle with icing if desired and serve while hot.

Orange-Almond Tea Ring

Basic Sweet Dough, page 203
½ cup sugar
Grated rind of 1 large orange
½ cup sliced or slivered blanched almonds
Butter, melted
Confectioners' Icing

Mix the sugar and grated rind together in a small bowl until well blended. Roll the sweet dough into a rectangle 10x17". Brush with melted butter to ¼" of edges. Spread the sugar mixture over the dough, smoothing evenly. Sprinkle the almonds on top. Roll from the long side, jelly roll style, and form into a circle. Join the two ends together by inserting one end into the other. Place on a baking sheet coated with vegetable spray. With scissors snip the top all around in one inch sections. Cover and let rise for 30 minutes. Preheat oven to 350°. Bake the cake for 30 minutes. Remove to a wire rack and cool. Spread with Confectioners' Icing flavored with orange liqueur. For Christmas red candied cherries may be placed in each one of the snipped sections. Serves 10.

Easter Bread

Divide the finished dough in two equal portions. Roll each piece into a 26" rope. Twist the two ropes together loosely beginning at one end. Form into a circle and join the two ends together. Place on a baking sheet coated with vegetable spray. Have 6 colored Easter eggs ready and place them in the twists snugly. The eggs do not have to be boiled as they are going to cook in the oven. Cover and let rise about 30 minutes. Preheat the oven to 350°. Press the eggs down again and bake the twist 30 minutes or until golden. Remove the bread to a wire rack to cool. The bread may be frozen until ready to use. Frost with a Confectioners' Icing flavored with lemon juice or vanilla. Drizzle with icing over the bread and cover with tiny sprinkles in Easter colors. The eggs are not to be eaten — just to be looked at.

APRICOT ORANGE BRAID

This beautifully designed coffee cake is easy to prepare — and it freezes well. The dough may be prepared the night before and tucked into a plastic bag, leaving room for rising. Close the top with a twist tie.

DOUGH:

3 tablespoons warm water

1 package quick-rising dry yeast

3 cups all purpose flour

3 tablespoons sugar

¼ cup cold butter, cut in pieces

1 large egg

Grated rind of 1 large orange

½ teaspoon salt

½ cup warm milk

APRICOT FILLING AND STREUSEL:

37 dried apricots

1¼ cups sugar

½ cup orange juice

1 large egg

TOPPING:

⅓ cup all purpose flour

2 tablespoons sugar

Grated rind of 1 large orange

½ teaspoon nutmeg

2 tablespoons cold butter

1 egg beaten with 1 tablespoon milk

Measure the water into a small bowl, sprinkle in the yeast and stir with a fork until dissolved. Set aside. To a food processor with steel blade in place add the flour, sugar, butter, egg, grated rind and salt. Blend mixture 5 seconds. With machine running, add the yeast mixture and the milk through the feed tube. Process until a smooth and resilient dough forms, about 20 seconds. Remove the dough to a lightly floured surface and knead 1 minute or until dough is a smooth ball. Place dough in a buttered bowl, turning to coat evenly. Cover loosely with plastic wrap and towel. Let rise until doubled, about 1 hour. Or place the dough in a plastic bag, seal and refrigerate overnight. The dough will slowly rise during the night and be ready for forming the next morning. To make the filling, in a saucepan combine 27 of the apricots, reserving 10, 1 cup of the sugar and the orange juice. Place over medium heat and stir constantly until the sugar dissolves. Reduce heat and simmer until the apricots are soft, about 7 to 8 minutes. Strain and pit the apricots if they are not already pitted, saving the juice for yogurt or ice cream. Place the cooked apricots in the clean bowl of a food processor with steel blade in place. Whirl 10 seconds. Add remaining 10 apricots, pitted, and finely chop with on/off turns. Add the egg and whirl until fairly smooth — the mixture does not need to be completely smooth as it needs some texture. Coat a large baking sheet with vegetable spray. Remove the dough to a clean surface and roll to a 12x15" rectangle. Transfer the dough to baking sheet. Spoon the filling down the center of the dough. With a sharp knife slit the dough at 1" intervals on either side. Fold strips across the filling at a slight angle overlapping as they are crossed. Cover and let rise until doubled, about 45 minutes. To make the topping, combine the flour, sugar, grated rind, nutmeg and butter. This may be done in a small bowl with a pastry blender, your fingertips or in the food processor. Brush the braid with the egg wash to hold the topping and sprinkle the streusel over the top of the braid. Bake in a preheated 350° oven about 30 minutes or until golden. Serve hot, warm, or at room temperature or cool and freeze for future use. Serves 12.

Variation: Blueberry Braid

2 cups fresh or frozen blueberries
½ cup sugar
3 tablespoons cornstarch
Grated rind of 1 lemon
2 tablespoons lemon juice
Dough for Apricot Orange Braid

Combine the blueberries, sugar, cornstarch, grated rind and lemon juice in a saucepan. Stir well and place over medium heat. Bring to a boil, stirring constantly — with frozen berries the time will be longer. Lower heat and simmer until thick, stirring occasionally. Remove from the burner and allow to cool.

Roll the Apricot Orange Braid dough in a rectangle as described, 12x15". Place the dough on a baking sheet sprayed with vegetable spray. Spoon the blueberry filling down the center of the dough. Cut as described in the Apricot Orange Braid and fold the strips over the filling. Cover and let rise 30 minutes. Brush with the egg glaze and sprinkle the top with the same topping. Bake in a preheated 350° oven about 30 minutes or until golden. When a dough is placed in the refrigerator overnight, remove at least 30 minutes before molding the cake. Sweet doughs respond quickly and are soft and easy to shape.

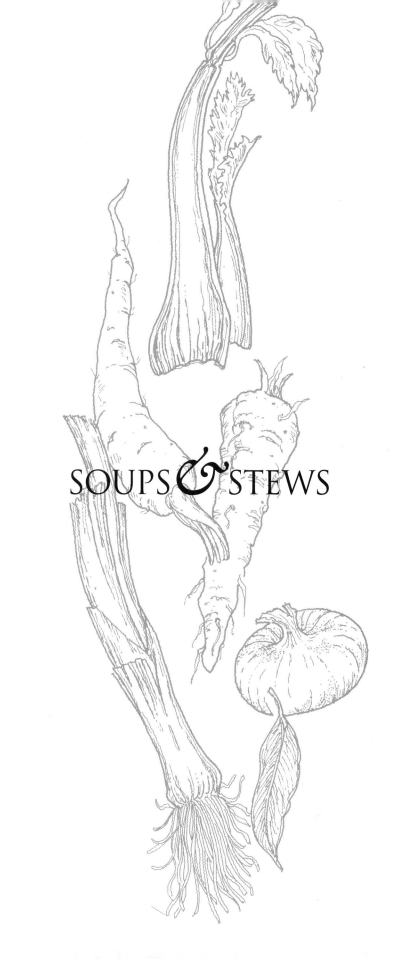

SOUPS&STEWS

Stocks, Broths & Light Soups

*O*ne theory about the origin of soup goes like this: Before primitive people had conceived of pottery but after they had discovered that fire enhanced the flavor of meat, they dug a shallow pit in the earth and lined it with rocks placed very close together. Then they poured water into the pit and added the game meat of the day. To cook the stew, they heated rocks in the fire and dropped them into the pit. As the rocks cooled, newly heated ones were added and although the water never actually came to a boil, the liquid was sufficiently hot to cook the meat. Over the centuries, they began to add herbs and grains to the pit stew. Ah, that intrepid cave woman, whose ingenuity was constantly at work!

Interestingly, I learned from my eldest son (who lived for a year with the Nunamuit tribe of Eskimos in northern Alaska) that well into the 20th century the Nunamuit cooked their primary food source, caribou, by placing it in a watertight wooden bucket along with heated stones. When hunters killed a caribou, it was immediately cut into pieces for easier transportation and then a small fire was built with scrub brush and the animal's liver was broiled and consumed on the spot.

Finally pottery was invented and early cooks began to simmer stews over a fire. Cooking had taken another big step forward. From the Amazon to the China coast, those who lived close to the seashore used conch, mollusk or

BASIC CHICKEN STOCK

Never throw away the carcass of a roasted chicken or turkey. Toss it in a large, heavy pot, cover with clean cold water, add a carrot, 2 blades of celery, an onion sliced in half and a bay leaf if desired (no need to peel them) and simmer 1-2 hours. Cool slightly, then pour through a large strainer, pressing on the bones to obtain all the flavor and goodness. The more meat is left on the carcass, the richer the stock will be. You can refrigerate the broth for a day or two, then make a soup with it, or freeze it in plastic quart containers for later use.

reptile shells for preparing stews. Many hunting tribes enjoyed the residue in the stomach of a large animal and thereby learned how strong the stomach's lining was and how to place stews in the stomach, tie it and hang it over a fire to cook. This is still the way Scotch haggis is constructed, using the stomachs of sheep. I tried haggis several times in the land of my forebears — once even with Scotch poured over it. I thought they were going to flame it but they didn't. When I returned home, my husband purchased a prize lamb at the fair so I asked for the lungs, liver and windpipe but decided to skip the stomach. The liver and lungs were placed in a pot of water and brought to a simmer and the windpipe was placed with one end in the pot and the other in the sink, supposedly to take off offensive gases. The whole mess gurgled away and I watched fascinated. Then it was just a matter of chopping the meat into tiny pieces, adding onion and oats and baking in a casserole. Well, we ate the haggis and I was satisfied that I had made it at least once.

Another son at 19 hitchhiked through the Middle East, lived in the desert close to Saudi Arabia, and dined with Bedouin tribes in Jordan and Syria. I questioned him about the stews he had seen. He said that the Bedouins had large pots made of copper or brass lined with tin and in those cooked a thick stew of lamb, goat and occasionally camel. Tiny birds were often boiled and eaten completely, bones and all. Rice was used to make stew thick enough to eat with flat bread, the knife, fork and spoon of the Arabs. All over Cairo there are vats of beans cooked much like stew. Traveling there myself once I saw the ghettos where families lived in doorless tiny rooms with dirt floors and sleeping benches. A small girl came running up to us clutching a steaming pot of beans and green onions and she was as happy as an American child with a double dip ice cream cone.

Soup and stews impart strength and a wonderfully soothing feeling. For thousands of years they have had a part in the history of every country and era. During the Middle Ages good broth from the cooking pot was sopped up in bread and speared with a knife. King Henry the VIII is said to have loved soups and to have used the newly invented fork to more easily spear a tidbit out of the soup kettle. Soup even helped give us the word "restaurant" which derives from the "restorative" soups made by a Parisian. Such soups became popular in the restaurants opened by chefs who had lost their jobs in the French Revolution.

During the 17th and 18th centuries soups were totally accepted by the upper classes of England and France. Often four or more soups would be served grouped in gorgeous tureens in the center of the table. In the American colonies, soup was truly a mainstay for early settlers had no ovens but most had a heavy pot that could be placed in the fireplace. George Washington's poor, ragged army was saved during a devastating winter at Valley Forge when the cook conceived the idea of "pepper pot soup," which included everything edible he could put his hands on, from tripe to peppercorns. During the Great Depression soup lines were a familiar sight in large cities. Itinerants who traveled by train made camps with a fire and a stewpot. Each new arrival who expected to eat would throw something into the soup.

When my sons were teenagers, I kept a stock pot simmering for two years. My stove had a well with a heavy kettle and into that I placed loads of bones, sometimes browned in the oven and sometimes just thrown in. I kept the bones covered with water and let them cook very, very slowly, for perhaps two days or until they literally fell apart. Then I discarded them and added chunks of good beef and vegetables. Everything from black-eyed peas to leftover carrots went into the kettle and there was always a big bowl of soup ready. The aroma permeated the air and when I baked bread for an evening supper, the kitchen was the most inviting room in the house.

Equipment for preparing soup stocks is simple. There are soup kettles of all sizes available. A large saucepan is necessary, a Dutch oven is superb for stews, casseroles are excellent for oven-baked stews, and a crockpot is perfect for a working couple. Just fill it early in the morning, plug it in and glorious stew will be ready at night. If possible, indulge in a food processor to cut and slice the vegetables — it will save more time than any other machine.

A hot aromatic soup encased in a handsome tureen accompanied with a basket of hot biscuits, fresh rye bread, slices of toasted muffin bread, or hot millet muffins will provide a convivial dinner party or a family supper. Guests will sit back with a deep sigh of happiness at being presented with such a meal. A salad and a dessert of cheese and fruit completes a perfect dinner.

BEEF STOCK

Any soup that requires beef or chicken stock is at its best with homemade broth. There is nothing difficult in the broth-making process except the time it takes. Beef stock simmers overnight, chicken is faster. Both stocks may be prepared, strained, placed in plastic containers with tight lids, labeled and frozen. Once I worked in a kitchen in the Sonoma Valley that had a soup pot big enough for me to sit in — except it was always filled with stock just barely simmering. All kinds of goodies were thrown into the soup pot and then stock was drawn from a spigot at the bottom. The aroma was delicious and so were all the restaurant's soups. My recipe comes from Michael Gubser's kitchen.

> 2½ pounds beef shank, cut in pieces
> 2½ pounds chicken backs, necks or wings
> 1 large onion, quartered
> 2 large celery ribs, sliced in large pieces
> 1 large carrot, sliced thickly

Preheat the oven to 450°. Place the beef and chicken bones in a large baking pan or roaster. Bake until brown and crispy, about 1½ hours. Place the vegetables in the pan the last 30 minutes — the onion, celery and carrot do not have to be peeled. If chicken backs are unavailable use any bony pieces such as necks and wings.

Transfer beef, chicken and vegetables to a large soup kettle or stock pot. Add 1½ gallons of water. Bring to a low simmer. Do not allow rapid boiling as this will cloud the stock. You should see just a few bubbles at a time. The stock should reduce no more than 2 cups. Allow the stock to simmer 10 hours, which can be done overnight. In fact, it is rather pleasant to awaken in the middle of the night and smell the lovely aroma from the stock pot. Remove from burner and strain through a fine sieve layered with cheesecloth. Cover the bone mixture again with water, about ½ to ¾ gallon, and simmer 3 hours. Strain the second broth and mix it with the first. Discard the bones and vegetables. Let broth cool and then freeze in 1 quart containers. Makes approximately 7 quarts.

CHICKEN BROTH

Chicken stock or broth takes little time to prepare. The leftover chicken can be made into a salad or sandwiches or put into a soup. You can also make chicken stock with the leftover carcass of baked chicken after the meat has been consumed, or with economical backs, necks, and wings. The only essential ingredient is chicken or meaty chicken bones; vary the rest to suit your taste.

> 1 three-pound chicken, whole or cut up
> Cold water to cover
> 2 bay leaves
> ¼ teaspoon basil
> ¼ teaspoon thyme
> Rind of ½ lemon (no white pith) in slices (optional)
> 2 medium carrots, cut in large pieces
> 2 celery stalks, cut in large pieces

Place the chicken in a large soup kettle and cover with cold water. Add the remaining ingredients (the vegetables do not need peeling) and slowly bring to a simmer. Slowly simmer until the chicken falls off the bone, about 1 hour. Place a piece of cheesecloth in a large colander or sieve over a large clean container. Pour the contents of the soup kettle into the colander and allow to drain. Debone the chicken for other uses and discard the bones. Chill the strained broth and skim off the congealed fat. The broth is now ready to use for soups or to place in plastic containers and freeze. Makes approximately 3 quarts.

VEGETABLE BROTH

For those who prefer it, a delicious vegetable broth is delightfully easy to prepare. Lots of good vegetables will yield an excellent broth. Use it immediately or freeze it for later use.

> ½ cup butter or margarine
> 4 onions, peeled and chopped
> 5 celery stalks with leaves, cut in large pieces
> 4 large carrots, unpeeled, sliced
> 2 large leeks, peeled and sliced
> 2 cloves of garlic, peeled
> 2 cups parsley, packed
> 3 parsnips, peeled and sliced (optional)
> 1 tablespoon fresh basil or 1 teaspoon dried basil, or to taste
> ½ teaspoon thyme
> 1 bay leaf
> 12 peppercorns
> 3 quarts water

In a large soup kettle melt the butter and sauté the onions until tender, about 10 minutes. Add the remaining ingredients. Stir to blend and bring to a simmer. Let cook at a bare simmer for 2 hours. I have added no salt as that should be done when the broth is used in a soup or stew. Strain through a fine sieve or a colander into a clean bowl. Transfer the broth to plastic containers and let cool. The fat from the butter may be skimmed before the broth is used or frozen.

Broth has many uses beyond the classic one of providing the liquid base for a soup or stew. It makes a flavorful cooking medium for rice couscous in place of water, and can be used to intensify the flavor of vegetables. Cook them, covered, in just enough broth to keep them moist until they are crisp-tender, then dress with a squeeze of lemon, some cracked pepper and salt to taste. For delicious pasta, first cook the pasta in a large pot full of boiling water, taking care to strain it from the water while it is not quite tender. Then place it in a saucepan full of hot broth and simmer until the pasta has absorbed all of the broth.

HONG KONG SOUP WITH POACHED QUAIL EGGS

A journey to the Orient ended in Hong Kong. The bar in our hotel was three stories tall with windows to the ceiling and from it we could watch the fascinating boat traffic. The bar served light food and to my delight I was given a small bowl of clear broth topped with a few chopped green onions and two tiny poached quail eggs. Each evening began with a bowl of this soup. Once I sent back the broth because it was lukewarm but I had eaten one of the tiny eggs so when a hot bowl arrived with two eggs, that evening I had three. Fresh quail eggs may be purchased through game growers and special Chinese shops.

> 2 quarts chicken stock
> 3 egg whites
> Egg shells
> ½ cup thinly sliced green onion
> ½ cup fresh bean sprouts
> 12 fresh quail eggs

Prepare the chicken stock. The stock can be made several days or even weeks ahead and frozen. Measure the chicken broth into a large saucepan. Beat three egg whites just until foamy and add them to the stock with the egg shells. Stir once and no more. Let the stock simmer 30 minutes without disturbing it. Place cheesecloth in a sieve over a clean bowl and strain the stock. Now it is clarified and ready to prepare this elegant little soup. Slice the onions, wash the bean sprouts and set aside. Select a small skillet and fill it halfway with water. Bring to a boil. Have six bowls ready, for the preparation goes quickly. If you can obtain 12 eggs, then each bowl will have two tiny poached eggs, if just six, then use one for each bowl. Breaking the eggs is tricky for the membrane is tougher than the shell. Using a sharp paring knife, gently cut through the shell and into the membrane. Place the eggs on a saucer. It is best to break three at a time. Remove the skillet from the hot burner so that the water stops boiling and gently slide the eggs in to poach. Prepare 3 more eggs and slide them into the water. Cover and let them cook just until the egg whites solidify. Pour hot stock into each bowl. Scoop up the poached eggs with a slotted spoon and place them in the bowls. Repeat with the next 6 eggs. Sprinkle with chopped green onion and sprouts. Serve immediately. This is truly a delight!

CONSOMME MADRILEÑA

The consommé calls for both tomato juice and fresh tomatoes. In the winter look for good tomatoes from our neighbors to the south. I have sometimes been able to obtain winter tomatoes that taste almost like tomatoes. The point is that the soup can be made at any time of year. When there was a severe illness in our family we discovered that this soup was easy to swallow — the patient would eat this soup and nothing else.

6 cups chicken broth
3 cups tomato juice
3 tablespoons powdered unflavored gelatin
2 egg whites, beaten until frothy
3 large tomatoes, cored and cut in pieces
¼ cup dry sherry
1½ tablespoons lemon juice
Grindings of black pepper (optional)
Salt to taste
Lemon or lime slices

Select a large soup kettle to allow room for boiling and add the broth, tomato juice, gelatin, beaten egg whites, tomatoes, sherry, lemon juice and pepper if desired. For an invalid omit the pepper. Heat through and allow to boil, stirring constantly, for 5 minutes. Lower heat and simmer 20 minutes without stirring. Taste for salt and adjust. Strain the soup through a very fine sieve layered with cheesecloth. Place in containers and cover tightly until thoroughly chilled, several hours to overnight. The soup will be semi-congealed. Serve in crystal bowls with a wedge of lemon or lime for a lovely light beginning to a dinner. Serves 12.

COLD BEET BORSCHT

My western Oklahoma friend Ginny Shelton suggested this soup for a hot summer day and it is indeed cool, refreshing and delicious. Not so in Russia. Traveling there we were served borscht with two meals a day. By the third day I felt certain we would have borscht for breakfast but that meal always consisted of two baked or hardboiled eggs, one tiny piece of very salty cheese or ham, a plum colored juice, and bread full of holes with plenty of very hot tea and coffee. In Georgia and Armenia we were relieved to find food much like that of the Middle East. Russian borscht contained lots of water and cabbage. Ginny's borscht is full of goodies and is beautiful in a white bowl.

> 4 cups canned tomatoes with juice
> 4 cups beets, finely sliced or grated
> ½ red onion, grated
> Juice of 3 lemons
> ⅓ cup sugar
> 2 cups sour cream
> Salt and grindings of black pepper

Cut the tomatoes in small pieces and place in a mixing bowl with the juice. Add the sliced beets (slivered canned beets are excellent and save a lot of time) and onion that has either been grated or whirled in a food processor until very finely chopped. Stir in the lemon juice and sugar and mix well. Blend in the sour cream and stir until smooth. More sour cream can be added if a thinner soup is desired. Taste for salt and add a few grindings of black pepper. Cover with plastic wrap and chill several hours. Accompany with Claremore Bread for a colorful summer luncheon. Serves 8 to 10.

GREEK LEMON SOUP

Traveling the length of the Italian boot by automobile, we stopped at a filling station deep in the south where a friendly attendant handed me two enormous lemons, as big as grapefruits. I gave one to a nephew in St. Louis who loves a lemon twist with his martini. That lemon lasted him three weeks. I had seen such lemons on a visit to the inner courtyard of a palace in Damascus. Later I learned that lemons apparently originated in what is now Pakistan, where the first really fine gourmet foods were served. Traders carried lemon seeds to Sumeria. But it was the infamous and brilliant Theodora who brought lemon soup to Constaninople from Cyprus. Theodora not only helped change laws to give more freedom to women but she also brought elegant food to the court of Justinian. Later the Moors brought oranges and lemons to Spain and from there they spread throughout the Mediterranean. Make a good chicken broth for this soup as it is delicate.

> 4 cups chicken broth, homemade
> ¼ cup rice
> Juice of 1 large lemon
> Salt to taste
> Pinch of cayenne pepper
> 2 egg yolks, beaten
> Croutons
> Sour cream or yogurt

Combine the chicken broth, rice, lemon juice and a touch of cayenne in a large saucepan. Bring to a boil and let bubble until the rice is tender, about 15 minutes. Taste for salt and adjust. In a separate bowl beat the egg yolks until frothy. Add a little hot soup to the eggs, blending well. Stir the mixture into the soup. Remove from burner and serve immediately. The soup may be topped with crisp croutons or a tablespoon of sour cream or yogurt. Serves 4.

Note: This is one recipe in which egg whites do not substitute satisfactorily for egg yolks.

ZUCCHINI SOUP

Very few calories are invested in this delectable, drinkable light soup.
Butter can be eliminated, or replaced with a little light margarine.

1½ pounds zucchini
4 cups chicken broth
¾ cups green onion, chopped
½ cup dry white wine
3 tablespoons butter
Salt to taste

Wash the zucchini, remove the ends and slice. Combine in a saucepan with the chicken broth and onion. Bring to a boil and cook uncovered over medium high heat until the zucchini is very tender, about 20 minutes. Whirl the soup in a blender or food processor and return to a clean saucepan. Add the wine, butter and salt to taste. Heat until simmering, pour into mugs and enjoy the fresh, de-lightful flavor. Serves 8.

One of the benefits of cooking vegetables in soup is that the valuable vitamins
and minerals which leach out of the vegetables during cooking are caught in the
rich broth or stock. When vegetables are simply boiled in a large amount of
water, then drained, the combination of high heat and water can cause a
dramatic loss of vitamins. Hard, long boiling in a quantity of water has been
shown to reduce the vitamin C content of cooked vegetables by 80% or more.
Many vitamins and minerals are simply poured away with the cooking water.

Creamy Soups

Most cream soups obtain their sensuous texture from a combination of butter, flour and milk or cream, diluted with stock. To add body to a creamy soup containing vegetables, first cook the vegetables in butter or a small amount of stock until tender, then whirl them in a blender or food processor. They can be blended to a puree or left chunkier, to suit your taste. You can strain them for a velvety texture or leave them unstrained for an earthier texture. The Chinese method of thickening soups is to add cornstarch dissolved in cold water instead of milk, cream or flour. The French often use potatoes as a thickener. This is a method you can always employ to thicken a vegetable-based soup to which you do not wish to add cream, milk or flour. Cook one or two all-purpose potatoes (peeled or unpeeled, depending on the soup and the desired result) until they are tender, then mash with a little of the cooking water and butter if desired, and add to the soup.

To lighten a creamy soup, you can substitute half-and-half, milk, 2% milkfat milk, or skimmed milk – in decreasing order of richness – for cream. Or use these in any desired combination. Sour cream may be replaced in whole or in part with plain yogurt. But remember to be very careful in cooking a soup containing yogurt, as it will curdle very easily if not handled gently over low heat.

CREAM SOUP VARIATIONS

Using a basic cream soup recipe such as the Cream of Cauliflower Soup on page 224, you can create a great variety of velvety, delicious cream of vegetable (or herb) soups. Select your favorite vegetable, or one that is in season and is especially flavorful. Or try a combination of vegetables and flavor them with your favorite herbs.

CREAM OF SPINACH SOUP WITH PINE NUTS

Pine nuts are used extensively in the Middle East and in China. I've found the Chinese pine nuts a bit less expensive, shorter and fatter in size but just the same in flavor as those from the Mediterranean.

One large bund fresh spinach or
    10-ounce package frozen spinach
2 tablespoons butter
½ cup butter
½ cup pine nuts
½ cup onion, chopped
7 tablespoons all purpose flour
⅛ teaspoon nutmeg
4 cups chicken broth
2 cups whole milk
Lemon juice to taste
Salt to taste

Cook well-washed fresh spinach in a heavy covered pot with just the water cling-ing to its leaves after washing until barely tender and drain in a colander. Or re-move frozen spinach from the box, place in a sieve and allow to thaw. Press out moisture. Melt the two tablespoons of butter in a small skillet over medium heat, add the pine nuts and sauté until lightly toasted. Be careful as these nuts easily scorch and become bitter. If this happens, throw them away and start over. Measure out six tablespoons nuts and chop finely. Set aside with the whole nuts. In a large saucepan melt the ½ cup of butter. Add the onion and over medium heat stir until limp; do not allow to brown. Add the chopped nuts, flour and nutmeg. Whisk until smooth. Add the chicken broth, stirring constantly to keep smooth. Allow to come to a boil, stirring constantly. Add the thawed spin-ach and milk. Bring to a simmer and let bubble lightly about 10 minutes. Re-move from the burner and whirl the contents in a blender until smooth. Return contents to a clean saucepan. Over medium heat, stir, add a few drops of lemon juice to enhance the flavor and taste for salt. Adjust to your taste. Add the whole nuts and serve in warm cream soup bowls topped with chopped nuts. Serves 6 to 8.

CREAM OF CAULIFLOWER SOUP

This light cream-colored soup, soothing and suave, is perfect for the first course of a special dinner.

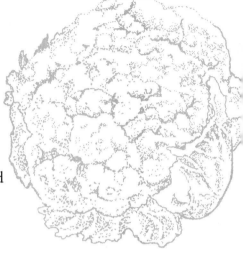

4 cups cauliflower flowerettes
⅔ cup butter or margarine
½ cup all purpose flour
3 cups milk
2 cups chicken broth
¼ teaspoon white pepper
3 tablespoons lemon juice
1 large clove garlic, peeled and crushed
¼ teaspoon Tabasco
1 cup half-and-half
Salt (optional)
Fresh chives or parsley, chopped

Cut off the flowerettes of the cauliflower heads, discarding wide, tough part of the stem. Divide the flowerettes into small pieces. In a large saucepan or soup kettle sauté the cauliflower in the butter until tender, stirring occasionally. Do not allow to burn and do not cover. (Covering brings out a cabbage-like flavor.) Add the flour stirring until well mixed. Blend in the milk and chicken broth and continue to stir until the mixture becomes slightly thickened and smooth. Add the pepper, lemon juice, garlic and Tabasco. Bring to a simmer and continue to cook until the cauliflower is very tender. Transfer to a food processor or blender and whirl until smooth.

Return to a clean saucepan. Stir in the half-and-half and taste for seasoning, adding salt if desired. Top with fresh chives or parsley. Serves 8.

WHITE GAZPACHO

This smooth, creamy, elegant soup is quite different from the usual red soup-salad. Placed in a lovely soup bowl and topped with ripe green avocado, it makes a pretty picture during the hot summer months.

3 medium cucumbers
1 clove garlic
3 cups chicken broth
1½ cups sour cream
1½ cups plain yogurt
3 tablespoons white vinegar
1 teaspoon white pepper
½ cup chopped green onion
½ cup fresh parsley, chopped
Ripe avocado

Peel the cucumbers, slice them down the center and remove the seeds (this is easily accomplished with a grapefruit spoon). Slice the cucumbers crosswise and place in a blender. Peel the garlic, slice in half and add to the blender. Add 1 cup of broth and blend until smooth. Measure in the remaining broth and continue to blend until creamy.

In a large mixing bowl combine the sour cream and yogurt. Slowly add the cucumber mixture to the bowl, whisking until smooth. Blend in the vinegar and pepper. Taste and add salt if desired. Although 1 teaspoon of pepper makes a zippy soup, ½ teaspoon more may be added if you like an extra filip. Cover and chill for 8 hours. Each bowl should be topped with a bit of green onion and parsley. Peel the avocado just before serving, cut into small pieces and add to the topping. Serves 10.

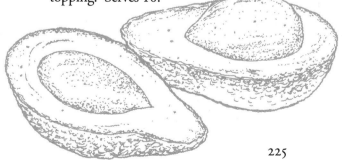

SENEGALESE PUMPKIN SOUP

My eldest granddaughter spent a month one summer with an American family in Senegal, which is a French speaking country. She brought back an account of the customs, the colorful clothes worn by both men and women and the food, which is often spiced with curry. Curry is a blend of spices originating in India. There are many variations, some so hot that they can cause a sudden sweat. In the U.S. curry is eaten a bit milder although if you prefer a spicier soup, add curry to your taste.

> 4 tablespoons butter or margarine
> 2 stalks celery, chopped
> Onion, chopped
> 1 medium apple (Granny Smith), peeled, cored and chopped
> 2 tablespoons all purpose flour
> 2 tablespoons curry
> 4 cups canned or homemade chicken broth
> 3 cloves
> 1 stick cinnamon
> ¾ teaspoon salt
> 2 cups canned pumpkin
> 1 cup half-and-half
> Fresh parsley, chopped

Melt the butter in a skillet or saucepan and sauté the celery, onion and apple until tender, about 10 minutes. Add the flour, stir well and blend in the curry, continuing to simmer lightly for 3 minutes. Do not allow to burn. Add the broth, cloves and cinnamon. Stir until there are no lumps. Bring to a simmer and cook uncovered 30 minutes. Strain the broth into a clean saucepan and replace on the burner. Add the pumpkin and salt and whisk until the mixture is smooth. Bring to a simmer and add the half-and-half, stirring constantly. Heat thoroughly but do not allow to boil. Serve in warm soup bowls with a sprinkling of parsley or serve in demitasse cups to begin a holiday dinner. Serves 8.

BROCCOLI SOUP

Broccoli is offered the year round, keeps well and is adaptable for salads and soups as well as for vegetable dishes. Members of the cabbage family such as broccoli should be cooked uncovered to keep the cabbage flavor from dominating.

1½ pounds fresh broccoli
5 cups chicken broth
1 cup celery, chopped
1 small onion, peeled and chopped
1 clove of garlic, peeled and minced
½ teaspoon dried basil
2 teaspoons lemon juice
1 tablespoon cornstarch
2 tablespoons water
1 cup light cream
Salt to taste

Cut away and discard the tough lower ends of the broccoli stalks. Select three-fourths cup of flowerettes, remove and cook in one cup of the chicken broth uncovered until barely tender. With a slotted spoon remove the flowerettes and set them aside. Cut up the remaining broccoli and place it in the saucepan with the chicken broth. Add the remaining broth, celery, onion, garlic and basil. Bring mixture to a boil and cook until the vegetables are tender. Whirl the soup in a blender, return it to a clean saucepan and add the lemon juice. Place over medium heat. Mix the cornstarch and water together. Add to the soup, stirring constantly. When the soup is quite hot, slowly stir in the cream. Taste for salt and more lemon juice, if needed. Serve in warm soup bowls topped with the whole broccoli flowerettes. Serves 10.

FRESH TOMATO SOUP

This creamy soup filled with the flavor of fresh tomatoes should be made in the summer when real tomatoes are available. However, you can make it in the summer and freeze it for a special delight in the winter. Many markets now sell fresh herbs but dried herbs will also work well.

½ cup butter or margarine
2 cups onion, chopped
1 sprig of fresh thyme
1 bay leaf
¼ cup fresh basil, packed or 1 teaspoon dried
Freshly ground black pepper
5 cups fresh tomatoes, peeled, seeded and chopped
   (about 3 pounds)
3 tablespoons tomato paste
¼ cup all purpose flour
4 cups beef broth or chicken stock
½ cup heavy cream (optional)
Salt to taste

Melt the butter in a large heavy saucepan. Add the onion, thyme, bay leaf, basil and pepper. Allow to simmer until the onion is clear, stirring occasionally, about 10 minutes. Add the tomatoes and tomato paste. Stir thoroughly and simmer 15 minutes.

Combine the flour and one cup of the broth, beating with a small whisk or fork until smooth. Stir the flour mixture into the soup and add the remaining broth. Return to a simmer and cook 30 minutes, stirring occasionally. Remove the bay leaf and whirl the soup in a blender. Strain into a clean saucepan. Bring just to a boil and serve hot. If a richer and creamier soup is desired, slowly add the cream and stir until the soup is hot. Taste and adjust for salt and additional pepper. Serves 6 to 8.

Soups with Fruit

*S*oups made with fruit are the most seasonal of the soups as their *success depends essentially on the flavor and perfection of the fruits, but when the fruit is firm, ripe and bursting with flavor, they are* almost foolproof. Most are served cold or at room temperature and can be made in advance, so they are an easy dish to add to a menu for entertaining. They are also versatile, and can be served for brunch with a selection of muffins or popovers with flavored butters, as a first course for dinner, or for dessert.

Fruit soups are amenable to a great number of flavorings and you may want to experiment with your favorites. Try freshly-grated nutmeg, cinnamon, a dash of brandy or rum, a squeeze of fresh lemon or orange juice, or the grated rind of either, or a tiny bit of fresh basil, ground cardamom, whole clove, or allspice.

To have a special treat during the cold winter months, freeze your favorite summer fruits, such as berries and peaches and melons, when they are at their peak, then thaw them to use for a jewel-like bowl of fruit essence in the depths of winter. Peaches and melons may be peeled and pureed or crushed in their own juices, packed closely into freezerproof plastic bags or other containers and frozen. To keep berries separated when freezing them, place them in one layer on a baking sheet in the freezer until they are frozen hard, then remove to a freezerproof container.

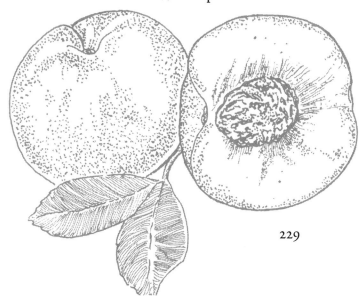

229

OAXACAN DRIED FRUIT SOUP

I once spent Christmas week in the old city of Oaxaca 400 miles south of Mexico City. A hotel room overlooking the central square of the city provided a perfect view each evening of the Festival of the Radishes and the procession of the Virgin Mary with Baby Jesus. It was entrancing. On Christmas Day I arranged a dinner for American friends that began with this superb dried fruit soup. No recipe was available but with a little experimenting I finally composed an excellent replica. Serve as a first course or as dessert.

  3 cups mixed dried fruits
   (apricots, pears, peaches, prunes, apples)
  2 cups orange juice
  3 cups water
  ½ piece of stick cinnamon
  2 slices of lemon
  ½ cup honey
  2 tablespoons quick-cooking tapioca
  ¼ cup brandy
  Plain yogurt, crème fraîche or stick cinnamon

Cut the dried fruits in bite-size pieces. Use fruits of your choice and measure the three cups pressing down so there is plenty of fruit! Place fruit in a large saucepan and add the orange juice, water, a small piece of stick cinnamon and the lemon. Bring to a boil, lower heat and simmer 10 minutes. Remove from burner and add the honey, tapioca and brandy. Stir well. Return to burner and simmer 15 minutes. Serve hot, at room temperature or even chilled. I love it best with a long piece of stick cinnamon to stir the soup, particularly if it is served in large pottery mugs as it was in Oaxaca. For variety, top with plain yogurt or splurge with a dollop of crème fraîche and a tiny bit of freshly grated nutmeg. Serves 8.

TOMATO ORANGE SOUP

This savory light soup can be served before a holiday dinner in small cups or cream soup bowls while the turkey is being carved. Or try it at a cocktail party after the period of serving drinks. Bring in trays of demi-tasse cups filled with this hot pungent soup. Your guests will appreciate such a thoughtful gesture.

4 cups chicken broth
3½ cups canned tomatoes, crushed
1 medium onion, peeled and sliced
1 carrot, cleaned and sliced
Grindings of black pepper
2" strip of lemon rind (no white pith)
1 bay leaf
½ teaspoon sugar
3 tablespoons butter or margarine
2 tablespoons all purpose flour
Grated rind of 1 large orange
½ cup orange juice
½ cup half-and-half
Salt to taste

Combine the chicken broth, tomatoes, onion, carrot, pepper, lemon rind, bay leaf and sugar in a large saucepan. Bring to a boil, lower heat and simmer covered 30 minutes. Remove lemon rind and bay leaf. Puree soup in a blender and remove to a clean bowl.

In a large saucepan melt the butter and whisk in the flour. Whisk constantly 2 minutes. Add the tomato puree, orange rind and juice, stirring until smooth. Bring to a boil, lower heat and bring to a simmer. Stir in the cream and simmer 2 minutes. Taste for salt and pepper and adjust. Serves 8 to 10 in soup bowls and twice that many if using demi-tasse cups.

CHILLED CHERRY SOUP

This wonderfully easy soup can be made several days ahead of a dinner party. Serve it at the beginning of a meal or for dessert. When my youngest son was a senior in high school we hosted a student from Sweden for the school year. He loved coffee cake and a cup of coffee for an afternoon snack. Finally he decided he should give up the coffee cake so I froze the ones I had on hand. Not long afterward when I checked the freezer I found that he was eating the coffee cakes frozen! His mother sent me two Swedish cookbooks, one of which contained this excellent Cherry Soup. I added the lemon and orange to enhance the flavor even further.

¾ cup sugar
1 cinnamon stick (3" long)
1 thick slice of lemon
1 thick slice of orange
1½ cups water
1 can tart pitted red cherries, drained
2 teaspoons cornstarch
1 tablespoon water
¼ cup half-and-half
¼ cup sour cream
½ cup dry red wine

Combine the sugar, cinnamon stick, lemon, orange and the 1½ cups of water in a saucepan. Bring to a boil and stir until the sugar dissolves. Add the cherries, lower the heat and simmer covered 10 minutes. Discard the cinnamon stick, orange and lemon slices. Stir together the cornstarch and the tablespoon of water in a small bowl. Add to the soup and stir constantly until it clarifies and thickens slightly. Place in a container with a lid and refrigerate. After several hours of chilling combine the half-and-half and sour cream, stir to blend and add to the cherry mixture along with the wine. Return to the refrigerator and keep chilled until ready to use. Serves 4.

FRESH CARROT ORANGE SOUP

Coriander, an ancient spice used extensively in the Mediterranean and the Middle East, gives the subtle flavor to this colorful soup. My middle son Peter hitchhiked through the Middle East at the age of 19. He was intrigued by the hospitable Bedouin tribes living in the black tents on the deserts who always served hot coffee from copper pots with spouts stuffed with hay to strain out the aromatic whole coriander seeds.

1 large onion, peeled and coarsely chopped
4 tablespoons butter or margarine
1 garlic clove, peeled and sliced
1½ teaspoons ground coriander
1½ pounds carrots, cleaned and sliced
1 large potato, peeled and cubed
7 cups chicken broth
1 cup fresh orange juice
Salt to taste
Grindings of white pepper
⅔ cup milk or heavy cream
Fresh parsley, minced or freshly grated nutmeg

In a soup kettle sauté the onions in the butter until tender, about 10 minutes. Do not allow to brown. Sauté the garlic two minutes, stirring constantly. Blend in the coriander. Add the carrots, potato, chicken broth and orange juice, blending the mixture well. Bring to a boil, lower heat to simmer and continue to cook until the vegetables are very tender, about 35 minutes. The timing will depend on how tender the carrots are — large winter carrots require longer cooking. Add salt to taste and the white pepper. Remove soup from the burner and puree in a blender. Return soup to a clean kettle, place over medium heat and add the milk. If you can take the calories, use cream but I love the soup just with milk. Bring to a simmer, taste again and adjust seasoning. Serve in warm soup bowls or for holidays in festive demi-tasse cups. Serves 8 in bowls, 16 in cups. Top the soup with either a sprinkling of parsley or nutmeg.

SWIRLED HONEYDEW AND CANTALOUPE SOUP

In the mid-1920s, a Tulsa oilman named Waite Phillips built an Italian Renaissance style villa on 23 acres of landscaped gardens and grounds. In 1939 he donated the property to the city of Tulsa to be used as a museum. For several years volunteers of the museum served luncheons and from one of those occasions came this elegant two-toned soup.

2 small or 1 large cantaloupe
2 tablespoons fresh lemon juice
1 large honeydew melon
3 tablespoons fresh lime juice
1½ teaspoons fresh mint, minced
Mint sprigs for garnish (optional)

Peel, seed and coarsely chop the cantaloupe. There should be sufficient cantaloupe to make 3½ cups when pureed. Combine the cantaloupe and lemon juice in a blender, whirling at high speed until very smooth. This will have to be done in several batches. Transfer to a pitcher and cover with plastic wrap.

Rinse and dry the blender. Repeat directions with the honeydew, combining with the lime juice and mint while blending at high speed until smooth. Transfer to a pitcher, cover with plastic wrap and refrigerate both mixtures. Chill at least three hours or preferably overnight. This is a bonus as the soup may be prepared a day ahead. If possible chill the soup bowls, then arrange in a row for easy preparation. Carefully pour the two soups together into each bowl so that the mixtures touch and swirl slightly. If desired garnish each with a tiny sprig of mint. The soup is especially lovely in white or light cream soup bowls. Serves 6 to 8.

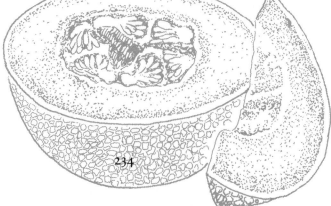

FRESH PEACH SOUP

Try this for Thanksgiving or Christmas dinner in demi-tasse cups while the turkey is being carved. When peaches are ripe in the summer, prepare extra — the recipe can be doubled or tripled. Tuck some in your freezer and your family will love you!

>   4 cups peaches, peeled and sliced
>   2 cups water
>   2 cups dry white wine
>   ¾ cup sugar
>   1 stick cinnamon (3" long)
>   2 tablespoons cornstarch
>   3 tablespoons cool water
>   Whipped cream (optional)

Combine the peaches, water, wine, sugar and cinnamon stick in a large saucepan. Bring to a boil, lower heat and simmer until fruit is soft, about 15 minutes. Remove from the burner and discard the cinnamon. Whirl the contents in a blender and strain through a sieve into a clean saucepan over medium heat. Mix the cornstarch with the water until dissolved and add the mixture to the strained peach mixture. Cook, stirring constantly, until the soup is thickened, about five minutes. Remove from the burner, cool, place the soup in a container with a cover and refrigerate until chilled. Adorn with whipped cream if desired. Frozen peaches may be used; add ½ teaspoon of lemon juice to bring out the flavor of the fruit. Serve 16 in demi-tasse cups or 8 in soup bowls.

ICED RASPBERRY SOUP

Mary Jane Kano, an intrepid cook, gave me this recipe years ago. I had forgotten it and so had she until I stumbled across a copy in her handwriting tucked in an old file. One evening I served a small group including Mary Jane this beautiful scarlet soup. She was delighted and asked for the recipe!

> 2 ten-ounce packages frozen raspberries
> 1 ¼ cups canned or homemade chicken broth
> ½ cup unsweetened pineapple juice
> 2 tablespoons sugar
> ½ cup sour cream
> Blanched almonds, toasted and chopped (optional)

Defrost the raspberries and whirl in a food processor or a blender. Strain into a bowl to remove the seeds. To the raspberry liquid add the chicken broth, pineapple juice, sugar and sour cream. Whisk until smooth, cover and chill for several hours. Serve in chilled soup bowls topped with chopped almonds. For another optional topping, remove two tablespoons of strained berries before continuing with the soup and mix with two tablespoons sour cream. Use to garnish each serving. Serves 6.

Note: The soup is excellent served plain in demi-tasse cups to accompany chicken salad and hot muffins.

Soups with Beans, Nuts, Grains and Pasta

For a soul-satisfying hot meal, especially in cold weather, it is hard to beat a steaming bowl of soup with the added flavor, texture and nourishment of beans, grains or pasta. And nuts, though they are not as common as beans and grains in the classic soups of America's melting-pot cuisine, are a wonderful soup ingredient, adding sophisticated flavor, substance and nutrition. Peanuts, or "ground nuts," for example, are a standard addition to the soups and stews of many African nations and have made their way into classic Southern cuisine of the United States.

Almost any kind of pasta will work beautifully in soup but the versions that are bite-size or smaller when cooked make for neater eating. There are many varieties available, in almost every shape imaginable from tiny corkscrews to miniature "elbows" of macaroni. You can experiment with high-protein pasta, whole-wheat pasta, or the recently-available array of spinach, tomato, or herb-flavored pastas.

Soups and breads, the soul of good eating, find some of their happiest marriages when the soup contains beans and the bread contains corn. Corn by itself has a scant supply of an important amino acid, lysine, that makes up part of the protein necessary for human life. But beans are well stocked with lysine, as well as tryptophan and niacin. Native Americans of the Southwest planted corn and beans side by side and often subsisted in good health primarily on these two foods. So, for both health and pleasure, pair any of the cornbreads with a pot of delicious soup containing beans.

ASPARAGUS SOUP WITH HAZELNUTS

A Venetian writer in 1475 said this about asparagus: "There are two kinds of asparagus, domestic and wild, the latter being more pleasing. Boiled asparagus is laid out on a platter and salt and oil and vinegar are added, some sprinkle with herbs. Eaten as a first course, they combat flatulence in the stomach, they help clear the eyesight, good for pains in the chest and spine and for intestinal complaints. If used too often they can be rather harmful, for they move the bladder quickly and make it sore which is a dangerous thing. The root of asparagus ground up and drunk in wine gets rid of stones. . ." and so it goes for 1475. Here at the end of the 20th century there is plenty of beautiful slender asparagus to cook in many ways without worry!

2 pounds fresh asparagus
¾ cup hazelnuts
Boiling water
4 cups chicken broth
1 rib celery, sliced
1 teaspoon dried basil
5 tablespoons butter or margarine
4 tablespoons all purpose flour
Cayenne pepper
Salt to taste

Clean asparagus and cut or break off tough ends. Cut into one-inch pieces. Cover the hazelnuts with boiling water and let stand about 5 minutes. Drain the nuts and place them in a thick turkish towel. Rub to remove the skin. Most but not all will be removed. Combine the chicken broth, celery, basil and asparagus in a saucepan. Place over medium heat and simmer until the asparagus is tender, approximately 20 minutes. The time will be regulated by the size of the asparagus. During the last five minutes add the hazelnuts. Puree the mixture in a blender and strain into a clean bowl — this will finish removing the brown skin of the nuts. Melt the butter in a pan, whisk in the flour until smooth and add the blended soup, stirring constantly until thick and smooth. Add a pinch of cayenne pepper and adjust for salt. Serves 6 to 8.

TERRY'S WHITE CHILI

Terry Davis is a full blood Cherokee Indian, an expert on chili, and the fine chef of Mary's Bread Basket in Tulsa. Terry's avocation is following chili contests in Arkansas, Texas, New Mexico, Colorado and Kansas. His cooking apparel is a handsome apron with Seminole patchwork in red and green and a big bright red pepper below the patchwork — and he wins those chili cookoffs!

6 cups chicken broth
3 cups navy beans (small white beans)
2 teaspoons cumin
1 teaspoon oregano
8 ounces canned green chilies, chopped
1 clove garlic, peeled and minced
1 cup onion, chopped
½ teaspoon white pepper
½ teaspoon ground cloves
1 pound cooked chicken, cut in pieces
Salt to taste

Combine in a soup kettle the chicken broth, beans, cumin, oregano, chilies, garlic, onion, white pepper and cloves. Place over medium heat and bring to a boil, then lower heat and simmer until the beans are tender, 1½ to 2 hours. When the beans are tender, add the chicken, bring to a simmer, and salt to taste. Simmer 10 to 15 minutes to allow ingredients to meld. Serves 10.

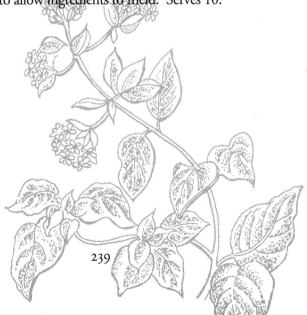

PEANUT SOUP

This delightfully simple soup can be made with ingredients right on your shelf. I encourage the use of a natural peanut butter with no additives such as Arrowhead Mills Creamy Peanut Butter.

1 cup onion, finely chopped
½ cup butter or margarine
3 tablespoons all purpose flour
1 cup creamy peanut butter
4 cups chicken broth
Grindings of white pepper
Salt to taste
Peanuts, finely chopped or croutons

Place the onions in a large saucepan over medium heat and sauté in the butter until soft and golden, about 10 minutes. Do not allow to burn. Whisk in the flour until smooth. Blend in the peanut butter and add the chicken broth, whisking until smooth. Bring the soup to a boil, lower heat and simmer 15 minutes. Blend in grindings of white pepper and salt to taste. Serve topped with finely chopped peanuts or crisp croutons. Serves 6.

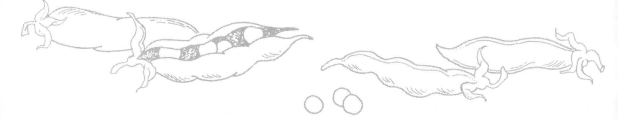

LOW CHOLESTEROL SPLIT PEA SOUP

For several years I have made split pea soup with chicken or turkey broth. Sometimes I simmer a chicken, use the broth for the soup and debone the chicken for salad. During holiday time I use the leftover carcass of turkey to prepare broth. Both are most successful in eliminating the usual ham.

1 pound split peas (2 cups)
3 quarts canned or homemade chicken broth
1 medium onion stuck with 2 cloves
2 cloves garlic, peeled and chopped
1 cup celery with leaves, chopped
2 leeks, cleaned and sliced, white part only
2 carrots, scraped, cleaned, sliced
½ teaspoon thyme
1 bay leaf
3 sprigs fresh basil or 1 teaspoon dried basil
Salt to taste
3 sprigs fresh parsley
Grindings of black pepper
⅛ teaspoon cayenne pepper (optional)
Yogurt
Grating of nutmeg

Combine the split peas with the chicken broth, onion, garlic, celery, leeks, carrots, thyme, bay leaf, basil, a touch of salt and parsley in a soup pot. Bring to a boil, skim, and lower heat. Simmer uncovered, stirring occasionally, for about two hours or until all the vegetables including the split peas are very tender. Discard the whole onion and puree the soup in a blender. Return soup to a clean pot, taste for seasonings and adjust. Hot split pea soup is delicious served with a dollop of plain yogurt and gratings of nutmeg. Or try grated skimmed milk cheese as a topping. Serves 12 generously.

LENTIL SOUP

Lentils in themselves can be bland but they have a marvelous quality of absorbing the flavors of supporting foods cooked with them. The ancients discovered this early for lentils are a very old food. A dish of ham and lentils was served in a Mesopotamian garden when Babylon was the center of the world. Lentils were the base for the "mess of potage" for which Esau sold his birthright. At the height of Rome's history lentil salad often was included in elaborate banquets. Lentils are full of vitamin B and obviously they give strength for the mountain-climbing Sherpas of the high Himalayas eat them too. I am pleased with the construction of this lentil soup whose flavor is unusually pleasing.

½ pound lentils
Water to cover
2 stalks celery
2 unpeeled carrots, cut in pieces
2 medium onions, peeled and chopped
2 teaspoons sugar
1 teaspoon thyme
⅛ teaspoon cumin
1 bay leaf
4 sprigs fresh parsley
2 garlic cloves, peeled and smashed
1 green pepper, chopped
8 cups beef stock
Meaty smoked ham hock

Wash the lentils well. Place them in a soup kettle. Add all the remaining ingredients to the lentils. Bring to a simmer and cook very gently until the lentils are very tender, about 1 hour. If not tender, cook a little longer. Discard the celery, bay leaf, parsley and remove the ham hock. Debone the hock, cutting the meat in bite-size pieces and discard the bone. Whirl the lentils and remaining ingredients in a blender and place in a clean kettle. If desired, blend three-fourths of the soup and leave the rest unblended for texture. Add the ham. If the soup is too thick, thin with a little beef stock. Serves 10.

SPICY CHICKEN TOMATO PASTA SOUP

Those who love pungent full meal soups with cornbread sticks or muffins will be warmed to their cockles when served this soup before a roaring fire in the mid-winter.

6 cups canned or homemade chicken broth
1 cup onion, chopped
1 cup zucchini, diced
½ cup carrot, diced
1 cup celery, diced
1 bay leaf
¼ teaspoon thyme
1 large garlic clove, peeled and minced
¼ cup parsley, finely chopped
Grindings of black pepper
3 sprigs fresh basil or 1 teaspoon dried basil
1 one-pound, 12-ounce can crushed tomatoes with puree
Approximately ½ cup Ro-Tel brand tomatoes
 and green chilies (½ of one 10-ounce can)
1 cup elbow macaroni or tiny pasta
2 cups cooked chicken, chopped
Salt to taste

Measure the chicken broth into a soup kettle, bring to a boil and add the onion, zucchini, carrots, celery, bay leaf, thyme, garlic, parsley, pepper and basil. Bring to a simmer and cook 15 minutes uncovered until vegetables are tender. Add the crushed tomatoes, Ro-Tel tomatoes and green chilies and pasta. (If a spicier soup is desired, add the remaining half can of Ro-Tel tomatoes and green chilies.) Bring to a boil, lower to simmer and cook gently 20 minutes until the pasta is tender. Add the chicken and simmer until thoroughly heated. If the soup becomes too thick after the pasta is added, add one to two cups additional chicken broth to suit your own taste. Adjust for salt. Serves 10 to 12.

CHICKEN AND BARLEY SOUP

Accompanied by a green salad and muffins, this superb soup makes a perfect and nourishing dinner. The recipe doubles easily and the cooked soup will keep in the refrigerator for a week.

2½ pounds chicken, whole or cut up
Water to cover
1 bay leaf
1 small onion, quartered
1 carrot, cleaned and sliced
1 stalk celery, sliced
½ teaspoon thyme
3 sprigs fresh parsley
6 cups chicken broth
Grindings of black pepper
½ teaspoon nutmeg
¼ to ½ teaspoon cumin (optional)
4 tablespoons parsley, finely chopped
4 tablespoons onion, finely chopped
4 tablespoons butter
1 cup pearl barley
2½ cups water
Salt to taste

Simmer chicken covered in a soup pot with the bay leaf, small onion, carrot, celery, thyme and sprigs of parsley. When the chicken is tender, remove and drain, saving the broth. Debone the chicken, discarding the bones and vegetables. Strain the broth into a clean soup kettle. If the broth does not measure six cups, add a good canned broth. To the broth add the chicken, pepper, nutmeg, cumin, the four tablespoons of parsley and onion. Bring to a simmer and allow to cook 15 minutes. Turn the burner off while preparing the barley. Melt butter in a large saucepan and sauté the barley for five minutes, stirring constantly. Add the water, cover, and simmer gently for 30 minutes. Stir occasionally. Add the barley to the soup in the kettle, place over the medium heat and bring to a simmer. Cook gently until the barley is tender, about 30 minutes. If quick barley is used the cooking time will be lessened. Taste for salt, pepper, nutmeg and adjust. Served in warm soup bowls topped with a sprinkling of nutmeg or freshly cut parsley. Serves 8 generously.

CHICKEN POZOLE

My first taste of pozole was on the Hopi Reservation in central Arizona. Mexican and Indian cuisine combined to produce this spicy, pungent soup. Hominy is of Aztec origin but used by American Indians in the East and West. Dried hominy is available in speciality stores and in some parts of the country — especially the Southwest — you can find frozen limed hominy called nixtmal in the supermarket. If the soup is made with hominy in these forms the cooking takes several hours. The following recipe calls for canned hominy as it is readily available in supermarkets. Both yellow and white hominy are used, along with chicken instead of the usual pork or lamb.

2½ pounds chicken pieces
2 tablespoons vegetable shortening
2 quarts chicken broth
3 tablespoons Masa Harina*
½ cup cool water
2 medium garlic cloves, peeled and minced
1 medium onion, peeled and chopped
1 tablespoon chili powder or 1 teaspoon crushed
dried hot red chilies (optional)
1 tablespoon brown sugar
1 tablespoon dried oregano
Grindings of black pepper
1 one-pound can white hominy
1 one-pound can yellow hominy
Lime wedges
Slices of ripe avocado

Sauté the chicken in the shortening in a heavy iron skillet until lightly brown. Transfer to drain on paper towels. Remove fat from the kettle. Return chicken to the kettle, add the broth and bring to a boil. Reduce heat until mixture is simmering. Mix the Masa Harina and the cool water with a fork, stirring until smooth. Blend into the soup until well mixed. Add the garlic, onion, the optional chili powder, brown sugar, oregano and pepper. Cover and simmer 45 minutes. Drain both cans of hominy and add to the kettle. Bring to a simmer again, skimming off any fat from the surface. Taste for seasoning and adjust salt content. Serve with lime wedges and slices of ripe avocado. Serves 8.

*Masa Harina is a finely ground corn flour available in many supermarkets and import stores.

BLACK EYED PEA SOUP

Tired of black eyed peas and ham hock for New Year's? Just a few extra flavors will take these good luck peas into another orbit.

1 pound black-eyed peas
4 cups beef broth
4 cups water
2 cups canned tomatoes with juice
1½ cups onion, chopped
1 clove of garlic, peeled and chopped
Grindings of black pepper
Meaty ham hock
4 slices canned jalapeños peppers or
one small fresh jalapeño, sliced

Wash the black eyed peas thoroughly and place in a large soup kettle. Add the beef broth and water, bring to a boil, lower to simmer and let cook 30 minutes. Cut the tomatoes in bite size pieces and add with their juice to the kettle. Add the onion, garlic and black pepper. Simmer for one hour or until the peas become tender.

In a separate pan cover the ham hock with water, bring to a boil, lower to simmer and let cook until tender while the soup is bubbling. When the ham is tender, drain, debone and cut in bite size pieces. Add the jalapeño peppers to the soup with the ham and simmer 30 minutes. Remove the soup from the burner and whirl one-half of it in a blender. Return to the soup kettle. Stir well, bring to a simmer and serve hot with any of the cornbreads. Serves 8 to 10.

MARY'S MINESTRONE

Every housewife and restaurant in Italy make a version of this magnificent soup. After traveling from the top of Italy to the end of the boot I decided to try my own version — and with two different endings. One is with pesto, the other with ham. Actually one could go whole hog and throw everything in.

2 cups dried white beans or an assortment of red,
black or white beans, lentils, and garbanzos*
4 large dried mushrooms
6 tablespoons olive oil
½ cup onions, chopped
4 cups eggplant, peeled and diced
2 cups zucchini, sliced
2 cups yellow squash, sliced
1½ cups celery, cleaned, cut diagonally
2 cups fresh green beans, broken in pieces
2 cups fresh tomatoes, peeled, seeded and diced
4 cups beef broth
4 cups chicken broth
¾ cup vermicelli
Salt to taste
Grindings of black pepper
  PESTO SAUCE:
¼ cup fresh parsley, packed
2 cup lightly packed fresh basil leaves or ¼ cup dried basil
2 cloves garlic, peeled
⅓ cup pine nuts
1 cup Parmesan cheese, freshly grated
6-8 tablespoons olive oil
2 tablespoons lemon juice
Optional Additions:
2 cups cooked ham, diced
Parmesan cheese

248

Wash the beans or combination of beans and lentils and cover with water to soak overnight. The next morning, drain the beans, place them in a soup kettle, cover with water and bring to a boil. Lower heat and simmer 1½ hours, skimming when necessary.

While the beans are simmering, prepare the vegetables. Wash the dried mushrooms, cover with warm water and allow to soak 20 minutes. Drain, slice and set aside. Heat 6 tablespoons of oil in a large kettle and sauté the onions 5 minutes. Stir in the mushrooms, eggplant, zucchini, squash and celery, stirring to coat with the oil. Add the tomatoes, the two broths and the beans. Bring to a boil, lower heat and simmer the soup 30 minutes. Add the vermicelli, salt to taste, and pepper. (Be careful in the addition of salt for the pesto containing Parmesan cheese is quite salty.) Stir, bring back to a simmer and cook until the pasta is tender and you are satisfied with the flavor and tenderness of the vegetables.

To make the pesto, combine the parsley, basil, garlic, pine nuts, cheese and 6 tablespoons of oil in a food processor. Pulse for several seconds, remove the lid and scrape down the sides. Add the lemon juice and whirl several seconds. A thick paste should form – if it is too thick, add a bit more oil. The pesto may be stirred directly into the soup but my favorite way of serving is to top each bowlful with a heaping teaspoon of pesto.

The ham may be added with the vermicelli. Its addition makes a full-meal soup that will serve 16. The pesto may be eliminated and Parmesan cheese passed separately in a bowl for a final topping.

*At most supermarkets jars or bags of assorted beans, lentils and garbanzos may be purchased. All these are excellent and save buying a large supply of each item. Minestrone may be varied in endless ways. Delete and add ingredients to your own taste. Enjoy!

Soups & Stews with Meat

earty meat stews are ancient, sustaining food. They pair beautifully with quick bread in the form of dumplings or noodles, or with hot cornbread or muffins, or a loaf of nut bread. Make them with your own stocks or use top-quality canned stock. To lighten meat stews, be sure to trim all visible fat from the meat.

Extending a pot of stew is easy: just add tomato juice or canned tomatoes when fresh ones are out of season, a potato, dry red or white wine, pasta, more dumplings, vegetables, extra broth. Or serve the thicker, richer stews over a bed of rice. Add more herbs and an extra bay leaf to intensify the flavors.

Avoid salting soups and stews until all ingredients are heated through and flavors have begun to combine, especially if you are using a presalted canned broth. For extra spiciness, add flakes of dried hot red pepper, readily available in the spice section of most supermarkets.

Leftover stews will keep in the refrigerator for 2-3 days and they freeze beautifully.

BREAD WITH STEWS

Kishk and Kibbe Soup with Pideh Bread

Steak Soup with Southern Spoon Bread

Greek Lemon Pork Stew with Applesauce Muffins

Oxtail Stew with Pumpernickel Bread

Gree Meat Ball Soup with Basic Nut Bread

Michael's Chili with Cheddar and Garlic Muffins and Spicy Corn Muffins

and the possibilities continue. . .

BEEF STEW WITH HERBED DUMPLINGS

¼ pound lean salt pork, cubed
4 pounds lean beef (chuck, preferably) cut in bite-size pieces
½ onion (3 tablespoons), chopped
1 carrot, cleaned and chopped
1 clove garlic, peeled and minced
2 tablespoons all purpose flour
Freshly ground black pepper
⅛ teaspoon nutmeg
2 cups dry red wine
1½ cups beef broth
1 bay leaf
Salt to taste

Brown the salt pork in a heavy iron skillet or dutch oven until crispy. Remove with a slotted spoon to paper towels to drain. Sauté the beef until brown, a small quantity at a time. Crowding the beef prevents browning. Remove to paper towels. Stir in the onion, carrot and garlic. Sauté for 5 minutes, stirring constantly. Return meats to the dutch oven or skillet, sprinkle with the flour and until meats are lightly coated. Add grindings of pepper and the nutmeg. Measure in the wine and broth and add the bay leaf. Stir until all ingredients are well mixed. Bring to a simmer, cover and cook 1½ to 2 hours or until the meat is very tender. Taste for salt and pepper and adjust.

Make the dumplings according to the recipe on page 253. When the stew is ready, drop the batter on top of it by the teaspoonful. Cover and cook over low heat for 15 minutes. Serves 8.

Dumplings for Stew

Dumplings resemble both biscuits and muffins in preparation. All purpose flour is combined with a leavening and butter or margarine is cut into it with a pastry blender. Liquid is stirred in quickly and the dumplings are ready to cook. When dumplings are cooked in stew, the lid is closed tightly so that steam will assist the dumplings to rise quickly and become tender.

Another method of preparing dumplings is to combine dry ingredients with liquid ingredients using the techniques familiar from muffin-making. These, too, are spooned immediately into the bubbling stew.

Basic Dumplings

1 cup all purpose flour
2 teaspoons baking powder
½ teaspoon salt
2 tablespoons butter or margarine, cut in pieces
⅓ cup milk
1 large egg

Combine the flour, baking powder and salt in a shallow mixing bowl. Cut in the butter with a pastry blender or a knife and fork until mixture is crumbly. Blend the milk and egg and add to the dry mixture. Stir rapidly until just well moistened. Drop by large teaspoonfuls atop a bubbling stew or soup, cover tightly, lower heat and simmer for 15 minutes. There will be enough dumplings to cover a stew in a large skillet.

Whole Wheat Dumplings:

Prepare Basic Dumplings using ½ cup whole wheat flour and ½ cup all purpose flour. Combine ingredients and cook as directed.

Herbed Dumplings

2 cups all purpose flour
4 teaspoons baking powder
1 teaspoon salt
⅛ teaspoon nutmeg
½ teaspoon thyme
⅓ cup minced fresh parsley
¾ cup boiling water
3 tablespoons butter or margarine, melted

Combine the flour, baking powder, salt, nutmeg, thyme and parsley in a mixing bowl and blend well. With a rubber spatula beat in the boiling water and butter. Stir quickly into a smooth batter. Drop dumplings by the teaspoon or tablespoon atop a bubbling stew. Cover, lower heat and simmer for 15 minutes. Serves 8.

Note: Herbed Dumplings may be made with any of your favorite herbs. Try finely chopped chives, oregano, dried or fresh basil or a bit of sage. Combinations should suit the stew being prepared.

Cornmeal Dumplings

¾ cup all purpose flour
½ cup cornmeal
1½ teaspoons baking powder
½ teaspoon salt
½ cup milk
1 large egg
2 tablespoons butter or margarine, melted

Combine the flour, cornmeal, baking powder and salt in a mixing bowl and blend well with a rubber spatula. In a separate bowl stir together the milk, egg and butter. Make a well in the center of the dry ingredients and add the liquids. Stir rapidly just until the mixture is well moistened. Drop by a heaping teaspoonsful atop a bubbling chicken stew. Cover tightly, lower heat and simmer about 20 minutes. Serves 8.

STEAK SOUP

A blazing fire one frigid evening and a tureen filled with piping hot Steak Soup, plus rice and a big casserole of Southern Spoon Bread, enticed my guests completely for nothing was left on a single plate. My first introduction to Steak Soup was in Columbia, Missouri several years ago in a campus restaurant close to the University of Kansas. Loving the unusual flavor of this beef stew, I found it originated in Kansas City, which certainly was logical. Some cooks use ground round but I prefer the richness of sirloin steak.

1½ pounds sirloin steak, trimmed and cubed
¼ cup light oil
8 cups canned or homemade beef broth
One 16-ounce can tomatoes and juice
Grindings of black pepper
1 cup celery, cleaned and sliced diagonally
1 cup carrots, cleaned and sliced thickly
1½ cups onions, peeled and coarsely chopped
½ cup soft butter or margarine
1 cup flour
Salt to taste

In a heavy soup kettle sauté the steak in the oil until browned. Drain off excess fat. Add 2 cups of broth, the tomatoes and black pepper. Bring to a simmer and cook 30 minutes uncovered. Add the celery, carrots and onions; simmer another 30 minutes. Combine 2 cups of the broth, the butter and flour in a blender. Whirl until smooth. Add to the soup, stirring until smooth. Blend in the remaining 4 cups of broth. Simmer for 15 to 20 minutes or until thick and bubbling, stirring occasionally. Serve in large warm soup bowls. Serves 8.

Kathy's Egg Noodles

I wish that I had paid better attention to my mother's cooking instead of just playing in the dough. She made wonderful noodles with no handy machines. I discussed this with my associate, Kathy Major, and she volunteered to create an easy recipe similar to my mother's except that we both agreed it should be made with a food processor. Try these with any meat stew instead of dumplings, or with Greek Meat Balls.

2 cups all purpose flour
1 teaspoon salt
2 large eggs
1 egg yolk
2 tablespoons water
2 tablespoons olive oil

Combine the flour and salt in a food processor with the steel blade in place. Pulse briefly to blend. In a measuring cup blend the eggs, egg yolk, water and oil, beating with a fork. Turn the food processor on and slowly pour the egg mixture through the feed tube, processing until the dough forms a ball. Continue to process 60 seconds. Remove the dough from the bowl and place in a lightly floured plastic bag to rest for 10 minutes.

Divide dough in half and place one piece back in the plastic bag to keep moist. Roll out the other half as thin as possible. Rub rolling pin with flour if the dough sticks. Loosely fold the sheet of dough lengthwise into thirds, like a letter, and cut into ¼" strips with a sharp knife. Separate the strips and set aside. Repeat directions with remaining dough.

The noodles are now ready to cook in chicken broth or in whatever way you choose, or to add to the soup of your choice. Fresh noodles cook quickly, so watch carefully. Bring broth, water, or soup to a boil, add noodles, bring to a boil again and cook about 3 minutes or until just tender. If noodles are cooked simply in water, drain and toss with butter or sauce. Serves 8.

OXTAIL STEW

Even though the tail is extraordinarily strong, its meat is some of the most delicious and tender of the whole animal — ox, cow or steer. The meat does have fat, but the cooked oxtails are refrigerated so the fat can be skimmed.

4 pounds oxtails, cut in pieces
Water
¼ cup all purpose flour
¼ cup light oil
2 quarts beef broth
1 bay leaf
3 sprigs fresh parsley
2 cloves garlic, peeled and sliced
½ teaspoon thyme
1 onion, peeled and stuck with 2 cloves
10 peppercorns
1 cup dry red wine
1 one-pound can tomatoes
2 celery stalks, chopped
2 leeks, split, cleaned and sliced
1 large carrot, cleaned and sliced
½ cup pearl barley (optional)

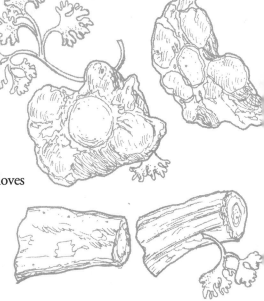

Place the oxtails in a large kettle and cover with cold water. Bring to a boil, remove from burner and pour the oxtails in a colander, discarding the water. Drain and dry the oxtails. Sprinkle the flour over them and then sauté in the oil in a large skillet until brown. Transfer to a heavy kettle such as a cast iron Dutch oven. Add to the oxtails the beef broth, bay leaf, parsley, garlic, thyme, onion with cloves and the peppercorns. Add wine to the skillet and bring to a boil, scraping the bottom, then add this to the kettle. Simmer slowly 2 to 3 hours. When the oxtails are very tender with meat falling off the bones, strain the broth. Separately cover the oxtails and the broth and refrigerate overnight. The next day skim the fat off the broth and combine the broth and oxtails in a soup kettle. Add the tomatoes, celery, leeks, carrots and barley if desired. Bring to a simmer and cook until vegetables are tender. Serves 8.

GREEK MEAT BALL SOUP

On a journey to Greece I fell in love with the country and the food in the Greek taverns. We dined several times with a young girl who had been an American Field Service student in Tulsa. I was touched when she and her mother brought red roses to our hotel and gave me a large beautiful copper pot with someone's initials on the side. I learned that when most apartments had no adequate stoves, people from the community brought their pots, filled with ingredients, to a local baker so their meal could be cooked on his stove. Thus, the initials on my copper pot. This is a wonderful full-meal soup, needing only a good bread and salad.

SOUP:

6 cups beef broth

One 28-ounce can crushed tomatoes
  with liquid

½ teaspoon oregano

1 bay leaf

1 large carrot,
cleaned and chopped

2 large stalks celery, cleaned
  and chopped

½ cup tiny pasta

MEAT BALLS:

3 slices white bread

½ cup milk

½ cup onion, chopped

1 garlic clove, peeled and minced

2 tablespoons butter or margarine

2 pounds lean ground beef

⅓ cup fresh parsley, chopped

1 large egg

1 teaspoon oregano

1 teaspoon salt

Grindings of black pepper

Parmesan cheese (optional)

In a soup pot combine all the above ingredients except the pasta. Bring to a simmer and cook 15 minutes. Add the pasta and simmer until tender, about another 15 minutes. In the meantime prepare the meat balls and add to the soup when finished. Place the bread in a shallow bowl and cover with the milk. Let soak 10 minutes until mushy. If not very soft, add a bit more milk. In a small skillet sauté the onion and garlic in the butter until golden, about 5 minutes. Place the beef in bowl of a heavy duty mixer with a flat beater or mix with a rubber spatula. Add the milk and on-ion mixtures, parsley, egg, oregano, salt and pepper. Mix until thoroughly blended. Place foil in a large baking sheet and coat with a vegetable spray. Roll very small meatballs — just bite-sized — and place on the baking sheet. Preheat oven to 400° and bake the meatballs 15 to 20 minutes or until they begin to brown. Add the meatballs to the soup and stir to distribute well. Serve the soup piping hot with the cheese as a topping if desired. Serves 8.

CHICKEN AND CORN SOUP

When I have leftover chicken, this is my favorite quick meal. It is perfect for luncheon or a light supper. Keep a can of cream style corn in your pantry and whenever there is leftover chicken and chicken broth, canned or homemade, you are set for an easy meal.

>3 tablespoons butter or margarine
>½ cup celery, minced
>½ cup onion, minced
>3 tablespoons all purpose flour
>2 cups chicken broth, canned or homemade
>2 cups milk
>1 one-pound can cream style corn
>1½ cups cooked chicken cut in bite-size pieces
>Grindings of white pepper
>Salt to taste

In a large saucepan melt the butter, then add the celery and onion and cook 5 minutes, stirring constantly. Whisk in the flour until smooth and bubbly. Do not allow to burn. Measure in the broth and milk, whisking to avoid lumps. Reduce heat, cover and simmer 15 minutes. Remove lid and add the corn and chicken. If more chicken is desired, add another half cup — personally I love lots of chicken and corn. Bring to a simmer, add the pepper and taste for salt. Adjust. Serves 6.

MOCK TURTLE SOUP

This soul-satisfying soup brings me pleasant memories of dining in the famous wharfside Bookbinders in Philadelphia, then wandering through the buildings where the U. S. Constitution was written and finally touching the crack in the Liberty Bell. It is a favorite meal for a cold winter's night. Serve in large soup bowls and pass a pitcher of a good dry sherry to finish the robust flavoring.

4 cups beef broth
4 cups water
2 pounds veal neck bones
1 large veal shank, cut in 2" pieces
1 large leek, white part only, cleaned and chopped
2 carrots, cleaned and sliced
2 large stalks celery with leaves, chopped
2 medium onions, each studded with 2 cloves
3 parsley sprigs
8 peppercorns
½ teaspoon marjoram
1 bay leaf
2 cloves garlic
2 cups tomato puree
Dash of Tabasco
¼ cup butter
½ cup flour
1 lemon, thinly sliced
Salt to taste

Combine the first 15 ingredients in a large soup kettle. Bring to a boil, skim, and lower heat to simmer. Allow to bubble lightly, uncovered, for two hours or until the meat is very tender. Remove meat and bones to a bowl and when cool enough to handle, debone the meat, discarding the bones. Dice the meat, cover and set aside. Strain the soup broth and discard the vegetables.

In a clean soup kettle, melt the butter and whisk in the flour, stirring until smooth and bubbling. Keep stirring until lightly browned. Add the strained soup and bring to a boil, stirring constantly to keep smooth. Add the meat, taste for salt content and adjust. Let the soup come just to a boil to heat the meat thoroughly. The soup is now ready to serve in two different presentations. You may add the sliced lemon to the soup or float two slices in each serving after ladling the soup into bowls. For those who like a final filip of flavor, pass a pitcher of dry sherry so that diners may splash the desired amount into their bowls. Serves 10 generously.

MICHAEL'S CHILI

Did you know that chili is the most popular stew in our fifty states? Chili cook-offs abound in every region, along with recipes for chili made with every kind of meat imaginable or even without meat. But I believe the best belongs to my son Michael. Much thought has gone into this chili which he serves frequently in his cafe-delicatessen called Mary's Bread Basket.

⅓ cup light oil
5 pounds beef chuck, chili ground
2 large onions, peeled and diced
4 cloves garlic, peeled and minced
3 to 4 tablespoons salt
1 tablespoon oregano
3 to 4 tablespoons cumin
6 to 9 tablespoons ancho chili powder*
1 tablespoon cider vinegar
3 cups beef stock
2 cups water
4 cups crushed canned tomatoes
3 tablespoons Masa Harina
Water

Heat the oil in a skillet, add the beef, and brown. Remove to a soup kettle using a slotted spoon. Add the onions and garlic to the skillet and sauté just until wilted — do not allow to burn. Add onions and garlic to the soup kettle with the salt, oregano, cumin, ancho chili powder, vinegar, beef stock, the two cups of water and tomatoes. Bring to a simmer and cook until the meat is very tender, 1½ to 2 hours. Adjust the spiciness, adding cumin and ancho chili powder to your taste. Add salt if needed. In a small bowl mix the Masa Harina in a small amount of water (¼ cup) and whisk into the chili to thicken. Simmer about five minutes to cook the Masa Harina. Now serve in big pottery soup bowls with a good cornbread. Serves 12.

*The ancho chili powder may be purchased at specialty stores (or see Sources of Supply, page 276) — Michael maintains it is the best and will use no other. Although still most commonly available in the southwest, various chilies such as the ancho are becoming more widespread in availability. The ancho chili is the dried form of the medium-hot poblano. Dried ancho chilies can be purchased whole or ground. If you cannot obtain ancho chili powder, use a good pure ground chili. The seasoning sold as chili powder is not pure ground chili but has been premixed with various flavorings, usually onion, oregano, garlic, cumin and caraway.

WINTER'S WINE STEW

When the weather map shows snow flurries and cold winds sweeping down from Canada, hurry to the market and purchase supplies for this hearty wine stew. With healthful brown rice and a salad the evening's meal is complete.

4 pounds lean stewing beef
3 cups dry red wine
1 medium onion, peeled and sliced
½ teaspoon thyme
1 bay leaf, broken in pieces
Grindings of black pepper
¼ pound lean salt pork, rind removed and cubed
1½ cups onions, coarsely chopped

3 large cloves garlic, peeled and chopped
¾ teaspoon dried thyme
½ teaspoon dried savory
1 whole bay leaf
2 thin slices orange peel
2 cups beef broth
¼ cup soft butter or margarine
¼ cup all purpose flour
28 small onions, peeled
Salt to taste

Place the beef in a deep earthenware or plastic bowl. Combine the wine, sliced onion, thyme, broken bay leaf and pepper. Stir well and pour over the beef. Turn the beef in the marinade — if it is not well covered, add more wine. Cover and refrigerate overnight. The following day remove meat from refrigerator, place a colander over a large bowl, pour in the beef and allow to drain. Transfer meat to paper towels. Reserve the marinade, discarding the bay leaf and onions.In a large skillet sauté the cubed salt pork until crisp and golden stirring constantly. Remove with slotted spoon to paper towels. Add the beef to the skillet a small portion at a time and sauté over medium high heat until browned. Transfer to a heavy casserole. Sauté the chopped onions and garlic in the same skillet until just wilted, about five minutes. If more fat is needed, add light vegetable oil. Transfer the onions and garlic to the casserole. Add the thyme, savory, bay leaf and orange peel to the casserole and stir. Pour the marinade into the skillet and cook over high heat three minutes, stirring to release the scrapings. Add to the casserole along with the beef broth. Cover and cook in a preheated oven at 300° for 1½ hours. At this point the stew can be cooled and refrigerated to finish the following day.

Cream the butter and flour together with a fork and add one cup of the hot juice from the stew, stirring until smooth. (Or combine one cup of hot juice, the butter and flour in a blender and whirl until smooth.) Remove the bay leaf and orange rind from the stew. Stir in the flour mixture until smooth. Add the small onions, adjust for salt, cover and bake one hour or until meat is very tender and the onions are done. The stew will be bubbling and thick, ready to serve over hot brown rice. Serves 10.

KISHK AND KIBBE SOUPS

The highway from Beirut to Damascus was both a perilous and beautiful drive even before the civil war began. The Mediterranean laps the front yard of Beirut while mountains ring the back in a semi-circle sometimes topped with snow — an exquisite sight from an incoming plane. The road through the mountains twists and turns making a thrilling drive for one never knows when a speeding bus will round a curve on the wrong side of the road. Then it winds out of the mountains and into the Bekaa Valley, rich with fruits and vegetables and into Zahle and through the small village of Hammana where Joseph Jabbour was born. But there was much for Joseph outside this small village. As a very young man he immigrated to the United States to study flying in Tulsa, Oklahoma where he met Judith. Judith and Joseph gave me a basic Yogurt Soup and with it the Lebanese Kishk and Kibbe soups. With Kibbe the soup becomes a complete meal. It is wonderful served with taboulie and toasted Pideh Bread (page 184).

Basic Yogurt Soup

> 1 clove garlic
> 1 tablespoon dried mint or 2 tablespoons fresh mint
> 1 tablespoon butter
> 4 cups chicken broth
> Kibbe Meat Balls (recipe following)
> 4 cups plain yogurt
> 1 large egg
> 2 tablespoons cornstarch
> 2 tablespoons water

Peel the garlic and crush in a mortar with the mint. Or grate the garlic in a small bowl and and mash the mint into the garlic with a fork. Sauté 2 minutes in the tablespoon of butter. Set aside. Heat the chicken broth in a large saucepan or small soup kettle until simmering. Add one-half the Kibbe Meat Balls. Bring back to a simmer and cook the meat balls 5 to 8 minutes. With a slotted spoon remove the meat balls to a bowl. Return the broth to the burner.

Pour the yogurt into a bowl and add the egg, beating until smooth. Add ½cup broth to the yogurt-egg mixture and stir well. Add another 1/4 cup hot broth, stirring constantly. Slowly add the yogurt mixture to the broth while bringing the soup just to a simmer – handle gently to avoid curdling the yogurt. Add meat balls and garlic-mint mixture. Stir gently until the soup is very hot or just simmering. Serves 8.

Kibbe Meat Balls

2⅔ cups bulghur wheat
Cold water to cover
1 large onion, grated
2 teaspoons salt
¼ teaspoon freshly ground black pepper
¼ teaspoon basil
⅛ teaspoon cinnamon
½ teaspoon allspice
2 pounds ground lean beef or lamb*

Place the bulghur in a large bowl and cover with cold water. Allow to soak 10 minutes. Drain the mixture in a sieve and then squeeze excess water out with your hands — thoroughly. Place the wheat back in the bowl and add the remaining ingredients. Knead this mixture together until very well mixed. Prepare small bite-size balls about the size of a walnut or smaller if desired. Add these to the yogurt soup and cook gently for 15 to 20 minutes. Serve with crisp Pideh Bread.

*If using lamb add ⅓ cup more bulghur. Bulghur wheat is available in some supermarkets and in health food stores, Middle Eastern import markets, and specialty shops.

Kishk Soup

1 large onion, chopped
3 cloves garlic, coarsely chopped
⅛ teaspoon freshly ground black pepper
1 tablespoon butter
2 cups kishk*
4 to 5 cups of water

Combine the onion, garlic and pepper in a medium size soup kettle and sauté in the tablespoon of butter until golden. Add the kishk and continue sautéing several minutes. Stir constantly to prevent scorching and lumping. Gradually add the water, continuing to stir until a smooth mixture is formed. Simmer 20 minutes until the soup is the consistency of a cream gravy. If the soup becomes too thick, add more water.

Variation: Prepare the Kibbe Meat Balls according to directions and add to the Kishk soup. Simmer over low heat for 20 minutes, stirring constantly.

*Kishk is a mixture of dried yogurt and wheat and is available in import stores.

Bulghur

Bulghur is the Turkish word for cracked wheat, a staple food in the Middle East. It is made by boiling, drying and grinding wheat grains. It is probably best known for its starring role in tabbouleh, a cold salad of bulghur, parsley, green onions, tomatoes, lemon juice and olive oil. Kibbe, classically made by pounding lamb into a paste with bulghur wheat, is often called the national dish of Lebanon. Cooked bulghur makes a delicious side dish with meats and vegetables instead of rice, potatoes or noodles.

SOPA DE LIMA

"Soup with lime" is a Mexican classic. I consider the soups to be the height of the national cuisine. This one can be started one day and finished the next.

One 3- to 3½- pound chicken, cut up

10 cups water

2 cups canned chicken broth

6 peppercorns

3 parsley sprigs

2 stalks celery, cut in pieces

1 medium onion, quartered

½ teaspoon thyme

2 tablespoons light oil

2 medium onions, peeled and chopped

2 large tomatoes, peeled, seeded and chopped

One hot green chile, canned or fresh (optional)

Juice of 2 large limes

3 tablespoons fresh parsley, chopped

1 teaspoon fresh cilantro, chopped

Freshly ground pepper

Salt to taste

8 tortillas

Place the chicken in a heavy kettle. Add the water, broth, peppercorns, parsley, celery, quartered onion and thyme. Bring to a boil, skim and reduce heat. Simmer uncovered, skimming when necessary, until chicken is tender, about 1 hour. Remove to a plate to cool. Strain the broth into a clean kettle. Debone the chicken and discard the bones. The broth and chicken may be covered and refrigerated overnight. Heat the oil in a skillet and sauté the chopped onion until tender, about 10 minutes. Add tomatoes. Add chile, if desired. Cook 5 minutes. Transfer to the chicken broth. Add lime juice. Stir in the chopped parsley and cilantro. Simmer 20 minutes. Add the chicken, heat to boiling and lower to simmer. Taste and adjust for salt and pepper. Fry the tortillas in oil in a skillet or toast in the oven until crisp. Break the tortillas into soup bowls and ladle soup on top. Garnish with thin slices of lime and chopped parsley. Serves 8.

CITY VEGETABLE SOUP

4 tablespoons butter
2 medium onions, peeled and sliced
2 teaspoons sugar
1 small leek, split, cleaned, sliced
1 carrot, cleaned, sliced
2 stalks celery, cleaned, sliced diagonally
2 large cloves garlic, peeled, minced
¼ pound sliced mushrooms, destemmed
¼ cup warm brandy
8 cups chicken broth
1 cup tomatoes, peeled, seeded, chopped
¼ cup dry sherry
2 teaspoons dry mustard
½ teaspoon thyme
⅛ teaspoon rosemary
⅛ teaspoon marjarom
⅔ cup young peas, fresh or frozen
⅔ cup broccoli florets
Freshly ground black pepper
3 to 4 dashes Tabasco
Salt to taste
Parmesan cheese (optional)

Melt the butter in a heavy Dutch oven or soup kettle over medium low heat, add the onion and sauté until soft, about 10 minutes. Add the sugar and continue sautéing until golden. Add the leek, carrot and celery and sauté 10 minutes. Blend in the garlic and mushrooms and sauté 5 minutes. Heat the brandy until just barely warm and pour it over the vegetables to "flame them," stirring constantly. Add the chicken broth, tomatoes, sherry, mustard, thyme, rosemary and marjarom. Simmer partially covered 30 minutes. Add the peas and broccoli and simmer 5 minutes. Season with pepper, Tabasco and salt to taste. Serve in warm soup bowls passing the Parmesan cheese as a topping. Serves 8.

GREEK LEMON PORK STEW

A piquant lemony stew that can be prepared with either pork or lamb. The stew may be made one or two days before and reheated. Add the celery, egg and lemon juice just before serving.

> 6 tablespoons butter or margarine
> 2 tablespoons light oil
> 2½ pounds lean pork, cubed
> 2½ cups onions, thinly sliced
> 3 tablespoons all purpose flour
> 1 teaspoon salt
> ¾ cup dry white wine
> ½ cup water
> 2 tablespoons parsley, finely chopped
> 1 medium size bunch of celery, sliced
> 4 egg yolks
> 4 tablespoons lemon juice

Melt butter with the oil in a skillet over moderately high heat. Sauté the pork until it is lightly colored. Transfer the meat to a casserole. Drain all but 2 or 3 tablespoons of fat from the skillet. Add the onions to the skillet and cook until soft, about 10 minutes. Whisk in the flour and salt, stirring until smooth and bubbly. Add the wine and water. Lower heat and simmer until smooth, stirring occasionally. Add the parsley. Pour the mixture over the pork and stir to mix well. Cover and place in a preheated 325° oven for 1½ hours or until the meat is fork tender. Clean the celery and slice the stalks diagonally in ½" pieces. Mince the celery leaves. Arrange celery and leaves over top of the stew, cover and bake 20 minutes. Beat the egg yolks with a whisk or electric mixer until they are thick and lemon colored. Slowly beat in the lemon juice. Add a few tablespoons of the hot broth from the stew. Pour the egg mixture into the casserole and stir it in well. Taste for salt and adjust. Turn heat off and place casserole back in the oven uncovered for 5 minutes. Serve over hot fluffy rice. Serves 6 to 8. The stew may be frozen but reheat slowly to avoid curdling the egg yolks.

Seafood Soups

Many seafood soups are very quickly made as the cooking time for the fish or seafood is very brief. The primary rule is not to overcook the seafood; if you do it will become tough and lose flavor. Shrimp, scallops, and lobster should be added at the end of the cooking time and only simmered gently four to five minutes. Another method of cooking them is to bring the soup to a boil, drop in the shrimp, scallops, lobster, or chunks of firm white fish, then immediately remove the kettle from the stove and cover it. The cool fish lowers the temperature of the pot and causes it to cease boiling. Within a few minutes the seafood will have cooked through gently. Seafood soups can be reheated the next day, but with great care not to overcook and toughen the fish.

Spiciness is a personal taste, but seafood soups may often benefit from a few dried hot red pepper flakes or a fresh hot chile pepper. Tomato-based seafood soups take especially kindly to the addition of some pungent element.

Soups with seafood and fish are delicious with popovers, scones, cornbread, slices of fruit and nut bread, buttered muffins or sliced and toasted cornbread muffins or Cornbread Loaf.

SALMON BISQUE

Ah, what can be accomplished with a good can of red salmon — from salad to soup. This is a favorite I love throwing together just for my own lunch or a quick dinner.   Serve hot biscuits or popovers as an accompaniment.

4 cups milk
1 bay leaf
1 garlic clove, peeled
3 sprigs of fresh parsley
1 clove
¼ cup butter or margarine
3 tablespoons onion, grated
3 tablespoons all purpose flour
1 one-pound can red salmon, deboned and flaked
2 egg yolks (optional)
¼ cup cream

Combine the milk, bay leaf, garlic, parsley and clove in a large saucepan. Bring to a simmer and cook 20 minutes. Remove from the burner and set aside. In a clean saucepan melt the butter and add the grated onion. Sauté, stirring, for 5 minutes. Add the flour and whisk until smooth. Strain the milk into the flour mixture and whisk vigorously until smooth. Add the salmon, stir to mix, and then put the soup in a blender or food processor and whirl until smooth. The soup is quite good at this point but for a smoother, richer soup, return the soup to a saucepan, beat 2 egg yolks with ¼ cup of cream, add a little hot soup and stir and then slowly add this mixture to the bisque. Heat thoroughly but do not allow to boil. The soup can be topped with fresh parsley or a few gratings of fresh nutmeg. Serves six.

SCALLOP CHOWDER

This chowder is perfection for a splendid dinner or special luncheon. I have been preparing it for a long time. You can omit the egg yolk but the cream should stay in.

2 medium potatoes, peeled and diced
1 small carrot, peeled and chopped
1 large stalk celery, chopped
1 medium onion, peeled and chopped
2 cups chicken stock
½ teaspoon salt
¼ teaspoon finely ground white pepper
½ bay leaf
½ teaspoon thyme
½ pound fresh mushrooms, sliced
1½ tablespoons butter or margarine
1 pound fresh bay scallops
½ cup dry white wine
1 cup heavy cream
1 egg yolk, lightly beaten (optional)
Parsley, freshly chopped

Combine the potatoes, carrot, celery and onion in a soup kettle, cover with the chicken stock and bring to a boil. Add the salt, pepper, bay leaf and thyme. Reduce heat and simmer, covered, until vegetables are tender. Remove the bay leaf and transfer the mixture to a blender. Whirl until smooth. Sauté the mushrooms in the butter until tender. Add the scallops and wine and cook one minute. (If large scallops are used, cut them in halves or fourths, depending on size.) Blend the cream and egg yolk and stir in the scallops. Combine the scallop mixture with the pureed vegetables and broth. Heat slowly until quite hot but do not allow to boil. Serve hot with a sprinkling of fresh parsley. Serves 10.

THE CELLAR'S NEW ENGLAND CLAM CHOWDER

One of the most charming gentlemen I've had the pleasure of meeting, Frank Hightower of Oklahoma City, established a fine restaurant called The Cellar. There he encouraged several young chefs who eventually branched out on their own, following Frank's precepts of classical cooking. Frank graciously gave me permission to share the recipe for his famous Clam Chowder.

6 ounces salt pork, finely diced

6 tablespoons all purpose flour

4 ounces butter

1 cup diced onion

3 eight-ounce cans minced clams and juice

2 cups water

2½ cups raw potatoes, diced

½ bay leaf

½ teaspoon thyme

2 to 3 cups half-and-half

White pepper

Salt to taste

Sauté the salt pork in a small skillet until brown and crispy. Remove with a slotted spoon and drain on paper towels. In a large saucepan or small soup kettle, combine the flour, butter and onion and cook together over medium heat for 4 minutes, stirring constantly. Add the clams and juice, the water, potatoes, bay leaf and thyme. Cover and simmer until potatoes are tender. Add the salt pork to the soup and slowly stir in 2 cups of the cream. Remove the bay leaf and bring the soup just to a simmer. Add more cream for consistency desired and the pepper and salt to taste. Serves 6 to 8.

CIOPPINO

The Portuguese are adept with fish in any form and their sailors have roamed the world for centuries. Naturally they found San Francisco as it awakened from a sleepy little village to a hustling city of men hungry for good food and gold. Some credit Portuguese sailors for this satisfying, flavorful stew.

1½ cups onions, chopped
2 cloves garlic, peeled and minced
4 tablespoons olive oil
2 cups canned tomatoes with juice
1 ten-ounce tomato puree
1½ cups dry white wine
1 cup water or clam juice
2 tablespoons red wine vinegar
½ teaspoon dried basil
½ teaspoon dried oregano
½ teaspoon dried marjoram
1 bay leaf
Grindings of black pepper
½ pound fresh mushrooms, sliced
2 tablespoons butter
1 pound scallops
1 pound lobster tails or a firm fleshed fish,
 such as red snapper or halibut
1 pound fresh shrimp, shelled

In a soup kettle sauté the onion and garlic in the oil until limp but not browned, about five minutes. Add the tomatoes, tomato puree, wine, water, vinegar, herbs, bay leaf and black pepper. Stir well, lower heat and simmer uncovered 40 minutes. In a small skillet sauté the mushrooms in the butter until they are limp and have given up most of their liquid. To the soup kettle add the mushrooms, scallops and lobster that has been removed from the shell and cut in bite-size pieces and the shrimp. *Do not overcook* or the fish will become tough. Cover and simmer 5 minutes. Remove from the burner and allow to sit 10 minutes. Serve in large warm soup bowls. Serves 8.

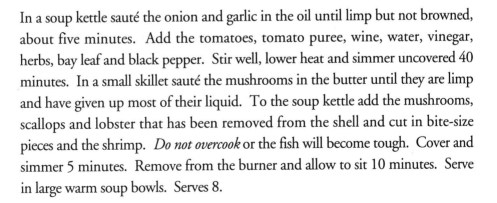

WITCH'S BREW

Salem, Massachusetts conjures forth visions of witches. Despite these gloomy stories I was served the very best chowder I've ever tasted in that city. A young black-clad waitress anxious to be of assistance scurried (or flew?) back to the kitchen returning with a list of all the ingredients but not how to put them together. So I whipped out my cauldron and carefully stirred everything together for a wonderfully complete meal.

¼ pound salt pork minus the rind, cubed in ¼" pieces
½ cup onion, finely chopped
1 garlic clove, peeled and finely chopped
2 cups water
2 cups new potatoes, peeled and cubed
1 bay leaf
¼ teaspoon thyme
1 twelve-ounce can evaporated milk
More milk sufficient to make 4 cups
¼ pound fresh lobster, cut in pieces
¼ pound halibut or haddock,
 deboned and cut in bite size pieces
¼ pound shrimp, peeled, cleaned and if large, cut in half
¼ pound scallops
¼ pound fresh clams or oysters
Fresh parsley, chopped

Sauté the salt pork in a heavy saucepan or soup pot until crisp and golden. Add the onion and garlic. Cook, stirring, until wilted, about 5 minutes. Add the water and potatoes with the bay leaf and thyme. Bring to a boil and let bubble until the potatoes are just tender. Combine the evaporated milk and regular milk and stir into the soup pot. Bring just to a simmer. Add all the fish except the oysters or clams and simmer five minutes. Do not allow to boil as this will make the fish tough. Stir in the oysters and simmer five minutes. Serves 10.

CREAM OF CORN AND CRAB SOUP

An absolutely delicious soup creamy with whirled corn, chicken broth, a little cream and just a hint of Tabasco if desired. Superb for a small luncheon with a fruit salad and hot bread.

2 cups canned or homemade chicken broth
2 cups cream style corn
1 medium onion, peeled and chopped
¼ cup butter or margarine
¼ cup all purpose flour
1 cup milk
1 cup half-and-half
6 ounces crabmeat, fresh or canned
Grindings of white pepper
Salt to taste
Tabasco sauce to taste (optional)

Combine the chicken broth, corn and onion in a saucepan, cover, bring to a boil and cook until the onion is tender, about 15 minutes. Whirl in a blender until smooth. In a separate saucepan melt the butter and whisk in the flour until smooth and bubbling. Continue to stir and add the milk until mixture is smooth and thickened. Blend in the half-and-half and add the corn mixture and crabmeat. Bring to a simmer, stirring, and add the pepper. Taste for salt and adjust. If desired add a few drops of Tabasco for piquancy. Serve steaming hot in warm soup bowls. Serves 6.

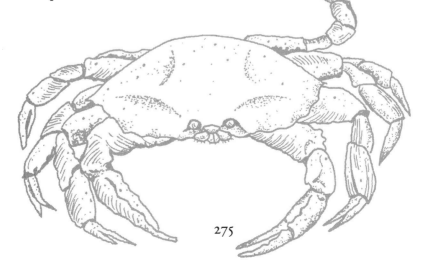

275

SOURCES OF SUPPLY

Akins Special Foods
65709 East 51st
Tulsa, Oklahoma 74145
Nuts, grains, specialty flours, health foods

Al's Food Store
6900 Greenville Avenue
Dallas, Texas 75231
Spices, specialty items, import items

Arrowhead Mills, Inc.
Box 2059
Hereford, Texas 79045
Flours and grains

B. F. Clyde's Grist Mill
R.F.D. 1A
Mystic, Connecticut 06355
Flours and grains

Brumewell Flour Mill
South Amana, Iowa 52334
Flours and grains

Burnt Cabins Grist Mill
Burnt Cabins, Pennsylvania 17215
Flours and grains

Caprilands Farms
Coventry, Connecticut 06238
Herb plants and seeds, herbal products

The Chef's Catalogue
3215 Commercial Avenue
Northbrook, Illinois 60062
Cookware, bakeware

The Chile Shop
109 E. Water Stret
Santa Fe, New Mexico 87501
Dried and ground chiles

Coombs Beaver Brook Sugarhouse
Box 503
Junction Routes 9 and 100
Wilmington, Vermont 05363
Flours and spices

Eastern Lamejun Bakers, Inc.
145 Belmont Street
Belmont, Massachusetts 02178
Spices

Elams Mill
2625 Gardner Road
Broadview, Illinois 60153
Flours and grains

Great Grains Milling Company
P.O. Box 427
Scobey, Montana 59263
Whole wheat flour

Kabani's
3207-A East Admiral Place
Tulsa, Oklahoma 74110
Orange blossom water, pine nuts, olive oils, spices, kishk

Mecca Coffee Company
3509 South Peoria
Tulsa, Oklahoma 74105
Specialty items, canned tomatoes, flavorings, imported food items

New Hope Mills
R. D. #2
Moravia, New York 13118
Flours and grains

Oklahoma Food Supply
5080 E. 50th St.
Tulsa, Oklahoma 74135
*Middle Eastern, North African, Indian
specialty foods, imported food items*

G. B. Ratto
International Grocers
821 Washington Street
Oakland, California 94607
International food items

Shiloh Farms
Sulphur Springs, Arkansas 72768
Flours

The Cedars Import Company, Inc.
5055 South Yale
Tulsa, Oklahoma 74135
Specialty foods, Middle Eastern items

The Mail Order Spice House, Ltd.
P. O. Box 1633
Milwaukee, Wisconsin 53201
Fresh whole spices, spice blends

The White Lily Foods Company
P.O. Box 871
Knoxville, Tennessee 37901
Cake flour

Thomas Market
2650 University Boulevard West
Wheaton, Maryland 20902
Spices

Walnut Acres
Penn Creek, Pennsylvania 17862
Flours

War Eagle Mill
Route 1
Hindsville, Arkansas 72738

Williams Sonoma
P.O. Box 7456
San Francisco, California 94120
*Lyle's Golden Syrup, specialty foods and
cookware*

INDEX

ABOUT THE AUTHOR

Mary Gubser, born in 1915 in a Methodist parsonage, is a native of Oklahoma. She began her baking career as a young mother when a post-World War II bakers' strike left the bread shelves of her local grocery store empty. In 1974 she wrote and published her *Mary's Bread Basket and Soup Kettle*, which was reprinted by William Morrow in 1975 and remains in print and in demand today. She followed that success with a second book on classic yeast breads, *America's Bread Book*. In *Mary Gubser's Quick Breads, Soups & Stews* the author brings her substantial knowledge of baking to the world of quick breads. Her humorous account of coping with rural life during World War II, *Back To the Damn Soil* (1986), is available from Council Oak Books. Mary Gubser lives and writes in Tulsa, Oklahoma.